The Voltage Effect

THE
VOLTAGE
EFFECT

*How to Make Good Ideas Great
and Great Ideas Scale*

JOHN A. LIST

CURRENCY | NEW YORK

Published in the United States by Currency, an imprint of Random House,
a division of Penguin Random House LLC, New York.

CURRENCY and its colophon are registered trademarks
of Penguin Random House LLC.

Library of Congress Cataloging-in-Publication Data
Names: List, John A., 1968- author.
Title: The voltage effect / John A. List.
Description: First edition. | New York: Currency, [2022] | Includes
bibliographical references and index.
Identifiers: LCCN 2021044408 (print) | LCCN 2021044409 (ebook) |
ISBN 9780593239483 (hardcover) | ISBN 9780593443521 (international
edition) | ISBN 9780593239490 (ebook)
Subjects: LCSH: Scaling (Social Sciences) | New products. | Strategic
planning. | Entrepreneurship. | Policy sciences.
Classification: LCC H61.27 .L57 2022 (print) | LCC H61.27 (ebook) |
DDC 300.72—dc23
LC record available at https://lccn.loc.gov/2021044408
LC ebook record available at https://lccn.loc.gov/2021044409

Printed in the United States of America on acid-free paper

crownpublishing.com

2 4 6 8 9 7 5 3 1

First Edition

Design by Fritz Metsch

To my truly inspirational scaling partner, Dana,

and our wonderful eight children:

Annika, Genevieve, Eli, Noah, Asher, Greta, Amelie, and Mason,

who have taught me the true value of scaling

Scalable ideas are all alike;
every unscalable idea is unscalable in its own way.

Contents

The Voltage Effect

t was never my plan to work for Uber. To be honest, it had never even occurred to me.

In the summer of 2016, I was busy with one of the most ambitious projects of my career. Six years earlier, alongside my teaching responsibilities in the Economics Department at the University of Chicago, I had led a team that opened a preschool for three- to five-year-olds that also functioned as a living research laboratory—a huge logistical and scientific endeavor I hadn't planned on undertaking and didn't exactly have the training for. While I had learned a few things raising five of my own kids, I had zero formal expertise in early childhood education. On the other hand, observing and studying people "in the wild" has been my lab for over thirty years now. And launching a preschool full of wonderful, crazy kids is as wild as it gets, albeit in a whole different sort of way.

Many people believe that the discipline of economics is all about money, or how capital flows through society. But my work as an economist doesn't involve things like analyzing fiscal data or predicting stock market trends. My specialty is conducting fieldwork in behavioral economics, going out into the real world to study the hidden, often surprising motivations behind big and small decisions we make every day.

This was why Tom Amadio and other administrators of the school district of Chicago Heights had approached me several years earlier. They knew about experiments I had done incentivizing people to adopt all kinds of positive behaviors, so they wanted to see if I might have any ideas on how to incentivize teachers and students in ways that would improve the students' performance. A town of close to thirty thousand people a half hour's drive south of Chicago proper, Chicago Heights is a place society has left behind. Boarded-up storefronts abound, and violent crime is disproportionately high compared to the rest of the United States. Today, over a quarter of the population lives below the poverty line, almost double the state-wide average of 13 percent when I first visited Chicago Heights. Un-surprisingly, these economic disadvantages take their toll on children there. High school graduation rates are low, and many high-schoolers are at a third- or fourth-grade level in reading and math. And this, of course, excludes them from numerous future opportunities; life is an entirely different game without a high school diploma.

Eager to get involved in a project that sought to reverse these trends, I teamed up with economists Steven Levitt (of *Freakonomics* fame) and Sally Sadoff (my PhD student at the time) in early 2008. Thanks to a generous gift from the Kenneth and Anne Griffin Foundation, we got to work conducting experiments with students and teachers at a Chi-cago Heights high school. Sure enough, our interventions produced gains in achievement standards and test scores, yet the results weren't as dramatic as we had hoped. We concluded that by working with high-schoolers we had missed a critical window in these kids' develop-ment, during which we could have altered their life trajectories. Show-ing up so late left much of their potential on the table; in fact, it had already been lost, years earlier. In other words, we were dealing with the wrong student population to truly tackle this problem.

So we proposed starting our own preschool, which would double as an experimental research lab on childhood education and devel-opment. We once again received support from our angel donor—a whopping $10 million from the Griffin Foundation—and that is how the Chicago Heights Early Childhood Center (CHECC) was born.

By the spring of 2010, we were on to the next phase of our work in Chicago Heights, and were joined by Roland Fryer, then a rising star at Harvard who studied the impact of economic inequality on academic performance, and Anya Samek, a postdoctoral student of mine. From 2010 to 2014, our preschool served nearly 1,500 students annually. The bedrock of our four-year pedagogical experiment was a curriculum that emphasized important noncognitive skills that have been shown to have a profound impact on later success in life, such as socialization, active listening, and delayed gratification. Our curriculum of choice was called Tools of the Mind. Crucially, we also had created a new program called Parent Academy, which incentivized parents to involve themselves in their children's early educational development in specific ways. Once the four years came to an end, we shuttered the school, as had always been our intent. But we continued collecting data on the children who had attended—and we plan to continue collecting these data for decades to come—to compare it against the performance of children who had the standard curriculum and whose parents did not receive any behavioral nudges from Parent Academy.

In other words, we had come up with a hypothesis about improving long-term outcomes for the children in Chicago Heights. We had designed a study to test it, and now we gathered and analyzed the results up to this point, which were quite impressive so far. "Our" kids were doing great and taking strong developmental strides. Ultimately, our goal was to take the key features of Tools of the Mind and combine them with our other findings to create a new curriculum model that we could expand to other communities in the United States, and even some abroad.

So in the midst of all this, when a recruitment officer from Uber called to explain that they wanted to interview me for the newly created position of chief economist, I dismissed the idea immediately. It would be one more set of responsibilities in my already jam-packed life. On top of the Chicago Heights research keeping me busy, I was about to remarry and would soon have a happy but frenzied new household full of eight kids, along with two grandparents. Plus, what did my research on early childhood education have to do with the pursuit of world domination by a ride-sharing company in Silicon Valley? The more I thought about it, however, the more I realized that my research project and Uber had one central goal in common.

Scale.

If you've spent any time around entrepreneurs, you're probably aware that "scale" has become a bit of a buzzword in the business world, where it typically refers to the process of growing a company. But scaling isn't just the domain of scrappy start-ups. It isn't simply about accumulating more users or capturing more market share. Defined more broadly, "to scale" means to achieve a desired outcome when you take an idea from a small group—of customers, students, or citizens, for example—to a much larger one.

Through my research and time working with policymakers, my personal credo had become that the only ideas worth pursuing are the ones with the potential to make a significant impact on human lives. And translating an idea into widespread impact requires replicating it at scale. The urgency of scaling up important ideas and enterprises impacts us every day, whether it's by protecting the health and safety of a community, improving the viability of a business, or enhancing the education and opportunities of a future generation, as I hoped to do in Chicago Heights by establishing a model that other school districts around the world might someday be able to implement.

Scale underlies all social and technological progress, since the innovations that change the world are those that reach the largest number of people. A social movement needs to scale to have an impact just as much as a new medical intervention does. But the scaling process isn't simple; there are pitfalls every step of the way, from the moment the seed of an idea is planted to well after you've launched a project, and even once you've successfully replicated that project again and again. Yet it wasn't until 2016 that I realized a secret had been hiding in plain sight in Chicago Heights: for several years, my research aimed at improving kids' educational outcomes had also been a study on scaling—why it sometimes worked, while other times it didn't. I wondered if working at Uber, a company that had managed to scale at lightning speed to some seventy countries and serve nearly 100 million customers, might reveal new insights that could be applied elsewhere.

I also knew that Uber had a whole lot of data, and for an economist like myself, big data isn't just my bread and butter. It's my professional playground. It was rumored that Uber even tracked the colors of customers' residences, which side of the backseat men and women sit in, and the friendship networks among riders. I wondered what secrets about scaling lay buried in all of that information that I could translate into academic research. Pretty soon I began to think that maybe working for Uber wasn't such an out-there idea after all. Also, I like a challenge, and the Uber recruiter had warned me that they had already interviewed several other economists for the position and none had made the cut, so I shouldn't assume I would, either. So I flew from Chicago to San Francisco for the interview.

After walking through the doors of the sleek, muscular building on Market Street that housed Uber's global headquarters at the time, I took the elevator up, and was promptly whisked into a conference room for my interview. That was when I noticed a slogan printed on pillars in Uber's offices: *Data is our DNA*.

I had thought such reverence for data was reserved for the ivory tower. Had I died and gone to heaven? This was clearly a place where the people spoke my language. I could immediately tell that just on that floor alone there was more science going on than at your average company.

Then the interview started and I no longer felt so at home.

During my opening presentation, one of the five executives in the room wouldn't stop interrupting me. He was a youngish guy, dressed in a T-shirt and jeans, with his hair beginning to show silver on the sides. After a few minutes, I realized it was Travis Kalanick, Uber's thirty-nine-year-old founder.

Travis struck me as the most confident person I had ever met. Which made sense; after all, you don't change the face of urban transportation worldwide and catapult a start-up to a valuation of

$66 billion in a mere seven years if you aren't confident in your ideas and, above all, your own instincts. He did have a charm to him, but nevertheless, he was making it hard for me to get through the Power-Point slides I had carefully prepared.

As I talked about different studies I had done on loss aversion—a favorite concept of behavioral economists, one that explains why loss is such a powerful motivator for decision-making—Travis inter-jected to question my results seemingly every other minute, all the while pacing at the back of the conference room like a lion poised to pounce on its unwitting prey. I was beginning to see why previous economists hadn't made it past the interview stage.

"That doesn't make sense," he said about an experiment I had done at a factory in China.

I told him he was wrong and explained why. I clicked to the next slide and began explaining another experiment. He interrupted me again as he continued to pace. I told him why he was wrong again. We did this cute little dance for about forty-five exasperating minutes. He got in his licks. I got in mine. Neither of us was backing down. Then, mercifully, the interview ended. I shook hands with everyone and left the conference room.

Well, that was a waste of time, I thought as I walked back to the lobby.

Just before I stepped into the elevator, one of the executives from the meeting rushed to catch up with me.

"Wait," he said, stopping the elevator. "Congratulations. We want to hire you."

Soon after, I began my tenure as the chief economist at Uber. This was how two drastically different worlds would intertwine for me—my long academic career in economic fieldwork and my new career in hyperspeed twenty-first-century business. This convergence would deepen my understanding not only of how to use data to evaluate the real-world viability of ideas but also of how to use data to scale those ideas to reach exponentially more people. Essentially, Uber became my new laboratory for studying the science of how to scale science.

Chicago Heights Early Childhood Center was a great idea. So was Uber. So are countless other ideas in countless other realms. But there is no rule anywhere that says a good or even great idea will meet its full potential. In fact, the one thing all great ideas have in common is that they are not guaranteed to succeed.

Be it a medical breakthrough, consumer product, technological innovation, governmental program, or any other enterprise, the path from early promise to widespread impact requires one thing and one thing only: *scalability*—the capacity to grow and expand in a robust and sustainable way.

Put simply: you can only change the world at scale.

The Voltage Effect

"To scale" has become a popular but imprecise term, too often used as a vague description or ambition when what we need is a clearly defined method with universal benchmarks. When is a thriving small business ready to open more locations? How does a tech start-up confirm that it has the right product / market fit? What are the signs for policymakers that an encouraging public health pilot project will succeed nationally? How do grassroots campaigns for change become national movements? Why is an organization's culture floundering? And most basic of all for anyone who throws themselves full-throttle into a dream: How can I grow my idea?

My work—and everything you'll read in the pages ahead—is about scaling in this broad and inclusive sense, toggling between the worlds of business, policy, and everything in between. In each domain, going from small to big is both the primary challenge and the primary opportunity.

My three decades in the field of economics have given me a unique and science-backed perspective with which to systematically answer these questions. When I completed my PhD in the mid-1990s, the social sciences were undergoing a credibility revolution, especially economics. At the time, much of the field dealt mainly in theories and computational models, but little of this research translated easily into compelling explanations of real-world phenomena. This was in large part because the evidence behind most advice was often based on arbitrary theories or correlations, rather than conclusions drawn from causal data on actual human behavior. This is where my specialty, fieldwork, came in.

My interest in this branch of economics grew out of something I'd been doing since high school: buying and selling baseball cards. Since the late 1980s, I had been studying the microeconomies of regional baseball card shows, a weird and wonderful little world. Analyzing this living and breathing market was how I came to see the world as my laboratory, and I soon began gathering scientific data in earnest from these markets. Studying real people making decisions out in the real world allowed me to arrive at credible conclusions about cause and effect and, in turn, better understand people and their motivations. Nothing was off-limits, from nerdy stuff like how markets can operate more efficiently to deeply pressing social issues such as why people discriminate.

Later I branched out and began studying myriad other behaviors across a broad range of people and populations. This research took me all over the world, from central Florida to Costa Rica, then to Africa, Asia, and finally Chicago. Sometimes my research flipped conventional wisdom on its head, overturning assumptions about gender (women aren't inherently less competitive than men; it's a socially conditioned trait), charitable giving (a charity will attract more donations in the short run *and* long run if they attract initial donors by promising to never bother them again rather than with the traditional strategy of constant follow-ups), and motivation (the fear of losing a reward we have already been given is a more powerful motivator than the promise of some future reward). I was content to continue in this academic vein, but my career took an unexpected turn when I was offered a job at the White House as a senior economist for George W. Bush in 2002.

Putting aside personal politics and all of the (legitimate) criticism President Bush and his administration brought on themselves,

I can say that one thing the Bush White House did right and rarely receives credit for was the emphasis it put on evidence-based policies. (Except—ahem—for the whole weapons-of-mass-destruction thing . . . major lack of evidence there! I should note that I was hired before that whole ugly mess but never played a role in that issue.) In other words, the administration wanted research to drive decision-making. In retrospect, this was a watershed moment for the relationship between science and government. And it was also how I ended up on a team focused on benefit-cost analysis for policies and programs implemented by the federal government. My work spanned several areas, including advising Colin Powell and Condoleezza Rice on the economics of tightening border control, and working with then-senator Hillary Clinton and her team to design the auctions for the Clear Skies Act.

At its core, even though I wasn't fully aware of it back then, the thread that connected all of this work was scale—how to design policies that would produce the greatest positive impact on the largest number of people in the most efficient manner.

Too often, policymaking is conducted in an information vacuum. A policy is proposed, voted on, and signed into law (or not), with little consideration given to the impact that policy will have—relative to the costs—when it is scaled up in the real world. Unfortunately, such oversights can come with grave real-world consequences, ranging from unequal outcomes, in which some populations reap more benefits of the policy than others, to massive cost overruns and budget shortfalls, for which lawmakers must compensate by cutting other vital programs and services.

Of course, neglecting to assess the scalability of one's idea can produce similar consequences in many realms beyond just policymaking or government. Here's a true story I witnessed firsthand (with the names changed). In the early 2000s, a small school district in the Midwest had been struggling with the kindergarten-readiness of its students for decades. Administrators felt they had tried everything, with little success, and the district superintendent, a tireless

woman named Greta, was at her wits' end. A new member of the
school board, Mason, who was a devoted follower of the science of
early education, had recently read about a new program producing
astonishing results in other districts. It had been peer-reviewed by
academic experts and reported large gains on several school-readiness
indicators. At the school board's last meeting of the year, as others
were lamenting the district's woes, Mason brought a welcome glim-
mer of hope. "I've found the silver bullet," he told the group. "The
benefit-cost ratio might as well be infinity, it is so high." The school
board promptly voted to adopt the program. Good move, right?

That fall the school district carefully introduced the new initiative
in an "experimental rollout" fashion so that it could credibly show
the community the benefits of the fabulous new curriculum. Greta
and Mason were so confident it would succeed, they mentioned it
at every fish fry and Rotary Club meeting they attended. "Just wait
until these students apply to college," Mason boasted at the Lions
Club pancake breakfast. "Our first Harvard matriculants are coming
soon." A year passed, and data on the benefits and costs of the intervention arrived. When Mason and Greta pored over the results of
the standardized cognitive and behavioral tests, they were shocked.
Much to their dismay, the program did not even *pass* a benefit-cost
test (i.e., the costs exceeded the benefits!), much less yield the hoped-
for silver bullet. Mason was speechless, only able to mutter, "I guess
the science got it wrong this time."

But in fact the problem wasn't the science; rather, it was that
the program, quite simply, *didn't scale.* Sadly, the story of Greta and
Mason is surprisingly common.

A pharmaceutical company develops a promising new sleep medication in its lab, but the drug doesn't live up to its promise in randomized trials. A small company in the Pacific Northwest successfully
launches a product, then expands its distribution only to find that it
sells poorly on the East Coast. A venture capital firm invests millions
in a new food-delivery app, which ends up only capturing the eyeballs

and clicks of a small slice of society. Scalability is critical not just for policy and science but for anyone who stands to benefit from the success of an idea. All too often, promising ideas collapse at scale.

These cases are all examples of a *voltage drop:* when an enterprise falls apart at scale and positive results fizzle. (The term "voltage drop" comes from the literature of implementation science and can be traced to the work of Amy Kilbourne and co-authors.) Voltage drops are what happens when the great electric charge of potential that drives people and organizations dissipates, leaving behind dashed hopes, not to mention squandered money, hard work, and time. And they are shockingly common. According to Straight Talk on Evidence, a venture created to monitor the validity of research across disciplines ranging from software development to medicine to education and beyond, between 50 and 90 percent of programs will lose voltage at scale.

The Voltage Effect is about the science of scaling: why some ideas fail while others change the world, and how to give every idea its best chance at success. Success and failure are not about luck. There is a rhyme and reason to why some ideas fail and why some make it big. Certain ideas are predictably scalable, while others are predictably unscalable. You will undoubtedly find much fortune and create impact if you choose to scale those ideas that are predictably scalable.

Most of us think that scalable ideas have some "silver bullet" feature: some quality that bestows a "can't miss" appeal. That kind of thinking is fundamentally wrong. There is no single quality that distinguishes ideas that have the potential to succeed at scale from those that don't. But there are five specific traits that scalable ideas must possess—the "key signatures" of ideas that scale, or what I call the Five Vital Signs. I call them Vital Signs because an assessment of the vitality of your idea is necessary before scaling, and I pinpoint five such vitals. A deficiency in any one can render an idea unscalable, even for the most ingenious among us. And no enterprise is immune to voltage drops—not successful companies like Uber, not the

U.S. government (or any government), and not well-meaning administrators like Greta and Mason, who make the all-too-common mistake of thinking that what works elsewhere works everywhere. The
consequences can be profound, which is why it is critical to guard
against voltage drops from first inspiration to launch, and even after
success.

But this book is not only about losses in voltage and how to avoid
them as you scale. The voltage effect goes both ways, which is why
I will also outline proven techniques for engineering *voltage gains at
scale*—types of incentives, cultural features, and economic principles
that will not only hold up at scale but allow your impact to multiply.
Ultimately, this book will offer a concrete, step-by-step guide for anyone who wants to cull bad ideas and scale great ones to their fullest
potential.

It should be clear why this is so important to me. I want Chicago
Heights Early Childhood Center and other initiatives like it to pass
the voltage test, bringing dramatic change on the largest possible
scale. I want innovative businesses to succeed and make our lives better and our economy stronger. I want government policies and programs to benefit all people equally, and cost taxpayers less. When
great ideas scale, we all win.

The evidence-based insights about scaling that I lay out in this
book are part of a new terrain that we are all charting together in the
twenty-first century. They are not only a product of a confluence of
research questions, business experiments, and urgent problems that
the world's smartest minds are trying to fix. The lessons about voltage gains and losses you will read about here are also the result of
the historical moment the entire human race is living through—the
age of big data. How we harness and use that data is up to us, but
one thing is clear: the vast quantities of data we are all able to collect
today on practically every type of human behavior, combined with
the computational capacity we now have to analyze it, can yield valuable insights for anyone attempting to scale their enterprise.

It is understandable that many people find the deep reach of big data disconcerting. It can feel like an invasion of privacy, especially with regard to the very serious concerns about what governments and companies can do with the data of their citizens and customers. But the innovations of big data also represent a seminal opportunity for humankind. Data-based insights into causes of death around the world, for example, have allowed us to scale new public health interventions that have improved the well-being and longevity of millions, perhaps even billions, of people. For the environment, big data can help to scale targeted programs to enhance household and firm-level energy conservation. Big data even reaches into our bedrooms. For example, roughly 10 percent of American women have fertility troubles. Biologically, tracking ovulation is one of the most effective ways for women to know when their body is ready to get pregnant. Big data is now used at scale to help women get pregnant by tracking critical fertility signs, and giving them the data they need to avoid costly, unnecessary trips to fertility treatment centers.

However, most people and organizations let data come to them—they make use of whatever data already exist. As a field experimenter using the world as my lab, I prefer to go out and generate data, leveraging partnerships with school systems, Fortune 500 companies, governments, nonprofits, and start-ups to try to learn the *whys* behind the data. Why do some people give to charity under certain conditions, while others don't? Why do some inner-city schools fail while others prosper? Why did one idea work at scale when another that was initially more promising failed? We can change the world by generating data to not only identify voltage gains and voltage losses but also understand why they occur.

The set of strategies you will learn in this book grow out of the marriage between big data and the economic way of thinking that has defined my research and my career. The book calls upon policymakers to move their attention from evidence-based policy to policy-based evidence. For entrepreneurs, *The Voltage Effect* lays out a set of scientific principles to guide decisions concerning which ideas have the best chance to scale.

The Living Lab

We all gain knowledge and wisdom over the course of our lives that we would like to share with others. So you can think of this book as my humble attempt at scaling the insights I have gained during my three decades as an economist. The core of these lessons emanates from a challenge. As we sat in a Market Street café a stone's throw from Uber headquarters in San Francisco, my wife, Dana Suskind, challenged me to produce science around scaling based on my previous experiences and past academic work. Never one to back down from a challenge, I accepted. But I knew that if I was going to succeed, I would need a few good partners. I chose Dana and my former PhD student and frequent co-author Omar Al-Ubaydli. In the past several years we have produced a series of academic articles on the science of scaling, complete with tedious math, plenty of Greek symbols, and obscure jargon. In this book, I've taken this new understanding and distilled it in a way that people everywhere can implement: from classrooms to boardrooms, nonprofit offices to research labs, the White House to your own house. In short, *The Voltage Effect* is for anyone who wants to increase the likelihood of their idea or enterprise succeeding.

This book is split into two parts. The first half will teach you that scaling is a fragile concept. It unpacks the Five Vital Signs, or the five key signature elements that will cause voltage drops and prevent an idea from taking off. The first is false positives—these are cases where there was never any voltage in the first place, though it appeared otherwise. The second is overestimating how big a slice of the pie your idea can capture. Often this is the result of failing to know your audience—or assuming that the small subset of people who have bought into your idea are more representative of the general population than they actually are, so that when you expand your idea it falls short for a broader set of people. The third is failing to evaluate whether your initial success depends on unscalable ingredients—unique circumstances that can't be replicated at scale. The fourth is when the implementation of your idea has unintended consequences, or spillovers, that backfire against that same idea. And the fifth is the "supply-side economics" of scaling—for instance, will your idea be too costly to sustain at scale? After you clear the hurdles of the Five Vital Signs, you will know you have an idea that scales.

The second part of the book is about how to produce voltage gains by adopting the practices necessary for maximum-impact scaling. It will unpack four proven techniques for increasing positive results at scale: using behavioral-economic incentives, such as the loss aversion principle, to create rapid gains; exploiting easily missed opportunities on the margins of your operation; knowing when to quit in the short term in order to win in the long term; and designing a high-voltage culture that is sustainable at scale.

Along the way, we will look closely at real-life stories that illustrate the lessons of the voltage effect. In the chapters ahead, you will gain a new perspective on how Theranos founder Elizabeth Holmes managed to defraud investors and deceive the public, why celebrity chef/ entrepreneur Jamie Oliver's restaurant empire collapsed, and why a well-intentioned campaign to improve automotive safety backfired after it reached a critical mass. I will tell you about behavioral nudges I designed to help the airline Virgin Atlantic save millions of dollars and the government of the Dominican Republic to collect $100 million more in taxes from its citizens. I will also relate the story of my time at Uber and give you my inside perspective on Travis Kalanick's downfall and what insights we can gain from it about building a scalable culture. And I'll tell you how I moved to Uber's rival, Lyft, where I gained other new data-based insights into scaling as Lyft's chief economist. These stories didn't play out in vitro—that is, in the lab. They are demonstrations of the science of scaling in vivo, with the world as my living laboratory.

The problems we face as individuals and as a global community in the twenty-first century are the direst and most far-reaching that humans have ever had to deal with. Which means we need innovations that work at scale if we are to solve those problems before it's too late. Whether you are a founder, an executive, a civil servant, a researcher, a concerned citizen, or a parent, you have ideas with the potential to scale positive change within your community, your company, your family, or society at large.

So let's begin turning up the voltage.

Part One

CAN YOUR IDEA SCALE?

DUPERS AND FALSE POSITIVES

On September 14, 1986, First Lady Nancy Reagan appeared on national television to address the nation from the West Sitting Hall of the White House. She sat on a sofa next to her husband, President Ronald Reagan, and gazed into the camera. "Today there's a drug and alcohol abuse epidemic in this country and no one is safe from it," she said. "Not you, not me, and certainly not our children."

This broadcast was the culmination of all the traveling the First Lady had done over the preceding five years to raise awareness among American youth about the dangers of drug use. She had become the public face of the preventative side of President Reagan's War on Drugs, and her message hinged on a catchphrase that millions of people still remember, which she employed once again that evening on television. "Not long ago, in Oakland, California," Nancy Reagan told viewers, "I was asked by a group of children what to do if they were offered drugs. And I answered, 'Just say no.'"

Although there are different accounts of where this infamous slogan originated—with an academic study, an advertising agency, or the First Lady herself—its "stickiness," to use the parlance of marketing, was undeniable. The phrase appeared on billboards, in pop songs, and on television shows; school clubs took it as a name. And in the popular imagination it became inseparable from what government and law enforcement officials saw as the crown jewel of the

Reagan-era drug prevention campaign: Drug Abuse Resistance Education, or D.A.R.E.

In 1983, Los Angeles chief of police Daryl Gates announced a shift in his department's approach to the War on Drugs: instead of busting kids in possession of illegal substances, the new focus would be on preventing those drugs from getting into their hands in the first place. This was how D.A.R.E., with its iconic logo of red letters set against a black background, was born.

D.A.R.E. was an educational program built on a theory from psychology called *social inoculation,* which took from epidemiology the concept of vaccination—administering a small dose of an infectious agent to induce immunity—and applied it to human behavior. The approach of the program was to bring uniformed officers into schools, where they would use role-playing and other educational techniques to inoculate kids against the temptations of drugs. It certainly sounded like a great idea, and the early research on D.A.R.E. was encouraging. As a result, the government opened its taxpayer-funded faucet, and soon the program was scaled up in middle schools and high schools across the country. Over the next twenty-four years, 43 million children from over forty countries would graduate from D.A.R.E.

There was only one problem: D.A.R.E. didn't actually work.

In the decades since Nancy Reagan urged the nation's youth to "just say no" to drugs, numerous studies have demonstrated that D.A.R.E. did not in fact persuade kids to just say no. It provided children with a great deal of information about drugs such as marijuana and alcohol, but it failed to produce statistically significant reductions in drug use when these same kids were presented with opportunities to use them. One study even found that the program *spurred* participants' curiosity about drugs and increased the likelihood of experimentation.

It is hard to overstate the cost of D.A.R.E.'s voltage drop at scale. For years, the program consumed the time and effort of thousands of teachers and law enforcement officers who were deeply invested in the well-being of our greatest natural resource: future generations.

Yet all of this hard work and time, never mind taxpayer dollars, was wasted on scaling D.A.R.E. because of a fundamentally erroneous premise. Worse, it diverted support and resources away from other initiatives that might have yielded real results. Why D.A.R.E. became the disaster that it did is a textbook example of the first pitfall everyone hoping to scale an idea or enterprise must avoid: a *false positive*.

The Truth About False Positives

A first truth about false positives is that they can be considered as "lies," or "false alarms." At the most basic level, a false positive occurs when you interpret some piece of evidence or data as proof that something is true when in fact it isn't. For example, when I visited a high-tech plant in China that produced headsets, if a headset working properly got marked as defective due to human error, that was a false positive. When I was called for jury duty, a false positive would have occurred had we determined that an innocent suspect was guilty. False positives also show up in medicine, a phenomenon that gained attention during the Covid-19 pandemic, when some test results for the virus turned out to be unreliable, showing people had contracted the virus when in reality they had not. Unfortunately, false positives are ubiquitous across contexts; consider a 2005 study that found that between 94 and 99 percent of burglar-alarm calls turn out to be false alarms, and that false alarms make up between 10 and 20 percent of all calls to police.

In the case of D.A.R.E., the National Institute of Justice's 1985 assessment involving 1,777 children in Honolulu, Hawaii, found evidence "favoring the program's preventative potential," and a subsequent study conducted soon after in Los Angeles among nearly as many students also concluded that D.A.R.E. led to a reduction in drug experimentation. These purportedly strong results drove schools, police departments, and the federal government to just say yes to expanding D.A.R.E. nationwide. Yet numerous scientific analyses over the following decade examining all of the known studies and data on the program yielded incontrovertible proof that D.A.R.E. *didn't* actually have a meaningful impact. So what happened?

The simple answer is this: it is not uncommon for data to "lie." In the Honolulu study, for example, the researchers had calculated that there was a 2 percent chance their data would yield a false positive. Unfortunately, subsequent research shows that either they underestimated that probability or they just, unfortunately, fell within that 2 percent. There was never any voltage in D.A.R.E.

How can something like this happen in the hallowed halls of science? First, I should clarify that when I say the data are "lying," what I'm actually referring to is "statistical error." For example, when you draw a sample of children from a certain population (i.e., children living in a single city in Hawaii), random differences among them might produce an "outlier group" that leads you to make a false conclusion. Had the researchers gone back to the original population of children in Honolulu and tested D.A.R.E. again with a new group of students, they would have likely found the program didn't work. (A related kind of inference problem is when the results from one group don't generalize to another; we take up this issue in Chapter 2.) Unfortunately, statistical failures of this sort happen all the time.

As we saw with D.A.R.E., false positives can be very costly because they lead to misinformed decisions with downstream consequences—time and money that would have been better invested elsewhere. This is especially true when the "lie" or error is missed early on, causing enterprises that were never actually successful to begin with to suffer an inevitable voltage drop at scale. In other words, eventually the truth will come out, as it did for D.A.R.E. when its critics produced overwhelming empirical evidence that the program didn't work. I have witnessed this firsthand in my own work in the business world.

In 2006, the newly christened CEO of Chrysler, Thomas LaSorda, was working tirelessly to try to save his company from bankruptcy. He reached out to me and two of my University of Chicago colleagues, Steve Levitt and Chad Syverson, to see if we had any ideas for how to increase profits, so we invited him and four top Chrysler executives to Chicago to meet. One idea that came out of our sit-down was to implement a wellness program. This might seem like an odd recommendation for a struggling auto manufacturer striving for a bigger slice of the pie in the marketplace, but improving the bottom line isn't always about sales.

Chrysler had an absenteeism problem. As a result, they were hemorrhaging money maintaining a "bullpen" of available work-ers to take the place on the assembly line of employees who called in sick on a given day. This might seem like a trivial expense for one of the world's biggest automakers, but in fact, a roughly 10 percent absenteeism rate cost them millions of dollars annually in these bull-pen wages. Moreover, when we examined defect rates from Chrys-ler's Sterling Heights plant, we found that over a three-year period a 5 percent reduction in absenteeism had decreased product defects by around five hundred per month! Beyond the absenteeism challenges, the company also struggled with high healthcare costs and "presen-teeism" (employees underperforming because of health conditions). Studies suggested that employee wellness programs could address these intertwined problems, so LaSorda believed—and I hoped—that instituting one grounded in the principles of behavioral economics would help Chrysler, too.

A company called Staywell Health Management, which handled programs and services relating to employee health and productiv-ity at Chrysler, agreed to partner with us on a pilot study: a seven-month intervention we called ANewHealthyLife. Conducted at one of Chrysler's thirty-one factories, the initiative used financial incentives (meaning we paid people) to get employees to engage in healthy activities. Initial results were promising. People in our well-ness program engaged in a greater number of healthy behaviors, had lower medical expenditures, and were absent at work less compared to employees who did not participate in the program. In short, our experiment appeared to have saved Chrysler a lot of money in a fairly short amount of time. LaSorda was impressed enough to commit resources for an expansion of the program across the remaining thirty plants.

Although my team and I were pleased with our results, we were more cautious. During my many years of conducting fieldwork and reviewing the research of others, I had seen my share of false positives. We argued that, since the evidence was just from one sample of workers from one plant, we should run one more pilot study before fully rolling it out. The company agreed, and we tried the same program with a new sample of workers from that same plant. This time the results were less thrilling. The employees who participated in the health initiative had no better outcomes than those who didn't across *all* of the main outcome metrics important to Chrysler: absenteeism, presenteeism, healthcare costs, et cetera. Uh-oh. It seemed the initial results were a statistical blip—a false positive.

In other words, the initial data seemed to be lying.

Just to make sure, we ran the program at two additional plants; twice more, our intervention didn't have an impact. The wellness program was just not as effective as the trial run's data had suggested. LaSorda was understandably disappointed, though not as disappointed as he would have been had Chrysler paid Staywell to scale up our intervention across all thirty-one of the company's plants. Detecting the false positive early on allowed us to pivot to a different wellness program that did end up proving effective.

The whole episode was a powerful reminder that when you draw a sample of people for a study, you must understand that it is just that: a sample. And samples are sometimes not representative of an entire population, meaning that sometimes the results you get from your sample will not be true for the entire population. In this case, it turned out that the employees who participated in the first pilot at Chrysler were not representative of all the employees at that plant, much less at all of the other plants. So while the early data appeared solid, clearly they did not tell the full truth.

The fact that statistical errors—like false positives—can occur even in well-designed research studies can be unsettling, especially for those of us (myself included) who see science as a bastion of truth. Yet remember what Winston Churchill once said about democracy: it's the worst form of government, except for all the others. Similarly, the scientific method is the "least worst" method we have for testing and refining important ideas. And as we will see later in this chapter, there is a method for avoiding the kinds of landmines in your data that prevent an idea from scaling.

Statistical errors, however, are only one of the reasons false positives can be found across so many domains. Another main culprit is biases hidden in the human mind.

Confirmation Bias, the Bandwagon Effect, and the Winner's Curse

In 1974, the psychologists Daniel Kahneman and Amos Tversky published an academic paper titled "Judgment Under Uncertainty: Heuristics and Biases." If you ever need a counterexample to the argument that good ideas will fail to catch on without good branding, this is it. In spite of the article's unsexy title—par for the course in academia—Kahneman and Tversky essentially launched a new field with its publication: the study of cognitive biases. With a series of ingenious experiments, they uncovered a constellation of hidden weaknesses in human judgment that steer us away from rational decision-making.

Cognitive biases are distinct from computational errors and other errors that result from misinformation. Mistakes that people make due to misinformation can be corrected by simply providing more accurate information, but cognitive biases are "hardwired" in the brain, which makes them difficult to change and impervious to correction, since the mind's faulty interpretation of accurate information is precisely the problem. Kahneman and Tversky's landmark collaboration has since been chronicled in multiple books—for instance, Kahneman's *Thinking, Fast and Slow,* Dan Ariely's *Predictably Irrational,* and Michael Lewis's *The Undoing Project*—and some of the cognitive biases they studied have even found their way into the cultural lexicon. One of these is called *confirmation bias,* and it helps to explain why innocent yet avoidable false positives frequently occur.

In the most basic sense, confirmation bias prevents us from seeing possibilities that might challenge our assumptions, and it leads us to gather, interpret, and recall information in a way that conforms to our previously existing beliefs. The reason we have this trapdoor in our thinking is that when individuals are presented with information, their brains are already filled with vast quantities of previously obtained information, social context, and history that project meaning onto the new information. Because we have limited brainpower to process all of this, we use mental shortcuts to make quick, often gut-level decisions. One such mental shortcut is to essentially filter out or ignore the information that is inconsistent with our expectations or assumptions. This is because science has taught us that reconciling new, contradictory information requires more mental energy than processing new information that is consistent with what's already in our heads, and our brains prefer the easier route.

This tendency might appear counter to our own interests, but in the context of our species's long-ago Darwinian history, confirmation bias makes perfect sense. Our brain evolved to reduce uncertainty and streamline our responses. For our ancestors, a shadow might have meant a predator, so if they assumed it was one and started running, this assumption could have saved their lives. If they stopped to gather more information and really think about it, they might have ended up as dinner.

While confirmation bias was useful for our species in the distant past and continues to be helpful in certain scenarios, for endeavors that require deep analysis and slow deliberation—like testing an innovative idea we hope to scale—it can be troublesome. It can hamper creativity and critical thinking, which are the pillars of both innovation and high-quality work. It can cause doctors to make lazy diagnoses and pursue the wrong treatment. It can drive policymakers, business leaders, administrators, and investors to pour massive amounts of resources into the wrong initiative or venture. And when it comes to interpreting information, whether in business or science, it can produce false positives.

The British psychologist Peter Wason's classic Rule Discovery Test from the 1960s illustrates confirmation bias in action. He gave subjects three numbers and asked them to come up with the rule that applied to the selection of those numbers. Given the sequence 2, 4, 6, for example, they typically formed a hypothesis that the rule was even numbers. Then the participants would present other sequences of even numbers, and researchers would tell them whether or not those numbers conformed to the rule. Through this process, participants were tasked with determining whether their hypothesis was correct. After several correct tries the participants believed that they had discovered the rule. But in fact they hadn't, because the rule was much simpler: increasing numbers.

The most interesting aspect of this study (and the many others like it) is that almost all subjects only tested number sequences that conformed to their personal hypothesis, and very few tried a number sequence that might *disprove* their hypothesis. Wason's experiment demonstrated that most people, regardless of intelligence, fail to examine their hypotheses critically. Instead, they try only to confirm them by "fast thinking," using quick heuristics, or mental shortcuts.

Another mental shortcut that has a knack for producing false positives is *bandwagon bias*. Also known as "herding" or "cascades," the bandwagon effect arises from social influences on our mental processes. Like confirmation biases, bandwagon bias interferes with our ability to accurately recall and evaluate information. But in this case, we are under the unconscious sway of the views and behaviors of others—the social side of decision-making. In 1951, the pioneering social psychologist Solomon Asch developed a now-famous laboratory experiment that can help us understand this kind of groupthink. He recruited students to participate in what they thought was a vision experiment. These students joined several other supposed participants—who were in fact experimental confederates, or scientists masquerading as participants—in a classroom.

Everyone in the room was shown a picture with three lines of varying lengths, in which one line was very obviously longer than others. Each person in the room was asked to state out loud which was the longest line. After the early confederates all identified the wrong line, more than a third of the participants, on average, went along with the clearly incorrect answer; over the course of twelve trials a whopping 75 percent went along with the obviously wrong answer in at least one instance. In contrast, when no confederates were present to tempt them to hop on their bandwagon, virtually all subjects chose the correct answer—demonstrating just how easily our independent judgment can be subsumed by our desire to "fit in" or be "one of the pack." Not only is this a disturbing blow to one's self-image as a freethinking individual, it also has unsettling implications for the science of scaling.

If you look at the bandwagon effect from the perspective of marketers, whose mandate is to create demand for products at scale, this quirk of the human mind is a godsend: the desire to conform that drives so many of our thoughts and actions can be converted into dollar signs. Indeed, there are mountains of research showing how the bandwagon effect shapes consumer choices, such as the clothing we buy (ever wonder why different colors and styles come into fashion every year?), the toys children ask their parents for (remember Tickle Me Elmo? For your sake I hope you don't), and the sports teams we root for and whose apparel we purchase (the top-selling basketball jerseys in the United States historically correspond to the star players of teams that make it to the NBA finals in any given year). The bandwagon effect—or social contagion, as it is sometimes called—can even influence our political leanings, and thus electoral results. While this is all well and good for marketers and strategists hired to nudge people toward certain choices over others, for those creating and launching innovations to benefit society, it can create false positives and lead to the scaling of bad ideas.

Bandwagon bias can lead to voltage drops at scale because it has the potential to relegate the selection of ideas to a few individuals rather than an entire team of freethinkers. In my own experiences, whether at a PTA meeting, a meeting in the West Wing, or a meeting in a boardroom, the exact same song and dance play out nearly every time. The leader, who usually is the most passionate, strong-willed person present, tends to talk first and loudest, setting the agenda, dominating the subsequent conversation, and influencing everyone else's opinions and decisions, either implicitly or explicitly. After all, we tend to want to align ourselves with the person who makes promotion and salary-raise decisions, though there doesn't need to be a power dynamic for the bandwagon bias to shape the dialogue—it can kick in anytime anyone makes their preferences known early on. So when an idea or intervention is vocally championed by a trusted or influential source (who isn't necessarily an expert and may have their own agenda), it can result in others jumping on board. In cases like these, what seems like an honest consensus is in fact a false positive, in that any number of people in the room might have opposed the idea were it not for their desire to conform with views expressed by others. The next thing you know, the group has voted to scale a bad idea, or to scale too soon, before additional research can be done. All of which could have been avoided had the leader instead listened carefully to others, understood that implicitly forcing a consensus is not the same as building a consensus, and been wary of bandwagon bias.

Recall how, in the case of D.A.R.E., the National Institute of Justice's favorable assessment in 1986 of the program's efficacy turned out to be a false positive, but this wasn't widely accepted until long after the program had been scaled nationwide. By then, D.A.R.E. already had a network of influential figures on its bandwagon: everyone from police chiefs to educators to community leaders to Nancy Reagan (certainly no expert, but trusted by millions of people), whose "Just say no" campaign had essentially gone viral. Moreover, by this point D.A.R.E. had also received generous funding, another form of social signaling that can help a dud of an idea be perceived as a seemingly scalable one.

The point here is that when bad ideas are endorsed by influential people and institutions, they can be contagious. And once a critical mass has climbed aboard that bandwagon, confirmation bias makes it much harder to convince people to change their now entrenched beliefs. This is why it took many years, and many misspent millions, for D.A.R.E. to abandon its flawed approach.

This unfortunate pattern can play out everywhere from education (e.g., the adoption of trendy but ineffective new curricular programs) to medicine (e.g., the widespread acceptance of medical procedures with dubious efficacy) and beyond. In all of these cases, bandwagon bias likely not only resulted in social and economic harm but also hijacked funding from programs or ideas that would have been more beneficial. Generations of people were robbed of ideas that might have worked.

There is one last set of hidden behavioral tics that often sabotage scaling: the *winner's curse* combined with the *sunk cost fallacy* (the latter of which we'll explore in depth in Chapter 7). As background, think of yourself as a private equity firm considering a purchase of a new company. You and several other companies enter into a bidding war; the highest bidder will win and be required to buy the company for that amount. Would you be tempted to bid more than the company is worth to ensure you come out on top?

I have simulated this scenario in a classroom experiment, only instead of a company, students bid on a jar full of coins. After everyone had written down their bids, I announced the winner—let's call him Eli—who had emerged as the high bidder at $25. I said, "Congratulations, Eli, you've just won all the coins in the jar for twenty-five bucks! How do you feel?"

"I feel pretty good," Eli said. Yet after we counted the change and learned that the jar contained just under $10 in coins, Eli no longer felt quite so good.

I have conducted this exercise for over a decade, and every single time students dramatically overpay, just like Eli did. This is because when everyone is guessing the value, some will inevitably guess too low and some too high. Since the highest bidder wins and has to pay up, the "winner" is guaranteed to lose money.

This is a classic example of the winner's curse. It happens all the time in just about every scenario that involves competitive bidding—venture capitalists vying for the chance to invest in a hot new app, Hollywood producers aggressively going after a buzzed-about screenplay, art collectors bidding for a Basquiat painting, you bidding on eBay, and so on. These are just a few examples illustrating a broader phenomenon: anytime there is competition over an asset of uncertain value, the party who wins the auction (or buys the idea, hires the worker, et cetera) oftentimes pays more than the asset is actually worth.

Seemingly scalable ideas are like that jar of coins. We overpay to get something off the ground, and later, when we find out that the idea really isn't very good, we ignore that truth and continue to scale because of cost bias: we don't want to admit we have just invested in a loser. Throwing good money at a bad endeavor, however, doesn't make a problem go away. It just compounds your losses. When you find yourself in such situations, the only time you should be comfortable being the highest bidder is if you have the secret sauce for making that idea great, or what economists call a "comparative advantage." This could come in the form of a patented technology that is necessary to scale an idea, ownership of a key resource necessary to operate at scale, or even personal expertise that will allow you to scale up that idea more quickly than competitors. Only then can you skirt the winner's curse, because you are winning by winning.

Whether it's due to statistical errors or errors in human judgment, the belief that an idea is more scalable than it actually is will almost always result in overspending and sunk costs. Fortunately, there is a method that can protect against these kinds of false positives. And we owe this method to, of all things, a cup of tea that changed the history of science.

The Revolution of Replication

In the early 1920s, a young, brilliant, and headstrong statistician named Ronald Fisher was working at the Rothamsted Experimental Station, an agricultural research center thirty miles north of London. One of his coworkers there was a brilliant biologist specializing in algae named Muriel Bristol. During afternoon teatime one day, Fisher made Bristol a cup of tea that she promptly refused. When he asked why, she explained that he had poured milk into the cup before the tea, and she liked the flavor better when the milk came second.

Fisher scoffed at the idea that the order in which the tea and milk were poured could make a difference in the flavor. It didn't make sense to him scientifically, since the molecular makeup of the final liquid would end up the same regardless. But Bristol doubled down, claiming that she could tell the difference between a cup of tea with the milk poured first versus one with the milk poured second. One of their colleagues, a chemist named William Roach, suggested that the three of them conduct an experiment to see who was right. With that, the stage was set for this epic showdown.

They ran the experiment in a very simple way: Bristol tasted eight cups of tea, four with milk poured first and four with tea poured first, in an order unknown to her. Then came the moment of truth. What happened?

She correctly guessed all eight.

Fisher was stunned. Bristol was vindicated. If they had been gun-slingers in the Wild West instead of prim scientists in England, she would have blown the smoke from her gun's barrel.

The important scientific breakthrough that came out of this encounter had nothing to do with milk and tea, however (though it would later be shown that milk globules *do* respond differently and produce subtly different flavors depending on whether tea is poured onto milk or the other way around). Its lasting legacy was this: in designing the eight-cups-of-tea test, Fisher realized that there was a real science to scientific experiments, and soon after, he set out to study it. (Well, that's not entirely true. As with any tale worth telling, there was also a love story here—William Roach and Muriel Bristol would end up getting married!)

In 1925, Fisher published the book *Statistical Methods for Research Workers,* and a decade later he published *The Design of Experiments,* both of which were regarded as groundbreaking and both of which became foundational texts. One of the key pillars of experimental design he established was *replication:* the idea that the act of repeating a test would increase the reliability of its results (which is exactly what Bristol did in the "lady tasting tea" experiment, as Fisher named it, by trying not two cups of tea but eight). By creating a larger data set, a researcher reduces the likelihood of variability, or statistical error, in the results. Indeed, galled by losing the tea argument, Fisher determined that they should have had Bristol taste *more* cups of tea to ensure that her correct guesses weren't a fluke. Put another way, he believed that the more the experiment was repeated, the lower the likelihood of ending up with a false positive.

But replication cannot in and of itself protect against false positives. You have to take the concept of replication one step further and seek an *independent* replication of your result. That is, a person or team with no vested interest in your success must test your idea to see if it replicates. This is precisely what *didn't* happen until much too late with the National Institute of Justice's report on D.A.R.E. Yet it is similar to what my team did do with the wellness program we created for Chrysler. If instead of replicating we had scaled a full rollout based on the hidden false positive, the company would have lost a lot of money, not to mention I would have lost my credibility. In this case, we caught the error without an independent replication, since we were motivated to doubt ourselves—if Chrysler had scaled the program and it failed, it would have hurt our reputations.

In order to replicate effectively, you must conduct the same successful study, program, or product test again with the same type of population, and ideally you must do so three or four times before you can be confident you have the truth. In some cases this might not be feasible, but my overarching point is that in those instances you should tread with caution rather than "move fast and break things." Otherwise you will soon be broke yourself.

This principle holds true beyond the realms of scientific research. We actually use the same basic approach all the time in our daily lives. Consider dating. At a party you briefly meet someone and feel a connection, and you consider going on a date. But you wonder: was the great rapport real, or—come to think of it—did the drinks you had at the party make the conversation seem better than it really was? Maybe the other person's jokes and stories (or your own) will lose sparkle after a few dates. There's one way to find out: only by spending more time with them will you know if you're truly compatible. This goes for trying out new restaurants, new apps, new hobbies, and so on; we know instinctively that one good experience could be a false positive, but three or four good experiences provide reliable data. In other words, replication is baked into human behavior.

Consider another real-life scenario in which a lot more is at stake. You go to the doctor and get a chest X-ray that reveals what appears to be a cancerous lesion in the upper lobe of your left lung. Uh-oh, big trouble. At this point, you can have your lung removed or you can see a pulmonologist, who will offer a second opinion, take a biopsy, and collect additional data to determine whether such a dramatic surgery should be performed. This "replication" might find the lesion to be just a harmless inflammation and the cancer diagnosis a false positive.

When it comes to matters of health, one could argue that getting a third or even fourth opinion might be warranted. If that suggestion sounds outrageous, consider an explosive study conducted by researchers at Johns Hopkins Medicine in 2016, which estimated that more than 250,000 Americans die each year from medical errors, making such errors the third-leading cause of death behind heart disease and cancer!

For businesses, false positives are usually easier to detect than in the world of medicine, simply by testing a product or feature out on a sample set of customers. For instance, when Lyft wants to test a new feature, they simply build it into the app and make it available to users, usually in just two or three markets to start. This gives my team ample data to analyze in order to determine if the new feature is worth scaling or not.

At the intersection of scientific research and public policy, however, garnering such data is trickier due to a lack of funding for independent replications and slow-moving assessments. Several years ago, a small pilot study of an educational enhancement program for children in Florida, Collaborative Strategic Reading, appeared to increase uptake of reading. It was scaled quickly elsewhere, only to fail miserably: in a series of tests in five different districts in Oklahoma and Texas, the program showed no discernible effect on reading and comprehension. A great deal of money would have been saved had they simply tested the program on a few groups of students in Oklahoma and Texas *before* scaling. Sure, it will take longer to get to the point where such programs can be widely implemented, but this might not be a bad thing.

In science, the practice of replication has become a hot-button issue, leading to what the media outlets are fond of calling the "replication crisis." Since the 2010s, researchers have set out to replicate several high-profile experiments—especially in psychology—that made splashes in major newspapers and on television, and found that the results failed to replicate. This emerging pattern even spurred one psychologist to organize an effort to replicate a hundred experiments whose results had appeared in prestigious academic journals. Shockingly—or perhaps not, considering what we have learned about false positives—only thirty-nine of the one hundred experiments produced the results reported in the published study. The replication crisis has, unsurprisingly, led to a credibility crisis, which scientists are working hard to address. I myself am involved in an effort to rectify what is known as the "file drawer problem"—the phenomenon of studies that failed to produce the desired results being relegated to the proverbial file drawer rather than being published. This is a problem, of course, because even such failures—or *especially* such failures—contribute to the ever-growing body of scientific knowledge, from which everyone benefits (that is, everyone except the researchers whose hypotheses fail, which explains why the results stay in the drawer). Replication is the key to making sure we learn from these failures, rather than waste time and resources pursuing ideas on the basis of faulty science.

As we have seen throughout this chapter, false positives are in most cases perfectly innocent, stemming from statistical errors or from the numerous cognitive biases that shape our perceptions and behaviors. But there is also a darker side.

This is where false positives cross into the realm of duplicity—another enemy of scaling and a problem that blights the noble intentions of science, while also wiping out billions of dollars for businesses and investors.

The Duper Effect

Brian Wansink was a rock star.

To the extent that a behavioral scientist ever attains mainstream cultural relevance, he was like the Mick Jagger of the food psychology world. As the director of Cornell University's prestigious Food and Brand Lab, he commanded attention both inside and outside academia thanks to his groundbreaking research on the intersection of environment, food consumption, and buying patterns. Over the years, he published a string of stunning findings demonstrating, for instance, that grocery shopping while hungry causes you to buy high-calorie items, that eating from a bigger bowl leads you to eat more, and that the classic cookbook *The Joy of Cooking* offered progressively less healthy recipes over the course of its many editions. Discoveries such as these, which garnered giddy coverage in the press, endowed him with authority and influence that stretched from the federal government to the corporate world. He helped the United States government issue new dietary guidelines, he consulted for Google and the

American military, and he published several popular books. People in positions of power trusted Wansink, so they invested resources to scale his ideas.

Then came the twist. It turned out that for years, Wansink had been falsifying results. His seemingly supernova career was built on corrupt science.

As of this writing, nineteen of Wansink's studies have been retracted, while dozens more are under review. In 2018, the *Journal of the American Medical Association* retracted no fewer than six of his studies in a single day. Even as Wansink defended his work, more and more evidence disproving the validity of his research continued to mount. Cornell launched an investigation, culminating in a damning press release stating that Wansink had engaged in academic misconduct, including "data falsification, a failure to assure data accuracy and integrity . . . inappropriate research methods, [and] failure to obtain necessary research approvals." In 2019, Wansink left Cornell and academia. His star had imploded.

Unfortunately, such behavior is more common than you might think. I wrote about this several years ago in an article titled "Academic Economists Behaving Badly? A Survey on Three Areas of Unethical Behavior." Using a randomized response survey technique (which is used when trying to obtain the truth pertaining to a sensitive issue), colleagues and I asked a thousand academic economists various questions about ethical behaviors. Shockingly, nearly 5 percent of respondents answered affirmatively to the simple question "Have you ever falsified research data?" In other words, 5 percent of respondents were in effect admitting to being what my friend Antonio Gracias, former chairman of the board of Tesla and founder of the billion-dollar investment firm Valor Equity Partners, calls a "duper"—a person who deliberately lies or misrepresents information to produce a false positive or to get what they want.

As an economist who studies incentives, I was interested in the question of what motivates people like Wansink to engage in such behavior, which was at best bad-faith science and at worst outright deceit. What could compel someone to risk their reputation and professional future in this way? The answer: the way the incentives are structured.

In academia, you only climb the ranks, get tapped to run a lab, and secure large grants (which usually increase your salary, and potentially your speaking fee) if you publish your research in marquee journals. And what gets you into those top journals? Fresh, exciting findings, and all the better if they're media-friendly. So when Wansink took shortcuts and even engaged in outright deception, he was in effect responding to the incentives built into academia. Of course, most top-tier scientists who reach Wansink's level of success do so through legitimate research, innovation, and elbow grease, but they're motivated by the same rewards. When you think about it this way, it's easy to see how someone could be tempted to try to give themselves a leg up by employing an approach that shows little respect for science and its ethical code.

The incentives to lie or cheat are even greater in business, especially in our world of inflated IPOs that turn struggling founders into millionaires or even billionaires overnight. A dramatic example is Elizabeth Holmes, one of the most notorious dupers of the twenty-first century. Her company, Theranos, raised over $700 million from investors and was valued at $9 billion thanks to its breakthrough blood-testing technology that was supposedly poised to revolutionize the practice of medicine around the planet. Of course, we now know that Theranos was in fact a ticking time bomb: its much-ballyhooed technology didn't actually exist. Once it became clear that the portable blood analyzer the company had raised billions of dollars to build was a dud, Holmes began faking it, by using machines made by other companies. Naturally, it was impossible for Theranos to scale its nonexistent technology, leading to one of the most severe and infamous voltage drops in business history!

Holmes's story is fascinating for a variety of reasons. First, it highlights a vulnerability at the heart of many high-risk investment ventures: people are betting on the person with the idea as much as on the idea itself. This was especially true in the case of Theranos's "moonshot" technology that "required" years of "research and development." In the absence of a market-ready product whose success could be measured, Theranos investors relied on *social proof* rather than hard data.

Holmes was smart and charismatic, allowing her to win over investors, who then vouched for her to other investors, leading to a bandwagon effect. Moreover, thanks to confirmation bias, investors with a financial stake in the company likely overlooked signs that ran counter to their expectation that the company would be a massive success. And these weren't people born yesterday—they included business titans like Rupert Murdoch, Carlos Slim, and Larry Ellison.

Could this debacle have been avoided? Or are some people simply bad actors whose duplicitous behavior can't be prevented? The answer comes down to incentives. Thanks to her stock options, Elizabeth Holmes had the most to gain from Theranos's success and would do anything for success. At one point those options were valued at over $4 billion! In other words, she had 4 billion incentives to pull off a win with the technology. But when it became increasingly clear that the promise of the company was unattainable—that the basic premise of this revolutionary blood-testing technology remained fictitious—the long-term incentive of financial success gave way to the short-term one of hiding the truth to put off the inevitable disaster. She was highly motivated to keep the plane in the air with new fuel (money) rather than making sure it could actually stay aloft with a real product and business plan. But fuel was not infinite, making a crash unavoidable.

But could it perhaps have been avoided if there had been incentives in place that encouraged other people in the company to notice—and speak up about—signs that something was amiss? Will employees possibly face repercussions if they surface information that runs counter to the desires of their superiors, as was the case at Theranos for employees who were attacked for raising red flags about problems inside the company, then threatened with lawsuits for speaking out publicly? If so, they may consciously or unconsciously alter their reports to protect themselves. But what if there were rewards, or at least a contractual guarantee barring punishment, for sharing data that challenged the company's assumptions or hopes? Then they would be incentivized to report the truth, which will eventually come to light one way or another. Theranos would have collapsed sooner and less disastrously had the company operated in this fashion.

The more general question of incentives for employees is a crucial issue for scaling up any product and initiative. When I was at Uber, if a manager had an idea that he or she thought had the potential to benefit the company, guess who was in charge of testing the idea? That same manager! Guess how people were promoted at Uber? By putting forth product ideas that were shipped!

Of course, showing data in a way that highlights the strengths of an idea or downplays the weaknesses is much different from knowingly falsifying data, but the solution to both is the same: independent replication, which is just as crucial for businesses as it is for scientists. If someone has an idea, it should be someone *else* with no stake in the idea and who doesn't stand to benefit financially who should test it out, or at least replicate it before it is shipped. Otherwise, incentives potentially conflict with full honesty.

So the best way to protect yourself from dupers is by keeping incentives top of mind. For example, someone thinking about buying a company should consider if the seller wants to stay involved or not. If the seller is planning to keep a stake in the company, they are incentivized to act in the company's best interests. If they don't want to keep a stake when they sell, this may be because they know negative things about the research, product, or market that you don't. Only they know how good the data truly are. I once conducted an experiment simulating this scenario with a group of MBAs playing the role of entrepreneurs with an idea to sell, but only they had the data indicating whether or not the idea was scalable. They were then presented with various deals from which they could choose. In one case the entrepreneur received immediate payment and went on their way. In others the entrepreneur's payment would depend on how well the product actually performed when it went to market (this is a form of "sharing profit flow," in the parlance of economics). As one would expect, the entrepreneurs who knew they had a losing proposition on their hands tended not to choose this strategy. Instead, they tended to opt for immediate payment, offloaded the idea, and washed their hands of it. They sold their (unscalable) idea at a handsome profit.

A general lesson is that beyond selling an idea, companies should engage in more profit-sharing with their employees, especially in those cases where their employees make key scaling and purchase decisions. Outside of the start-up world, this is rare, but there are many cases where linking compensation to some metric of future performance (for example, buyers at a retail chain or acquisitions editors at publishing houses having their compensation linked to sales of the products or books they choose) more accurately aligns incentives within organizations and will lead to fewer scaling errors.

Second, if you're in a leadership position, you should also incentivize your staff to be "bias disruptors." As we have seen, organizations don't always incentivize employees to speak the truth, and in many cases the person who comes up with an idea is also the sole tester of the idea. This speaks more broadly to the need for every business and organization to have a devil's advocate deputy, team, and/or function built into its structure—in other words, a force that is always pushing for more data, more proof. A truly good, scalable idea will hold up even under the closest scrutiny.

*   *   *

BY NOW I hope it's clear that the most hazardous obstacle to successful scaling is not ignorance. It is the illusion of knowledge, arising from either misleading data, hidden biases, or outright deception. Luckily, as we've seen, these hurdles are all surmountable. Yet even solid data that have been independently replicated, trustworthy people, and the right incentives do not guarantee that an enterprise or idea will scale.

Even if your idea has proven itself among certain groups, it doesn't necessarily mean those results will hold up for the general public. Are those who gain from your idea or product representative of a large enough group to merit scaling? The answer to this question can make or break your enterprise.

KNOW YOUR AUDIENCE

I n the spring of 2018, nearly two years after my interview in San Francisco, I left Uber to work for its ride-sharing rival Lyft. A strange quirk in California labor laws allowed me to do so without much time on the sidelines: I left Uber on a Friday, took the weekend off, then started at Lyft the following Monday as their chief economist.

Travis Kalanick himself had left Uber the previous summer amid a string of scandals (more on this in Chapter 9), and after witnessing the near-implosion of the company, I was ready for a change. I wanted to either retreat back to the relative calm of the academic world or pursue a different kind of Silicon Valley experience. That was when I was introduced to Lyft's cofounder and CEO, Logan Green.

A pensive introvert with a playful sense of humor—hence Lyft's trademark pink "carstache" that graced the fronts of its drivers' cars for several years—Logan is cut from a different cloth than Travis. I noted this within the first ten seconds of meeting him in person, when he shook my hand, began asking me questions about myself, and quietly waited for me to finish each of my answers. Yet Logan and Travis did share the same missionary zeal for changing the face of urban transportation.

A native of Los Angeles (just like Travis, as it happens—surely no coincidence), Logan had grown up sitting in bumper-to-bumper traffic, gazing into the windows of cars with miserable-looking people trapped inside. The drivers were paying hefty sums for gas and insurance, not to mention the cars themselves, and for what? To waste time and pollute the environment! It didn't make any sense to him. He wondered if there couldn't be another way of doing things: one that structured cities around people rather than around cars. After finishing college, Logan came up with an answer: a ride-share company that functioned as a kind of matchmaker for people looking to carpool long distances securely. So in 2007, two years before the founding of Uber, Green and his friend John Zimmer founded Zimride, the company that would soon be rebranded as Lyft.

As with most Silicon Valley companies, Lyft's approach to scaling was data-driven, so I felt right at home, just as I had initially at Uber. Equally important, Lyft had a positive work culture that reflected Logan's genuine desire to improve customers' lives. But the company still had to jockey for position in the marketplace and turn a profit, which was no easy feat with a competitor as aggressive and effective as Uber, even with Travis Kalanick no longer at its helm. When I joined Lyft, Logan was in search of a breakthrough innovation that would allow it to more quickly scale. And in late 2018, about six months after I jumped ship to Lyft, Logan felt he had found the golden ticket that would lock in more customers by providing special benefits: a membership program.

Logan had arrived at this idea in part because he understood the power of the loyal consumer. And as a devoted member of Costco, he saw how these consumers are more than willing to pay for membership in order to gain access to the bulk quantities, low prices, and large selection of supermarket and department store products that differentiate Costco from its "big box" competitors. Logan admired Costco's highly profitable model—in 2018, for instance, its net earnings would top $3 billion—as well as their customer experience, which he himself enjoyed. He didn't want to make membership a requirement at Lyft, but he believed it had great potential as an option for habitual riders and/or passengers who liked the idea of getting special access to bonus services.

Such models aren't at all rare in the transportation industry. Many businesses around the world, ranging from airlines to gas stations to railway companies, offer paid memberships in exchange for perks such as upgrades, discounts, and add-ons (like the cushy, exclusive waiting lounges at airports). Logan thought that, if designed right, a similar model could work for Lyft, and maybe even become a long-term strategy that would make ride-share users as devoted to Lyft as Costco's 100 million customers were to the retailer. Before developing such a program, however, Logan sought opinions on his new idea from employees, including me. And boy, did I have opinions. To put it simply, I didn't think a paid membership program could scale.

As it turned out, my view was in the minority. Over the course of the following months, I duked it out affably with various executives. I recall four different meetings that felt to me like town hall debates. Dozens of employees attended and watched us spar on the issue. Was I the bull and Logan and the other key executives the bullfighters, or was it the other way around? I wasn't sure at the time, but it certainly made for good entertainment.

I agreed entirely with Logan's point that product differentiation and loyalty had to be the linchpins of Lyft's strategy for competing with Uber both then and in the future. This was because the only way to maneuver away from cutthroat price competition with a formidable foe like Uber is to focus on something *other* than price. But we disagreed on how to use these two pillars to drive a new strategy for the company. Logan was confident that memberships were the answer. I was confident that they were not. My argument hinged on the unique baseline vulnerabilities that made Lyft different from companies like Costco or Netflix. My thoughts were that a subscription model could scale only if it gave access to goods or services that *weren't* readily available and accessible without a subscription. That was the secret sauce of successes like Costco, where shoppers need to present a membership card to get in the door, and it was at odds with our market, where an Uber or Lyft arrives in seconds at the touch of a screen and riders can easily access other low-cost options like a taxi or train. In a nutshell, as I contemplate buying a pound of chicken breast at Costco, I cannot tap an app and have Sam's Club put a chicken breast in my basket.

Moreover, because of the economics for food products and department store goods, prices and products tend to be the same everywhere all the time, which is how Costco ensures that the selection and savings it offers are not readily available at other retailers. Ride-sharing, meanwhile, is a dynamic product operating in micro-markets where price, demand, supply (of passenger-ready cars), and arrival times fluctuate constantly. If one company's supply of drivers thins out so its fares surge or wait times balloon, it's very easy for people to switch to a competitor. In fact, many people "dual-app"—they have both the Uber and Lyft apps on their phones, and swiftly check the wait times and price on both before making the choice. Switching is nearly effortless; you just tap a different app on your phone for an estimate, then request a ride. Tap—tap—done.

Costco's model doesn't function this way, and neither do subscription (read: membership) services like Netflix, where viewers generally don't impulsively cancel their subscription and switch to another streaming service on the spot—you have to go through the process of setting up an account and entering credit card information. Plus, with streaming, people often pay for more than one platform simultaneously in an effort to receive a richer set of choices.

Likewise, just because you're a member of Costco doesn't mean you don't also shop elsewhere. You might buy all of your household items at Costco but buy your groceries at stores with other selections of products or brands. With ride-sharing, there is no such differentiation. In many cases, the car that pulls up has both Lyft and Uber stickers on its windshield. The drivers themselves are dual-apping! And while even products as similar as Coke and Pepsi have different branding, the fact that Lyft and Uber drivers largely don't makes it that much harder—but also that much more important—to inspire loyalty in customers. It also explains why I so strongly believed that unless we could somehow add related goods or services to the ride experience that weren't readily available without a membership (think of a partnership with United Airlines that gave free upgrades to loyal Lyft customers only), scaling would be difficult, if not impossible. And these challenges weren't my only concern.

The Disneyland Dilemma

Economists have studied the pricing of membership programs ever since pioneering economist (and Nobel laureate) Arthur Lewis's 1941 paper on "two-part tariffs"—economese for a business requiring customers to pay an entry fee to gain access to products they then pay for. While that may sound like a raw deal, in some circumstances this arrangement makes sense. It is Costco's model, and you'll find this approach in other contexts as well.

Take the famous Rose Bowl Flea Market, held at the eponymous stadium in Pasadena, California, on the second Sunday of every month. To gain access to the eccentric variety of antiques and rare goods the vendors peddle at their stands, visitors must first pay an entry fee. Since competition for premium finds is fierce, pricing is tiered, starting with VIP admission from 5:00 to 7:00 A.M. at $25, then dropping to $18 from 7:00 to 8:00 A.M. and $14 from 8:00 to 9:00 A.M. before falling to a $9 general admission price beginning at 9:00 A.M.

In a 1971 paper titled "The Disneyland Dilemma," economist Walter Oi provided the theoretical conditions for when it made sense for the amusement park to charge guests an entry fee as well as separate fees for every ride—or in other words, whether the revenue from the additional tariff was worth losing those customers unable or unwilling to pay the additional cost of entry. In the end, Disney opted for just the one tariff; as many parents of young children are all too aware, visitors pay for entry, but once inside the park, rides are free. (Though in semi-monopolistic micro-markets like Disneyland, food, souvenirs, and other offerings function as a profitable second tariff. This isn't exactly an example of a membership program per se, but it highlights the fact that businesses can get away with exploitative pricing in situations where consumers have no other readily accessible options.)

In Lyft's case, the membership program wasn't meant to be exploitative. Logan wanted to make one set of prices available to everyone *and* offer riders the option to buy a membership and gain access to special accommodations, like discounted prices or preferential dispatch (getting a car earlier). As a general rule, consumers are willing to pay for a membership as long as the benefits they gain from having the membership (i.e., lower prices, faster service, and other perks) are worth more than the cost of it. If they aren't, the program won't scale.

In this sense, there are two types of consumers who consistently buy into membership programs. For the first type—let's call them JoGoods—the better deals incentivize them to purchase *even more* products (or more rides, in Lyft's case). Psychologically, the more they take advantage of the discount, the more the initial tariff feels worthwhile, even if they are actually spending more than they would have otherwise. This behavioral pattern explains why "buy one, get the second half off" supermarket deals work so well: consumers want to take advantage of the discount, so they end up buying two of a product they actually only need one of. This is the sweet spot for companies, and it's what Logan was banking on happening with Lyft—consumers would get a good deal, enjoy the service even more, and take more trips. A true win-win all the way to the bottom line.

However, there is also a second type of customer, whom we'll call NoGoods. They buy the membership because it is a good deal, but unlike JoGoods, they don't increase their number of trips. In their case, the membership is valuable because they ride a lot, and the discount applies to all of the purchases they would have made anyway. This is the unsweet spot for Lyft: people who are taking the same number of trips but paying less for each of them, and the membership fee Lyft collects from the NoGoods doesn't make up for it.

The challenge for any company that wants to provide a scalable membership program is the same: there must be an attractive ratio of JoGoods to NoGoods, otherwise you will lose money. Which is to say you must thoroughly think through which of your customers are most likely to want the membership.

This was my key objection to Lyft launching a membership-pricing program. My intuition was that the majority of riders who would embrace a Lyft membership would be the ones who were taking frequent trips already. These are the people who would benefit the most but not ride more—in other words, the NoGoods. If I was right, these customers could not just erase any profits from the membership program but wind up costing the company more.

Sure, membership would inspire loyalty and make Lyft more attractive to a lot of people, I said in the meetings, but it could also lead to a balance-sheet disaster. And what's the point of loyalty to a company if it then goes under? In the end Logan felt it was important to test out his idea with a soft launch. I still had my reservations, but the wisdom of running a pilot program and gathering data before scaling the idea more widely was something we could both agree on!

So the company set up an experiment where different riders were offered a monthly subscription with varying discounts and up-front costs. For about two weeks in early March 2019, roughly 1.2 million people were given the opportunity to buy one of six randomly assigned membership deals:

1. $5 up front for 5 percent off all rides
2. $10 up front for 5 percent off all rides
3. $10 up front for 10 percent off all rides
4. $15 up front for 10 percent off all rides
5. $20 up front for 10 percent off all rides
6. $25 up front for 15 percent off all rides

During those two weeks, Lyft riders who took up one of these six offers crisscrossed their cities, leaving behind a trail of data. Untangling the patterns behind each group's behaviors would be the key to determining if the membership model indeed had potential at scale, and if so, what the ideal price point and discount rate were, for both the company and its customers.

Believe me when I say that I took no joy in the fact that, after tussling with all of the data, we discovered that I had been right: of the six different pricing structures we tested, not a single one would scale.

To unpack why, let's return to our two types of customers, the JoGoods and the NoGoods. After all, those 1.2 million experimental users weren't a monolith. They had different riding needs and income levels, not to mention different tendencies in how and when they spent money. And these idiosyncratic consumption styles would lead them to use the membership differently. Some would spend more; others would save more. So my team dug in and looked for groupings in order to establish patterns. With this, we could extrapolate which types of members the company would be likely to lose money on and which it wouldn't.

The results were stark: the NoGoods were nearly three times more prevalent than the JoGoods, meaning that the vast majority of core customers who bought memberships didn't increase their number of rides. Rather, they were taking the same number of trips but at a discounted fare (a good deal from their point of view, but not so great for us). Sure, there was increased ridership overall thanks to the JoGoods, but the key to judging the scalability of membership was a matter not simply of counting the number of rides but of figuring out *who* was riding more. The data suggested that at a three-to-one ratio of JoGoods to NoGoods, the more we expanded the program, the more money we'd lose on the NoGoods relative to what we'd earn from the JoGoods. This would be unscalable.

Going back to basic economics, this meant that we needed to change the benefit-cost calculus, either by changing the up-front cost or by making the membership benefits more attractive. In terms of the former, by digging into the data from the experiment, we found that, overall, when the up-front cost was higher and the discount was the same, fewer people opted in than when the discount was higher and the up-front cost was the same. Had we simply been trying to maximize the number of people who joined, the solution would have been obvious: increase the discount. But remember that we weren't concerned with how many people joined; we cared about *who* joined. We needed to find a structure that attracted more JoGoods and fewer NoGoods.

Our analysis of all these data showed that the optimal membership was not one of the memberships initially considered, but one that had a 7.5 percent price discount per trip for an up-front cost of $19.99. Under this pricing framework, fewer customers would buy in (in fact, just a tiny slice of Lyft customers would), but we could actually *increase profits*.

Once we figured out the pricing and discount structure, Logan knew that if we wanted the membership program to scale, we'd also need to increase the number of potential customers, and we'd have to include in the membership program more attractive benefits—importantly, ones that weren't available without a subscription. Through customer surveys and conjoint analysis, we learned that beyond a safe, reliable, and low-priced ride, customers liked priority airport pickups, surprise discounts, cancellation fees waived, and exclusive savings deals.

We put all this together, and at the end of 2019, Lyft Pink was born. Recommended for customers who took two to three rides per week, the members were promised an "elevated" experience at $19.99 per month: 15 percent off unlimited car rides, priority airport pickups, three waived cancellation fees per month (if riders rebooked within fifteen minutes), waived lost-and-found fees (for belongings left in cars), surprise discounts and exclusive savings, and three half-hour bike or scooter rides (through Lyft's bike-sharing service) per month in select markets. The ride discount was the ice cream, and the other offerings were the cherries on top. Logan believed that the extra perks combined with the 15 percent discount on rides (rather than the 7.5 percent discount we'd initially calculated) would motivate more JoGoods to join.

It was an enticing suite of perks—enticing enough that three months later thousands and thousands of Lyft users had signed up. But then, as we all know, the coronavirus hit, and in mid-March 2020 nearly the whole world shut down. Ride-sharing ground almost to a halt, and even after reopenings began, business still wasn't the same for Lyft. The company scrambled to shore up operations, from the cost side to the customer side. It was believed inside the company that Lyft Pink would now play an even more prominent role. At the time of this writing, as we are beginning to emerge from the pandemic, only time and data will tell whether Lyft Pink is scalable. I remain optimistic, but the proof will be in the pudding. Ultimately, the relative number of JoGoods to NoGoods will be the deciding factor in whether Lyft Pink can hold up at scale.

Know Your Audience

The story of Lyft Pink illustrates a challenge for scaling enterprises of all varieties: knowing your audience. This matters because if you don't truly understand the different types of people you serve now, you can't accurately predict who will respond to a product, service, or intervention at scale. So once you've cleared the false-positive hurdle we discussed in Chapter 1 and have reliably demonstrated the efficacy of the endeavor you hope to scale, the next step is to answer the question "How *broadly* will the idea work?"

In general, when you scale an idea or enterprise across cultures, climates, geographies, and socioeconomic groups, it's inevitable that different people will make vastly different choices. And there's always a risk that the people who participate in a pilot or soft launch will behave in ways that are particular to a specific place or culture. To take an absurdly obvious but illustrative example, a new line of beachwear might fly off the shelves in Southern California, but it's probably not going to scale along the whole Pacific Coast up to Alaska. Similarly, earthquake kits sell very well in parts of the United States vulnerable to earthquakes but not so well elsewhere, so scaling up a new advertising campaign everywhere in the country wouldn't make sense.

As an analogy, think of comedians. For a comedian to kill it, she has to *know her audience.* Jokes that bring down the house in one setting likely fail in another. Likewise, an idea that succeeds with one group might fall flat with another. This is why you have to know your audience—that is, exactly whom your idea is for—in order to assess its potential to succeed at scale. For example, the social media platform Pinterest is used primarily by women, which puts a cap on its user base and revenue potential. Of course, many businesses simply have built-in limitations, and that's fine. Your idea can still serve a purpose and make money even if it has a ceiling. Take dating apps. They scale very well, but only up to a point. From the start these companies know that they will never scale for people in committed monogamous relationships. (Meanwhile, the app Ashley Madison, with its slogan "Life is short. Have an affair," claims to have tapped into an unspoken but 70-million-strong market of people who are in relationships but not actually committed to them.)

When conceiving a product or program to scale for maximum impact, however, ideally you want to serve as many people as possible. The more universal the appeal of the idea, the better it scales. With this in mind, you must take into account that consumers have different needs, spending habits, and behavioral tendencies, and find the point where the most interests and benefits converge. After all, in the land of Cyclopes you're not going to sell normal eyeglasses.

If the specific needs and demands of unique groups or customer segments are ignored, voltage drops are sure to occur. For a textbook example of this at work (I actually wrote about it in an economics textbook), look no further than the tale of Kmart's Blue Light Special.

In 1965, the store manager at a Kmart in Indiana had a bright idea—literally. He rigged a flashing blue police light above an assortment of items that were failing to sell, cut their prices, and then turned the light on as an employee came on the loudspeaker announcing something to the effect of "Attention, Kmart shoppers! Men's winter jackets in aisle three are 50 percent off. Get there fast before they are all gone!" This spectacle grabbed the attention of shoppers, who dashed over to snag the savings before it was too late. And just like that, Kmart's famous Blue Light Special—one of the first incarnations of what's now known as a "flash sale"—was born.

Word of the technique spread, and soon every Kmart across the country began running Blue Light Specials with similar success. As a promotional innovation, it scaled brilliantly. The eye- and ear-catching hyping of the sale and the sense of urgency it fostered among customers were part of the brilliance. The other part was that the choice of the products on sale was up to the individual store managers, who knew their customers. They talked to them, plus they also lived in the same communities and had certain shared experiences. So pretty soon the Kmart managers began selecting not only items that were languishing on the shelves but also products catering to the needs of the particular shoppers at that particular place and time, like shovels or ice-melting salt the morning after a heavy snow. Sam Walton, founder of Walmart, called the Blue Light Special "one of the greatest sales promotion ideas ever."

Then Kmart screwed the whole thing up. Instead of permitting each individual store to choose the goods to be discounted, all goods sold on Blue Light Specials would now be dictated months in advance from the corporate office in Hoffman Estates, Illinois. This meant that on any given day, the same exact goods were sold as Blue Light Specials regardless of whether the store was located in Laramie, Wyoming; Sarasota, Florida; or Seattle, Washington. So when a summer heat wave hit Sarasota or a rainy spell hit Seattle, managers in Florida and Washington no longer had the autonomy to tailor the promotion to better serve their customers. By ignoring the unique needs of different customer segments, this new policy short-circuited the proven scalability of the program.

From Selection Biases to WEIRD People

The inevitable variability across different audiences and customer segments poses another challenge for scaling. To truly achieve widespread impact, it's not enough to understand how your current customers or audience differs across geographies, demographic groups, and so on. You also need to think about how your current audience might differ from your future one.

Put another way, is the initial audience—or test subjects, or market segment—that yielded your early success a representative snapshot of the larger group of people whom you hope to serve at scale? When looking at results in the early stages of any enterprise, you must check that you're correctly gauging what scientists call the *representativeness of population*.

Non-representativeness can occur either accidentally or through willful selection of the sample. When it occurs accidentally, it is a phenomenon known as *selection bias*—when people opt in to programs in a non-random way. This is problematic because people who choose to participate in a pilot program or study are the most likely to benefit. Of course insomniacs flock to the medical trial for a new sleeping pill! But when a disproportionate part of the sample is made up of people who opt in because they are most likely to benefit, this has the potential to distort the results, painting a more optimistic picture that wouldn't hold up at scale—what scientists call a "selection effect." Similarly, the people who opt in to a health program may be more motivated to improve their health—and therefore more likely to engage in any number of other healthy behaviors—than those who did not opt in. In these cases you might incorrectly attribute improved health outcomes to the intervention instead of to other healthy habits: a false positive. If the research and development team for the new sleep medication, for example, fails to anticipate and correct for selection bias, the results may indicate the medication is effective, when in fact it's effective only for a subset of the population, not the whole group. This is bad for the company that invested in the sleep medication and will now lose money on it, and also it's bad for the people in need of a new drug to help them sleep better.

My talented former student Tova Levin leads experimental strategy at Humana, a healthcare company that makes decisions through rapid testing and therefore relies on well-designed studies to ensure that the desired effects hold up at scale. For example, in a few different studies looking to improve social determinants of health, such as loneliness and food insecurity, Tova's team designed studies comparing statistically significant, randomized populations across the country, thereby ensuring that the results weren't just a fluke or a product of the selection effect.

This can happen elsewhere in the business world, too. In the mid-1990s, McDonald's did extensive focus-group testing on a new item it would hail as a more sophisticated and slightly more expensive hamburger: the Arch Deluxe. The people who participated in the focus groups liked it, so scaling it across the United States seemed like a sure bet. But in fact, the Arch Deluxe turned out to be a deluxe failure. It didn't scale.

How did this massive misfire occur? The people who participated in the focus groups weren't a faithful reflection of McDonald's customers as a whole. After all, a person who signs up to take part in a McDonald's focus group is probably someone who is crazy about McDonald's, or loves all kinds of burgers, or both. But the average person, it turns out, goes to McDonald's for the Big Mac, not a fancier version of one. The lesson here should be clear: don't assume that your initial audience is necessarily representative of the population as a whole.

In the preceding examples, the selection effect resulted from a non-representative sample of people opting to participate in the trial. However, the threat of the selection effect unraveling your scaling hopes can also occur in sample populations that have been deliberately selected. Take what happened when researchers set out to find a treatment for the iron deficiencies that result in anemia, which is a widespread problem in India and elsewhere. People who suffer from anemia are short on the healthy red blood cells that shuttle oxygen to the body's tissues, resulting in fatigue, inflammation, and other effects damaging to one's health and quality of life. As a possible path toward remedying this problem on a large scale, researchers ran pilot studies measuring the benefits of consuming iron-fortified salt. The study participants who received the treatment showed dramatic improvements, so the program was scaled up. However, it turned out that the fortified salt had no effect on the policy goal of reducing the prevalence of anemia in the larger population. Voltage nosedived. Why?

The researchers had specifically sought out adolescent women to participate in the original studies. While the treatment benefited their particular physiology, these health gains didn't manifest at a larger scale with a broader population. Not everyone with iron-deficiency anemia is an adolescent girl, so if the intervention wasn't meant exclusively for them, it never should have been tested exclusively in them in the first place. Similar failures have occurred elsewhere attempting to scale initiatives to decrease rates of STD transmission and promote safe sex, due to variations in community mores related to sex.

This example highlights that there is always the risk—or temptation—that researchers may deliberately seek out a specific population that stands to benefit most from the program, product, or medication in order to show large effects, since this can increase the chance of public recognition and further funding or investment. Likewise, it may be less expensive to convince people to participate in a study if those people expect to benefit from it. So some researchers might see it as a win-win: better results at a lower cost.

Contrast this with an initiative by the Nurse-Family Partnership, which tracked the impact of home visits by registered nurses on prenatal care and pregnancy outcomes for first-time mothers; it also looked at whether the nurses' visits could reduce child abuse and neglect, and improve school-readiness. To ensure their sample was as representative as possible, the program's founder, David Olds, ran pilot programs in three cities: Memphis, Tennessee; Denver, Colorado; and Elmira, New York. These three locations provided variation in household demographics: Memphis had a large Black population, Denver was ethnically very diverse, and Elmira was a traditional manufacturing town with mostly white residents.

The positive interventions proved very valuable. Mothers saw decreases in their prenatal cigarette smoking and health problems, in addition to fewer closely spaced subsequent pregnancies. They also got more paying work, relied less on government assistance, and had more stability in their intimate relationships. As for the children, those enrolled in the program excelled academically compared to peers who didn't receive nurse visits, and they had better language and self-control skills. Best of all, these benefits replicated in follow-up work both within these cities and beyond.

An even better solution is to test only a *random* sample of people. The sample must not be cherry-picked; cases of deliberate cherry-picking take us back to the moral quagmire of duping, which does happen. That said, more often than not, the selection effect is simply the result of carelessness. This is why randomized trials are the proverbial gold standard for pharmaceutical research.

In 2008, Opower, a customer-engagement platform for utility companies, launched an energy conservation program that involved sending customers letters showing their electrical usage compared to that of other people in their communities. The idea was that they would be motivated to save more energy if they knew how much more or less their neighbors saved. Opower carried out this behavioral "nudge" in 111 randomized control trials involving 8.6 million households across the United States. The brilliant young economist Hunt Allcott pored over the data and found that the initial results were stunning, with big energy savings. Furthermore, those results held up after several replications. It would be a sure win at scale across the whole country, right? Wrong.

Even though the first set of results showed the program to be quite effective across millions of households, the truth of whether it could scale lies in the actual sample of utilities that participated in the original nudge program and its replications. Utilities in more environmentalist areas were more likely to be in these trials, and their customers were more responsive to the nudge. As the program moved to places where people tended to have different values and priorities, however, the letters didn't move the needle on conserving energy. The initiative succeeded spectacularly in the original markets but had much less voltage in others. So scaling nationwide would have been a colossal mistake, or at least would have suffered from a severe voltage drop.

The company hadn't filtered out "site selection bias," nor had it foreseen its own bias in reading the data incorrectly. Failing to fully understand how the different segments of your sample population may differ from your audience at scale is one reason we oftentimes miscalculate how representative the sample is of the overall population. I saw this issue firsthand in Chicago Heights. On average, our Parent Academy improved education and developmental outcomes for children. That was a huge success. But when we dug deeper into the data, we discovered that was the case *only* for Hispanic families, not for Black and white families. The key was that having a multigenerational family unit mattered a great deal, and within Chicago Heights, the Hispanic families, on average, were much more multigenerational and intact than Black and white families. This meant that when Mom or Dad couldn't make a meeting or help their child with homework, an aunt or uncle, grandparent, or cousin could readily step in and not miss a beat. In this case, it was important for scaling purposes to have drawn a random sample of families into the original study to ensure we understood which type of families were helped by the intervention (rather than follow Opower's strategy and have people self-select into the program, because in that case we would have had mostly Hispanic families).

These challenges have even shaken the foundations of social science, which underpin much of our contemporary understanding of human nature. Over the last hundred years, psychologists and scientists from numerous other disciplines (including economics) have conducted experiments from which they have extracted purportedly universal findings about human nature—for example, what motivates people to engage in cooperative acts, the inner workings of markets, why people discriminate, and much more. These discoveries influenced everything from the design of exchange institutions to federal equal employment laws. The data were there, the replications were there, so what could possibly go wrong? As a matter of fact, everything.

In the mid-1990s, Joseph Henrich was a bright PhD student in anthropology. For his research he went to Peru to conduct field research with an indigenous Amazonian community. He decided to run a behavioral-economics experiment to uncover whether the people in the community demonstrated the same attitudes about fairness that scientists took for granted as a basic component of human cognition—namely, our belief that people who act selfishly (in this case, by failing to distribute money equitably in an experimental game) deserve to be punished. To his surprise, the Peruvian participants didn't respond this way to the game, opting *not* to punish other players who had shorted them unfairly. This finding raised a question that Henrich would spend the next twenty-five years examining: Could it be that the purportedly universal insights of the social sciences were applicable only to what he has termed "WEIRD" people—people in Western, educated, industrialized, rich, and democratic societies? Were many Western scientific findings in fact unscalable throughout the world?

The answer, devastatingly, appears to be yes in many cases, a finding that has forced scientists in numerous fields to question bedrock assumptions. At this point you might be wondering how so many scientists could have overlooked the seemingly obvious (in hindsight) impact of culture on human behavior. The answer lies in the simple fact that historically, the vast majority of research subjects have hailed from Western cultures. In fact, most social science researchers in the United States harvest their campus community for study participants—and suffice it to say that American college students (pass the beer bong!) are not exactly the most representative sample of the mind-bogglingly diverse range of humans that populate our planet.

This immense scientific blind spot suggests that many seemingly unimpeachable findings may not in fact be applicable (or "scalable") to non-WEIRD populations. For example, in my own field research, I've discovered that widespread cultural assumptions in patriarchal Western societies about women being intrinsically less aggressive than men did not hold up in a matriarchal society in India. Under the right conditions, women are just as competitive, dominant, and hungry for power as men! Moreover, men in this society behave more like the Western stereotype of women.

In short, if we in the social sciences wish to create impact on the largest possible scale, we have important work to do. We should conduct new research on broader samples of participants in diverse communities around the world, and we should do much of this work through "natural field experiments"—in environments where the subjects are naturally undertaking certain tasks, and where they are not self-selecting into the experiment. Such an approach combines the most attractive elements of the experimental method and naturally occurring data. In many cases, we need to move from a mentality of creating evidence-based policy to one of producing policy-based evidence.

Businesses can—and increasingly do—apply this approach by testing their ideas or products on more culturally diverse groups, and by moving from focus groups to experiments conducted "in the wild." Think back to how we tested Lyft Pink—it was simply a natural field experiment.

The big-picture lesson here is one you ignore at your own peril: when assessing early responses to your idea, look under the hood and make sure the people in that group are representative of the larger population you ultimately hope to reach. To uncover true actionable knowledge, it is important to recognize heterogeneities rather than hide them. In fact, I'd suggest going even further: do everything you can early on to uncover and examine hidden differences in the people you eventually hope to serve at scale, not only because this will likely yield valuable insights about the scalability of your idea but also because it is what will set you apart from competitors. These differences can involve anything from geographic location (as we saw with Kmart) and family structure (as with Parent Academy) to behavior patterns (like the ones we observed when we tested our membership program at Lyft) and cultural attitudes and norms (such as gender roles or what constitutes "fairness")—and everything in between.

If you're a high school principal considering implementing a seemingly impressive new intervention—say, to increase students' admittance to four-year colleges—investigate whether students in existing program locations might have socioeconomic backgrounds that differ from those of your own students. If you're a venture capitalist considering investing in a promising company, find out exactly where the business model is succeeding and with whom precisely. In short, think about your audience. Then, once you're ready to raise your voltage, look for people you aren't currently serving but could if you tweaked your model.

Which brings us to an important question: what should we do if we discover that our current model will not scale past a certain point, and yet we still have ambitions to expand?

Broadening Your Audience

Rafael Ilishayev and Yakir Gola really liked smoking hookahs.

As sophomores at Drexel University in Philadelphia in 2013, the twenty-year-old friends liked to sit around talking and puffing late into the night—that is, until they ran out of tobacco or got hungry for a snack. Then they would have to trudge to the nearest convenience store that was still open, or worse, just call it a night. This predicament they kept finding themselves in gave them an idea.

Using seed money from a used-furniture business they had created together, Rafa and Yakir started a new company with a simple premise: a *convenience store that delivered*. They created an app for users to place orders, and soon the two were working hundred-hour weeks driving around Philly delivering everything from hookah tobacco to chips, six-packs to gummy worms, ice cream to microwavable taquitos. Aptly named Gopuff, their company was like Amazon for the college munchies set, but with deliveries arriving within thirty minutes.

From these humble beginnings Gopuff scaled up at breakneck speed. Rafa and Yakir landed early investors, hired a team of employees, negotiated wholesale deals with brands, hired their own drivers, and used social media to playfully market to millennials. Their enterprise was eminently scalable because they knew their audience so well.

They expanded their operation to other cities, and pretty soon Rafa and Yakir had carved out a nice share of the rapidly evolving new food-delivery niche. As of this writing, Gopuff has some 7,000 employees and is active in more than 650 cities; in 2019 it generated over $250 million in revenue. In 2019, the Japanese conglomerate Soft-Bank reportedly invested $750 million in the company. Whether the two founders realized it at the outset or not, Gopuff was perfectly built to scale to a specific customer base, and it was one they knew well: people like them. Like many great ideas, theirs came from identifying what they themselves wanted, which, as it turned out, many other people did as well.

Yet as profitable as Gopuff was, Rafa and Yakir realized that there was a cap to their market. Most adults don't have the lifestyle of college students. This meant that there was an enormous potential customer base they were currently ignoring. They had the distribution infrastructure already in place to keep scaling, but in order to do so, they needed to rethink what they were offering—and to whom.

In 2020, Rafa and Yakir contacted me to discuss how to roll out Gopuff in new markets. I told them that their expansion had the potential to fall apart if they didn't properly account for the realities of target customers in different (read: older) demographics. Rafa and Yakir wisely decided that they would need to offer a wider array of products if they wanted to capture new and different customers. In other words, what they needed to do was diversify. To cater to older customers, for example, they would need to be an instant-delivery pharmacy rather than just a convenience store. To attract new parents, they would need to offer 24/7 delivery of diapers, baby food, wipes, and so on. And to make these new, more mature customers aware of their new offerings, they would need new marketing approaches. They executed all these changes, and then, in 2020, came an unexpected boon for business: the coronavirus pandemic. In the first half of 2020, their sales jumped by 400 percent.

Gopuff scaled meteorically not by replicating their early success and giving the same customers more of what they wanted. Instead, they expanded by offering a larger suite of products meant to enlarge their customer base. With this approach they scaled up their customer base big-time simply by giving different people different options.

Fast-food restaurants do this all the time by adding new items to their menus, and often this works out much better than things did for the Arch Deluxe. For example, in 2018, Taco Bell introduced Nacho Fries, which soon became the most popular item in the chain's more than half-century-long history. While Nacho Fries were already a staple on many of Taco Bell's international menus, their U.S. debut excited habitual customers and reeled in new ones as well.

What if expanding your product offerings proves too complicated or expensive to sustain at scale? Try keeping the product the same but experimenting with ways to make it cheaper or easier to produce (for example, look at better production or distribution models). You can also look at taking the product to a potentially better market where it will find more people who need and can afford it. But if none of these tweaks work, then it might be time to quit or pivot.

Similar principles apply to nonprofits and public policy initiatives. When I partnered with the Sierra Club to help them raise money, I learned from my field experiment that men were compelled to give more money when we included a matching gift (think "If you give $100 today we will match your $100 with an anonymous donor's

$100"). Women, however, were not moved by the match. Of course, I didn't want to abandon female donors, so I explored other avenues, such as small donor gifts. Likewise, when we discovered that our Parent Academy in Chicago Heights worked only for Hispanic families, we didn't stop there. We began to develop programs—effectively "product tweaks"—such as an all-day preschool program that did turn out to work among Black and white families.

When scaling programs like these in the messy world, you may have to look beyond a one-size-fits-all approach. So be prepared to make adjustments to ensure that *all* groups are being served.

*   *   *

WHETHER IN THE realm of business, scientific research, education, or policymaking, even the best ideas will lose voltage at scale if the needs of their future audience haven't been properly accounted for. But as we're about to learn, circumstances—the third hurdle in the Five Vital Signs—are just as important.

IS IT THE CHEF OR THE INGREDIENTS?

When the boyish British celebrity chef Jamie Oliver opened the flagship location of his restaurant Jamie's Italian in the United Kingdom in 2008, it appeared he had the perfect recipe—not just for healthy and scrumptious Italian food at a reasonable price but also for a chain that had the potential to scale up fast.

By this time, Oliver was already well known around the world. After being discovered by a BBC film crew in 1997, the telegenic young sous-chef soon had a hit show of his own, *The Naked Chef,* followed by a bestselling cookbook of the same name ("naked" referred to the stripped-down style of cooking that Oliver preached, not an ill-advised choice regarding his wardrobe). He prized fresh yet inexpensive ingredients and simple recipes over rare delicacies and sophisticated techniques, and he showed people that you didn't have to have extensive training or aspire to culinary greatness in order to cook tasty, nourishing food at home. This approach had mass appeal, winning over viewers of all ages, men and women alike.

More Jamie Oliver TV shows and cookbooks followed, along with the admirable efforts of his foundation, which sought to reduce obesity and food-related diseases by promoting cooking and nutrition education in British schools. He also created a nonprofit training program to turn young people from disadvantaged backgrounds into skilled chefs, which not only put them on a path to a promising career but also injected new diversity into the restaurant industry. Oliver had scaled not only his approach to cooking but also a set of values and a hopeful message—that food could be a pathway toward positive social change. It seemed that the only goal this apple-cheeked kid who had grown up chopping onions and pulling pints in the kitchen of his parents' village pub had left was to conquer the highly competitive restaurant world. And who was to say he couldn't pull it off? If anything, Oliver's career to this point had demonstrated that he was the kind of person who could build an empire and make it look easy.

So no one was surprised when the first Jamie's Italian, in Oxford, drew large crowds of hungry diners upon opening its doors. It received an admiring review from *The Guardian*. Most importantly, it served high-quality food at prices that didn't break the bank for the average person. It seemed that Oliver's Midas touch would keep on turning food to gold. Yet he had an ambitious expansion plan for Jamie's Italian that would put his business acumen to the test. As the critic for *The Guardian* put it, "If Jamie can replicate this early Oxford form, he will soon be driving a prize herd of recession-proof cash cows across the land." In other words, if he could scale this initial proof of concept, Jamie's Italian could be unstoppable. This was Oliver's ambition, yet as we have already seen, scaling up often reveals the hidden fault lines in an enterprise. So would Jamie's Italian be able to crank up the voltage and live up to the hype? Or would it suffer a crushing voltage drop?

Oliver's new chain was so successful that within a few years it expanded to seventy locations in twenty-seven different markets, many of them abroad. That he was able to scale the enterprise at lightning speed was especially impressive because, as a general rule, a chef's special touch in the kitchen is unscalable. A person's unique magic at any given specialized skill isn't something that can be mass-produced, for one simple reason: that person can't be cloned. To put it in classical economic terms, supply (of singular cooking talent) is limited no matter how high the demand, which makes scaling a losing bet unless a chef is able to sufficiently pass on her magic to protégés or employees—something that is very hard to do. This explains why so few truly exquisite restaurants ever open in more than one location, or if they do, the quality tends to plunge and soon after so does the number of customers. Human talent is difficult, if not impossible, to scale. The restaurant industry has learned this lesson the hard way, which is why so many of the best chefs in the world are wise to measure the success of their enterprises on the basis of reputation and quality rather than scalability.

The chef Ferran Adrià's one-of-a-kind El Bulli in Spain epitomized this kind of success; this bold experiment in molecular gastronomy relied entirely on his unique expertise and gifts. Adrià's creative process was so intense that for many years he closed the restaurant for up to six months at a time to invent groundbreaking new dishes. Not exactly efficient, but he knew his limitations and played them to his advantage. In the final years before the restaurant closed its doors (by choice) in 2010, it was reported that 1 million people annually tried to make reservations at El Bulli for only 8,000 spots (showing that scarcity and exclusivity sell). Adrià was well aware that if he had tried to scale his innovative menu—with its pioneering white bean foam and deconstructed liquid olives—in kitchens he didn't oversee, he almost surely would have seen a huge drop in voltage and a huge drop in quality. In other words, he understood that he, as the chef, was the secret ingredient in El Bulli's success.

So how did Oliver bypass this obstacle and manage to scale the unscalable?

To begin with, the formula of Jamie's Italian scaled so well from the get-go because Oliver's name and face served as a brand that got people in the door. Fame and brand recognition are extremely scalable if people like and trust you, and Oliver wasn't just a celebrity but a celebrity chef with earned credibility. However, this alone wouldn't have guaranteed that the chain would thrive at scale. Countless restaurants owned by celebrity chefs—and just plain celebrities—have failed even before scaling up. What kept customers coming back and new ones coming into Jamie's Italian was that, like the recipes in his cookbooks, the dishes relied on fresh ingredients simply prepared, rather than on extravagant ingredients or a laborious creative vision. Put simply, Oliver wasn't a Ferran Adrià type of chef. His brilliance in the kitchen wasn't an innovative or technical style; it was his everyman approach. This meant that other chefs could easily replicate his cooking, while also allowing a price point for dishes that kept demand high. In this way he had circumvented the Catch-22 that makes most great chefs unscalable. While Adrià's secret ingredient was the man himself, Oliver's secret ingredient *was* his ingredients. And unlike humans with special talents, ingredients are eminently scalable.

Yet such rapid, large-scale expansion would catch up with Oliver. What he failed to understand was that there were other, less visible ingredients so essential to his empire's recipe for success that if they changed, the whole franchise would fall apart. Which is precisely what happened.

The first was managing director Simon Blagden. A seasoned executive, Blagden had been running business operations for Jamie's Italian since the chain's inception and was almost eerily adept at knowing where, when, and how to open new locations. It was a unique and hard-to-scale skill, one that involved leveraging his years of experience in the restaurant industry to determine exactly whom to choose as franchise partners—ideally, business partners whose values aligned with Oliver's and who would prioritize sourcing good organic ingredients and maintaining high food quality, even if it meant lower profits. Blagden also oversaw a positive company culture that kept the retention rate of the kitchen staff high, no easy task in an industry in which fast and frequent turnover is the norm. Blagden's business instincts had been honed over time, particularly when it came to hiring and working with the right people. He was indispensable to Oliver's enterprise as it began to scale.

Then there was Oliver himself. Even as the chain grew, he had tried to stay as present as possible in overseeing its operations. His spirit and mission were part of his culinary brand, and this part of him was scalable. Even though Oliver wasn't the one cooking the food that was served under the banner of his name around the world, his impact on each one of his restaurants could be felt. Unfortunately, Oliver underestimated his own importance to his chain.

Things began to unravel in 2017, when Blagden left Jamie's Italian along with two other top executives. In replacing them, Oliver made the mistake of elevating someone new to his company who was woefully unqualified to keep a restaurant chain functioning well at scale: his brother-in-law, Paul Hunt. A former stockbroker, Hunt had been fined for insider trading in 1999, suggesting he wasn't the best fit for the values-oriented culture of Jamie's Italian. More importantly, Hunt hadn't logged the years of experience in the restaurant industry that the job required. Hunt was good at taking an axe to those branches of Oliver's business empire that had run into debt and were hemorrhaging money, but he lacked Blagden's magic touch when it came to the critical task of selecting new sites and partners for expansion. As the future CEO of Jamie's Italian would say in a public postmortem, "We were opening too many restaurants, too quickly, in the wrong places."

Hunt wasn't very good at retaining employees, either, which made him unprepared to maintain the positive company culture at scale. Former employees of Oliver's company would later describe him as a bully and a sexist, which torpedoed company morale. (For the record, Oliver publicly defended his brother-in-law and sought to diminish Hunt's blame.)

To make matters worse, by this time Oliver had overstretched himself and was only able to devote a limited amount of time to Jamie's Italian. His absence, combined with Hunt's limitations, resulted in a leadership void that prevented the company from adapting agilely to a changing market being undercut by app-driven food-delivery services. This is a useful reminder that being successful at scale isn't just about maintaining productivity, distribution, and demand. It's also about being nimble enough to adapt when the landscape starts to change. And if key people are spread too thin—remember, humans don't scale!—an enterprise can become sluggish.

But then the worst thing that can happen to any restaurant—even worse than losing ground to new competitors—happened to Jamie's

Italian: the quality of the food tanked. Abominable reviews piled up online ("Absolutely terrible food and service," wrote one customer on Tripadvisor, echoing the sentiments of countless others) and in the press. By the time the influential *Sunday Times* critic complained about Jamie's Italian, writing that the experience made her want to scream and kick things, Jamie Oliver himself probably felt like kicking and screaming, too. At the start of 2019, the chain was $100 million in the red, forcing Oliver to shutter twenty-five restaurants in the United Kingdom and lay off a thousand employees. In 2020, Oliver had no choice but to close still more locations, including ones in Taiwan and Hong Kong.

For a few years, Oliver pulled off what few chefs ever can: success at scale. But in the end, the voltage gains proved unsustainable, and the enterprise ultimately failed.

Negotiables Versus Non-negotiables

The collapse of Jamie's Italian didn't stem from a false positive (taste buds don't lie) or from the company not knowing its audience (both the menu offerings and prices were designed to appeal to middle-class diners). Rather, it occurred because Oliver didn't seem to fully understand the reasons for its ascendancy to begin with. He didn't appreciate the relevant conditions that had led to its success at scale—and which needed to *stay in place* in order to sustain high voltage.

In Chapter 2, we saw that loss of voltage can result from misjudging the degree to which one's audience or customers are representative of the larger population. But anyone wishing to scale an idea or enterprise must also take into account the *representativeness of the situation,* or the circumstances needed to scale. Were Jamie's Italian's situational conditions at scale similar to those that were present at the chain's inception? The answer was yes . . . until certain indispensable pieces shifted.

For any idea or enterprise—not just restaurant chains—to hold strong at scale, you need to know what the drivers of high performance are and do everything in your power to keep them in place. To achieve this, before anything else you must determine if your secret sauce is the "chef" or the "ingredients." In other words, does your success at small scale rest largely on the people indispensable to your idea or product— say, the engineer who built the platform your business runs on, or the celebrity spokesperson who fundraises for your nonprofit—or is it the idea or product itself? If it involves people, a key piece to understand is whether those responsible for implementing the idea will be faithful to its ingredients (this is called "political will" in policy circles). Knowing this isn't half the battle. It's the whole battle.

If your answer is the "chef" (people), there will likely be a limit to how big you can get, since, as we've seen, people with unique skills are inherently unscalable. However, that doesn't mean you can't be profitable, provided that you recognize your scaling limitations from the beginning. List Trucking is one of countless examples. My gramps started our family business, and he was a one-man show: one guy, one truck, one good living. My dad took it over and expanded a little, but he still had just a few trucks, with him running things solo. Then my brother took it over, and now it is basically him and one other guy. My gramps, dad, and brother are all great men and hard workers. But guess what? They don't scale, because they are in the chef business rather than the ingredients business. Of course, there are trucking companies that have scaled to hundreds or even thousands of trucks and employees, but for many small companies the personal touch is the key, if an unscalable one. And that's okay. The men in my family accepted that they would run a small firm their whole lives, and they have been happy and successful doing so.

The point is simply that you need to know if your idea is of the mom-and-pop variety or the Uber variety. If yours hinges on a combination of both chef *and* ingredients, like Jamie's Italian, you need to determine the relative importance of each. When it comes to ingredients, you must know your *negotiables* and *non-negotiables,* then figure out whether your non-negotiable ingredients—the ones your enterprise can't survive without—are in fact scalable.

Consider the publisher of this book, Currency, which is an imprint of Penguin Random House. Their distribution network is a key ingredient of their business, and it's scalable, because there are systems and infrastructure in place such that if two hundred new bookstores were to open all across the country, the publisher would be able to ship books to them almost overnight. But another key ingredient is great content, which doesn't scale because there are a limited number of great ideas and writers in the world (just as there are a limited number of world-class chefs). So if they plan to scale further, they first need to identify which of the key ingredients are scalable and which aren't. In this case, if they were to double in size, they wouldn't be able to maintain fidelity for content, yet they could for distribution.

If you slow down and take a look around, you'll see that the idea of negotiables and non-negotiables is everywhere. When you break down the component parts of a car, it's fairly easy to see what's negotiable and what's not. For an automobile to serve its purpose, four tires and an engine are non-negotiables, while a state-of-the-art navigation system and TV screens for the backseat passengers are not. In economics, the practice of valuing such component parts is known as *hedonics*. Making similar hedonic assessments of your idea is a central feature of the science of scaling.

Non-negotiables have infinite value, since your enterprise will not function at scale without them. Negotiables, meanwhile, have finite value. Scaling can succeed only when the non-negotiables remain in place. In general, a growing enterprise will begin to lose voltage once it reaches the point where its non-negotiable ingredients no longer scale.

Keeping the Faith

As the preceding examples showcase, to achieve high voltage as you grow you need to maintain *fidelity* to your scalable, non-negotiable sources of success. In the case of Airbnb, for example, its non-negotiables when it started out were its digital platform and network of hosts, and the company has been able to sustain these elements at scale (though this hasn't prevented them from also launching experiments scaling other services). As you grow, you may also establish new non-negotiables, either in place of or in addition to others. Take Netflix. In its early years, its non-negotiable ingredients included the shipping infrastructure needed to operate its DVD-by-mail service. Today, that infrastructure remains relevant but arguably negotiable, while new non-negotiables include its library of streaming content and the online platform through which that content is delivered.

Staying faithful to your non-negotiables, however, often presents difficulties as you scale. One of the clearest illustrations of this issue is the long-standing challenge for medical practitioners of getting patients to consistently take medications—what is known as medication compliance (or "adherence"). Prescribed medication is a non-negotiable for the effective practice of medicine. Patients need it in order to heal. That fungal rash isn't going away if you don't apply the ointment, and your strep throat won't clear up quickly without antibiotics. Naturally, then, a patient who doesn't consistently take medication as prescribed (with the exception of experimental medicines without established efficacy or drugs with a high risk of interactions or intolerable side effects) won't receive the needed or even lifesaving benefits.

Yet noncompliance with treatments plagues medical professionals around the world. In fact, doctors have been trying to understand this phenomenon for over a century. You can't scale medical knowledge and advances if the patients they are meant to benefit don't properly administer them. So recalcitrant patients are a consistent obstacle to scaling.

Lack of compliance can present a significant challenge to scaling policies and public goods as well. Think of it this way: a community doesn't benefit from building a new park if no one uses it. Similarly, there are zero benefits to a back-to-work training program that no one enrolls in. These individual examples may seem inconsequential, but imagine five hundred parks that no one uses or five hundred back-to-work training programs with no enrollment. These represent shattering failures at scale.

Compliance—another way of simply saying "use"—is a non-negotiable ingredient for just about every policy, program, or enterprise at scale. Just as focus groups need to be wary of misrepresenting who the population will be at scale, so designers of pilot studies have to look out for whether compliance levels might drop with an expansive rollout. This hidden trap crosses over to the business world as well.

There is a reason there is so much research on compliance in the field of medicine. Sure, the medical establishment cares about the well-being of patients, but because the profit motives for big pharmaceutical companies are immense, those companies have a strong vested interest in getting people to take their meds. It shouldn't be a surprise, then, that many studies in this area are funded by Big Pharma. Insurance companies, too, have a clear profit motive: they want you to take your meds and get healthier so you have fewer claims! The same goes for life insurance: the longer you keep living, the more premium payments accrue to the insurer, and the further out they can push the final settlement payment.

Any business that is built on recurring purchases and consumption runs into this compliance conundrum—that to scale you need people to not only come to what you've built but also actually use it and receive enough of a benefit that they'll use it again and again. Trader Joe's can't get you hooked on one of their dips if you don't try it and like it first. (The same goes for products that are actually physically addictive, like cigarettes.) Similarly, if you don't show up on the first day of the back-to-work training program and find it useful, you're not likely to stick with it, and if you don't take the medication for a few days but still start feeling better, you're less likely to complete the full course of treatment. So for an idea or product to succeed at scale, it's not enough to simply find your audience; you also have to make sure your audience actually engages in the desired fashion with what you have to offer. This isn't up for negotiation.

Naturally, the question of why people don't take medication that will benefit them is more baffling and psychologically complex than why people don't buy this or that dip at Trader Joe's. The difference is that with most medications, the cost is immediate, while the benefit—feeling better—comes in the future. But with the dip from Trader Joe's, you experience the tasty benefit the moment you ingest the product. Since humans tend to have present bias (we place higher values on immediate things), it's not easy to get people to consistently take a medication if the benefits won't kick in for weeks or months. Yet ultimately the challenge is identical because in both cases (and everything in between) success all comes down to getting the incentives right. With the Chicago Heights Early Childhood Center educational curriculum, I saw firsthand what happens if you fail to do this.

By the third year of our experiment at CHECC, we had designed a program that produced impressive gains for the children. The curriculum itself had two non-negotiable pillars: explicit instruction time devoted to developing both cognitive and noncognitive skills, and the guided involvement of parents. We knew we faced a dual challenge in getting parents first to sign up for Parent Academy and then to comply with its protocols, as a variety of life circumstances made it difficult for many parents in the community to be involved in the way our program called for. So we decided we would offer cash incentives to ensure their participation.

While many of us might have romantic notions about how money shouldn't be necessary to motivate parents to get more involved in their children's schooling, my research had shown financial incentives like these to be a powerful behavioral nudge, especially in underserved communities in which parents are frequently overworked and struggle to afford basic necessities. In Chicago Heights, the payments were essential and we knew this. But we didn't know exactly how essential until a school district in London contacted us to say they had read about the success of our CHECC curriculum and wanted to implement it themselves.

As my colleagues Robert Metcalfe, Sally Sadoff, and I helped the London school officials prepare the curriculum, we discovered a catch: the school district had a policy that prohibited giving parents financial incentives for involvement in their kids' education. The administrators had their reasons for instituting this policy, all of which made sense to me. But this didn't change the fact that payment to parents was a non-negotiable for scaling our program. We explained this to the school officials, but they insisted on implementing the Chicago Heights curriculum anyway.

Just as I'd feared, parents were loath to sign up—mostly because they couldn't afford to devote the time—and those who did sign up had even worse attendance than what we observe among the most truant students in the lowest-performing school districts in the United States. Unsurprisingly, their kids didn't benefit from the curriculum. How could they? They never received a non-negotiable component of the program. This would be akin to not taking your medication at the height of hay fever season but still expecting your allergies to get better.

The point here is that you don't have full control over how people will engage with your idea or enterprise when it is expanded; you can sometimes incentivize people to comply with the non-negotiable components, but you can't force them. Sometimes this failure to meet a requirement is dramatic, as was the case in London, where removing the financial incentives for parents was like taking the wheels off a car—a fatal hedonic mistake.

In other cases, the lack of fidelity to non-negotiables is more subtle or nuanced. This leads to *program drift* (also called *mission drift*), which is starkly different from noncompliance in that the lack of fidelity stems from the behavior of the idea's implementors rather than the behavior of its users. With program drift, the non-negotiables are not fulfilled at scale either because of organizational constraints that weren't present in the small scale or because implementors either won't or can't replicate the program faithfully. This causes an entirely different program to be provided at scale. Program drift is akin to a restaurant chain putting a lobster dish on the menu at its first few locations, then continuing to offer the item at new locations nationwide—only instead of lobster the dish is made with crab. For a more consequential example of program drift, we can look at the U.S. government's national Head Start program.

Head Start was launched in 1965 as part of Lyndon B. Johnson's Great Society, a sweeping social initiative that included legislation for the War on Poverty. A key component of the program, Head Start sought to mitigate a host of adversities facing low-income communities, everything from early childhood education to health and nutrition. Thirty years later, a new, more narrowly focused program came into being under the Head Start umbrella. Early Head Start grew out of a recent leap in the scientific understanding of child development—specifically, how much development occurs between birth and age three. As a result, its programs were tailored for the unique needs of infants and toddlers and focused on promoting their physical, cognitive, social, and emotional development through safe and enriching caregiving. It has since grown to be one of the largest federally funded early childhood interventions in the world. Starting with sixty-eight programs in 1995, it has grown to more than 1,200 programs, and as of 2019, 3 million children and families have gone through Early Head Start.

Following the Head Start model already established, Early Head Start aimed to support parents in taking a more active role in their children's educations. One of the linchpins (read: non-negotiables) of Early Head Start is its home visit services. Twice a month, a worker visits each family for about an hour and a half and helps parents find ways to stimulate their child's development. In the years after Early Hard Start launched, the home-visiting program yielded significant gains in school-readiness and strengthened parenting practices. A win all around—at least when done on a small scale. However, when the program scaled, it experienced considerable voltage drops, specifically with home visits for at-risk families. Upon closer scrutiny, it turned out that there was significant variation in the quality of home visits across the country. More people served at scale meant more opportunities for the quality to slip.

The problem was, the more at-risk families Head Start workers visited, the more they were greeted by parents facing many more distractions than the typical parent has to deal with. These parents understandably had much less time to devote to their kids' schooling; they were too busy keeping food on the table and making sure the bills got paid. Basically, life was getting in the way. As a result, the home visits "drifted" away from Early Head Start's method and mission. It was no longer Early Head Start as originally designed and tested. It had morphed into something that sounded the same but was actually quite different and less effective.

The home visit services ceased to maintain fidelity to their non-negotiables at scale because Early Head Start didn't fully understand those non-negotiables—parents having the time and focus to engage with their kids' learning—to begin with. The consequence was a drop in participation, which only further isolated many children from services that might have benefited their development and future lives.

With programs where academic research intersects with governmental/philanthropic funding and nonprofit implementation, program drift is quite common. Often this is due to funding coming from multiple sources, each with their own priorities and agendas—for example, a foundation whose donors want improved test scores from everyone, a school district that requires no child to be left behind, and university researchers who want publishable results. Each party might impose demands that dilute the non-negotiables. Voltage drops in such situations are especially insidious because properly evaluating programs that are scaled in the public system takes a long time, which allows failure to go unchecked for years. Thus lots of money and human effort are misspent before the problems are identified, understood, and rectified.

The concept of drift isn't exclusive to the slow-moving world of policy interventions and academic research. It plagues businesses as well, especially when the quality of a product fails to maintain the standards of customers' satisfaction. At Jamie's Italian, for instance, the combination of poor management and overstretched resources caused the quality of its food to deteriorate—what the author Paul Midler calls "quality fade." Interestingly, the place where mission drift has drawn the greatest scrutiny is at the intersection of nonprofit and for-profit enterprises.

Over the last several decades, businesses have increasingly reoriented to include social impact in their strategic priorities, while many nonprofit entities have simultaneously had to develop for-profit arms to sustain their operations. What this means in practice is that we now see venture capital firms trying not just to make truckloads of money but also to improve the world while doing so, while nonprofit groups try to support their programs with for-profit businesses— for example, the American Association for Retired Persons (AARP) funds its advocacy with an insurance-based business that generates more than $1 billion annually. Researchers have found that in both social and commercial enterprises, these dual pulls of "serving two masters" often lead to mission drift. When generating both profit *and* social good is non-negotiable, resources are often spread too thin to provide the necessary support to each.

So how can an organization combat noncompliance and drift? Addressing the economic and psychological incentives in each is a meaningful place to start. For better compliance, we need to find ways to make benefits more immediate and visible, while making compliance less costly. For drift, we have found that having people with a personal interest in maintaining the fidelity of an idea—say, the company's founder, or the original scientist who discovered the medical breakthrough—on the implementation team minimizes program drift. Short of that, if the implementors understand the *whys* behind the mission, they will be much more faithful to it.

In the world of twenty-first-century business, however, the loss of fidelity to non-negotiables that leads to the steepest voltage drops at scale frequently has nothing to do with drift. Instead, it often results from the introduction of a wonderful new ingredient that appears to scale beautifully: an innovative new technology.

Smart Technologies, Dumb People

Most digital technologies are inherently scalable. Strings of code are infinitely and instantaneously replicable, and people are going to "comply" with your product because it is precisely what they paid good money for. So if a new technology is the foundation of your enterprise, you might think that your non-negotiables are secure at scale because each copy is identical.

Not so fast.

Recall the utility engagement platform Opower from Chapter 2. In 2010, two years after launching their energy-saving initiative, the company had a new data set that my brilliant postdoctoral student Rob Metcalfe offered to analyze for them with the help of our team. Working with Honeywell, Opower had recently created what they hailed as a game-changing smart thermostat. To conserve energy, it could do things like modify home temperatures when the occupants were at work or asleep and reduce costs by purchasing more power during off-peak hours and less during peak times. It was also linked to an app so that customers could easily adjust the thermostat wherever they found themselves in the house, as long as they had their phone on them.

It had all the makings of a winning product. After the smart thermostat passed every engineering test and performed exceptionally well as a prototype, Opower rolled it out widely in areas of central California. Inexplicably, the anticipated energy savings never materialized. That was when our team (Chris Clapp, Rob Metcalfe, Michael Price, and me) came on board to figure out why.

Looking at the data from nearly two hundred thousand households, we determined that the explanation for this voltage drop was simple: adoption doesn't always equal compliance. Sure, the smart thermostat had been installed in customers' homes and its app downloaded to their phones, but this didn't mean that customers were using it properly. The default settings produced savings gains, but in practice customers gradually undid the default settings and went back to their habitual usage patterns, which undercut the promised advantages.

The problem was that the engineers hadn't modeled how actual humans behave. In essence, the promising conservation gains they predicted assumed the "perfect" customer who used the technology in optimal ways. In reality, however, their customers were humans, and humans are impulsive, error-prone, and heuristic-driven, have a proclivity for short-term gratification, and aren't always very good at understanding or following instructions. Maybe customers didn't want their dogs to be stuck in a cold house when they were away at work, or perhaps they liked coming home to a warm house instead of one still warming up. Human incompetence, laziness, and wastefulness should not be underestimated—especially at scale! The engineers should have built and tested the thermostat precisely with these tendencies in mind. Without properly testing the product with real users, it would have been impossible to guess the myriad ways in which customers misused the innovation and entirely unraveled the intended gains.

In short, they may have built a smart thermostat, but the humans who used it were certainly not so smart. In fact, Opower's problem wasn't all that different from patients not taking their prescribed medications, since pills and innovative technologies are both perfectly scalable ingredients in theory, but only with proper compliance. My team has since designed fieldwork to show how to incentivize stronger customer engagement with the smart thermostat, and initial results are promising.

Of course, with 20/20 hindsight, the better move for Opower would have been to avoid disappointing performance altogether by anticipating and addressing compliance challenges during the design phase of the device. This takes both imagination and beta-testing with people who aren't tech-savvy engineers. Top tech companies like Apple often do this. Continuing the legacy of Steve Jobs, Apple has a beta program that lets users try out prerelease software to identify glitches. Registered users get early access to new software Apple is about to release and can give their feedback.

In contrast to innovations like the smart thermostat, which had a steeper learning curve, user-friendly technologies are generally much easier to scale right out of the gate. Look at Instagram. It's incredibly straightforward to use. You take a picture and post it, and then others see it. No instructions needed, and even people who don't post pictures can use the app as voyeurs. This simplicity and ease of use are non-negotiables for Instagram, and the app works just as well with the more than one billion people globally who use it today as it did with its first one hundred users.

One last example of a recent technology that scaled exceptionally well comes not from business but from social activism. In the days following the murder of George Floyd by Minneapolis police officer Derek Chauvin in the spring of 2020, before anyone had been charged with a crime, the Grassroots Law Project organized a call drive to flood the phone lines and answering machines of public officials in Minnesota to demand justice. All volunteers had to do was call the number the Grassroots Law Project provided, which played a message coaching them on what to say, then transferred them to the office of a public official. After they spoke to someone or left a message, volunteers simply pressed the star key and would be automatically rerouted to the next official. Volunteers hit the star key again and again and left message after message, making sure their voices were heard. Great innovations like this one add new efficiency to an already existing need. Within days, Derek Chauvin was arrested and charged, with the other officers who had been involved being arrested days later. While numerous factors played into this win for justice, the automated phone drive technology clearly helped. And it will continue to be a valuable tool for activists wishing to reach large numbers of people with their message, because easy-to-use technology scales.

The lesson here is to make compliance easy. It might take more time, money, legwork, and creative energy early on to both design and test a new technology with a wide range of average people. But given that—to invoke Murphy's law—what can go wrong almost always does go wrong at scale, it will be worth it.

To avoid voltage drops that come from circumstances shifting when an enterprise scales up, I advocate flipping the traditional research and product development models. This means you should *start* by imagining what success would look like at scale, applied to the *entire* population with their varying situations, over a long period of time. To accomplish this goal, you need to identify your non-negotiables from the start. For example, if an education project relies on having fifty thousand teachers at scale, you should not cherry-pick the ten best teachers for the pilot study; top-tier teachers will not be representative of the 49,990 additional second- and third-tier teachers you will ultimately have to hire. Similarly, if the likes of Albert Einstein are necessary to make the curriculum work, then develop a technology that can scale Einstein-caliber teaching, because the curriculum won't scale otherwise. For policymakers, this means flipping the script from evidence-based policy to policy-based evidence.

If there are certain organizational constraints at scale—ranging from building size to available technologies to safety concerns to intrusiveness—test whether those are negotiable or not in the original study. If they are non-negotiables but aren't available at scale, then you don't have a scalable idea. This general approach is called "backward induction," and we will take it up again in greater detail in Chapter 5.

*   *   *

ONCE WE ACCEPT the realities of what our ideas have to offer, we can more realistically scale them for success. We need to understand our constraints in ecologically valid settings before we can begin to work inside of those constraints. This doesn't mean slowing down your pace. It means figuring out which way to run before sprinting ahead.

I have worked hand in hand with a lot of fast runners in the business world, and even the fastest among them never win when running in the wrong direction.

But what do you do when you uphold your non-negotiables, only to discover that scaling up successfully creates unintended consequences that threaten to undo all your hard work?

4

SPILLOVERS

n 1965, the legendary consumer-rights crusader Ralph Nader, a thirty-one-year-old lawyer at the time, published his first book, *Unsafe at Any Speed: The Designed-In Dangers of the American Automobile*. An explosive and unexpected bestseller, Nader's book took a gloves-off approach from its very first sentence: "For over half a century the automobile has brought death, injury and the most inestimable sorrow and deprivation to millions of people."

In each chapter that followed, Nader unpacked a different facet of car design that needlessly or excessively endangered drivers, passengers, and pedestrians. He examined the science of collisions, for example, and showed how manufacturers were ordering engineers to prize style over safety; he discussed air pollution caused by cars in traffic-heavy cities like Los Angeles. His jeremiad was an impassioned call for regulation—and it worked. Within months of the book's publication, the usually sluggish U.S. government moved quickly to create the National Highway Traffic Safety Administration. By 1968, a flagship federal law was passed requiring all personal vehicles to be outfitted with seatbelts.

On the surface, it appeared that Ralph Nader had succeeded at making America's roads safer. Or was it more complex than that?

Flash forward to 1975, when my adroit University of Chicago colleague Sam Peltzman published a paper titled "The Effects of Automobile Safety Regulation." The unassuming title belied Peltzman's striking conclusion: the decade of measures spearheaded by Nader to increase automotive safety hadn't actually made people safer at all. As Peltzman put it, "The one result of this study that can be put forward most confidently is that auto safety regulation has not affected the highway death rate." More surprising than this, perhaps, was his explanation for why. Drivers felt safer because of the legislated measures put in place to protect them, so they took *more* risks while driving, and in turn had more accidents. *Since I'm so safe with my seatbelt,* a driver might reason (consciously or not), *why not lay the pedal to the metal?* Seatbelts make any individual driver safer in the event of an accident, but at scale, they also appeared to lead to more total accidents. It was as if one voltage gain had been wiped out by a consequent voltage drop—an unintended and shocking consequence.

While Peltzman's paper was controversial at the time— unsurprisingly, it was politicized by pro- and anti-regulation advocates—much research in the intervening years has borne out similar conclusions in other domains. It turns out people have a tendency to engage in riskier behaviors when measures are imposed to keep them safer. Give a biker a safety helmet and he rides more recklessly—and, even worse, cars around him drive more haphazardly. And a 2009 study directly following the line of research pioneered by Peltzman found that NASCAR drivers who used a new head and neck restraint system experienced fewer serious injuries but saw a rise in accidents and car damage. In short, safety measures have the potential to undermine their own purpose.

This phenomenon—which came to be known as the Peltzman effect—is often used as a lens for studying *risk compensation,* the theory that we make different choices depending on how secure we feel in any given situation (i.e., we take more risk when we feel more protected and less when we perceive that we are vulnerable). This is why, in the wake of the 9/11 attacks and the rise in fear of terrorists gaining access to nuclear weapons, political scientist Scott Sagan argued that increasing security forces to guard nuclear facilities might actually make them less secure. The Peltzman effect also reaches into insurance markets, whereby people who have coverage engage in riskier behavior than those without coverage, a phenomenon known as *moral hazard*. Clearly, this pattern of human behavior has potentially huge implications when taken to scale.

The most obvious takeaway here is that seemingly free-will choices we make every day may in fact be shaped by hidden effects we are not aware of. (Also, you should wear a seatbelt *and* drive safely!) But in the context of scaling, this illuminates another cause of voltage drops that we must avoid: the *spillover effect.* This is the unintended impact one event or outcome can have on another event or outcome, a classic example being when a city opens a new factory and the air pollution it produces impacts the health of residents in the surrounding area. That this effect occurs speaks to the inescapable web linking events, the things humans create, and the natural world. The term "spillover effect" has been applied in fields as far-ranging as psychology, sociology, marine biology, ornithology, and nanotechnology, but for the purposes of this book we will define it in a human sense, as the unintended impact of one group of people's actions on another group. And nothing makes spillovers more likely and visible than scaling an endeavor to a wide swath of people. Remember the Murphy's law of scaling: anything that can go wrong will go wrong . . . *at scale*. Or to put it slightly less memorably, something unexpected has a much higher probability of occurring at scale than not at scale.

Spillovers That Emerge at Scale

The spillover effect falls under a larger umbrella category popularly known as the law of unintended consequences. The idea is self-explanatory: sometimes an action with a planned outcome creates a subsequent surprise outcome. As we saw with Ralph Nader's well-intentioned campaign for automotive reform and regulation, just because you design something to have one effect doesn't mean it won't yield other effects, too. And this phenomenon usually becomes most visible at scale.

One of the ways that spillovers can perilously flood a scaled-up operation results from what economists call *general equilibrium effects,* a term describing shifts in an overall market or system that likely don't manifest on a small scale. In economics, general equilibrium effects refer to the self-adjusting relationship between supply and demand that is shaped by developments in the marketplace. More broadly, this simply means that when the equilibrium of a system is disrupted in one area, the system will adjust itself in other areas until that equilibrium is restored. One tweak ends up tweaking the entire system.

We see many examples of this in the job market. Let's say that in a certain year, 50 percent of all college sophomores decided to change their major to economics. What would happen a few years later when they entered the workforce? Assuming no sudden spike in employer demand for economics majors, a large influx of new economists on the market (increased supply) would cause their wages to plummet—a huge voltage drop. However, let's say I conducted an experiment where I randomly chose just one hundred college sophomores, forced half of them to change their major to economics, then looked at how much they were earning in their first job. These additional new majors would not have a negative impact on their earning power at all, because a mere fifty students is not enough to disrupt the equilibrium of the job market overall.

Here is the rub: our experiments typically give us answers along the lines of my small-scale experiment. They don't speak to large movements, such as everyone, or even 50 percent of college sophomores. Yet, in a very real sense, this is exactly what we want to know before we scale, especially in the policy world: what are the total effects of my idea in a world where *everyone* changes and *anything and everything* else can change? Ideas don't exist in petri dishes. And an innovation can have negative consequences that are at odds with its purpose but *only become visible at scale.*

You can imagine a similar outcome with large-scale job-training programs intended to give people more opportunities. They seem great in theory, but in reality, the more people who become highly skilled, the greater the competition for those high-paying jobs. This competition has the potential to lower wages for all high-skilled workers, making job-training initiatives problematic and less attractive, or at the very least a mixed blessing, at scale. Once again, general equilibrium effects can upend expectations.

The world of ride-sharing is another perfect laboratory for uncovering general equilibrium effects. For example, when I was at Uber, Travis Kalanick agreed to try to raise drivers' incomes by increasing their base fare. It sounded like a logical approach—higher fares equal more money, right? Yet looks can be deceiving.

When economists Jonathan Hall, John Horton, and Daniel Knoepfle examined Uber base fare increases across thirty-six cities over 105 weeks, they found an interesting pattern: the rise in base fares led to significant increases in driver earnings for several weeks, but by week six, driver earnings had dropped to just slightly above where they had been before the base fare increase, and by the fifteenth week, the earnings increase had disappeared entirely. Why? Because the fare increase made driving for Uber a more attractive proposition, which incentivized existing Uber drivers to offer more rides, while also attracting new drivers. As a result, the supply side of the market became more competitive, which meant that on average each individual driver got fewer trips overall, erasing the intended gains from the wage bump. The unintended consequence—or spillover—of the increased base fare on drivers at scale thwarted the well-intentioned deed by Uber.

I later observed a similar spillover effect among Uber riders in Seattle. What happened was fairly simple. We gave one group of Uber users $5-off coupons for rides on a specific Friday afternoon, then we compared their behavior on that Friday afternoon to that of users who hadn't received the coupon. Sure enough, the couponers took more rides than the no-couponers, and the increased earnings from those rides were more than enough to offset the discounts the coupons provided. On the surface, it seemed like we'd hit the jackpot: a tiny tweak with the potential to generate big bucks.

Buoyed by this early success, we scaled up the $5 coupon initiative to include a much larger group of Seattle riders. Instead of leading to more gains, however, this expansion produced a punishing voltage drop. The coupons increased the number of rides immediately; just as they had in our initial test run. But then came market imbalance, the number of trips fell suddenly, across the whole city. It appeared that the initially attractive offer had turned repellent overnight, like a delicious plate of food that is left out and spoils. Why had this happened?

When we looked at the data, the reason became crystal clear. It wasn't that our first small-scale success had been a false positive, nor was it because the riders who took part in the pilot didn't accurately represent Seattle riders as a whole. At scale, the coupon deal initially caused demand to spike to the point of reducing the available supply of drivers. The shortage of drivers resulted in an increase in fare prices and wait times, which in turn decreased overall demand. The living, breathing market was simply settling into a new equilibrium. While the strategy had seemed foolproof among a small subset of users, it shape-shifted into a failure at scale. To borrow Malcolm Gladwell's term, there was a tipping point at which a good idea became a bad one.

Even at the most macro level, spillover effects work in the same way. For example, epidemiologists commonly report that many air and water pollutants are harmless; because they are present at such low levels, the body's natural protective mechanisms can repair any damage, so there is no ill effect. Yet if the power plant that emits those pollutants expands, or a new one comes online, the critical threshold might be exceeded. Or just look at our history with automotive and air travel. These technological innovations in transportation have wonderfully revolutionized human life. Our ancestors from the nineteenth century would marvel at how easy and fast it is for us to see places and visit people all over the world. But at scale, over time, our advances in transportation technology have also vastly contributed to climate change, which threatens to radically alter human life on our planet.

While we tend to focus on the unforeseen problems that can arise from spillovers, unintended effects aren't by any means all negative when it comes to scaling. In the world of international development, there has been much concern over the downstream impacts that foreign-aid organizations can have on local communities. In particular, in development economics, cash transfers to residents in poverty-stricken locales are an area of worthwhile scrutiny. For example, a nongovernmental organization eager to stimulate the local economy by giving money or microloans to a significant number of residents would want to be aware of any possible spillovers. Will this scaled-up infusion of cash trigger inflation, or might class stratification increase?

In 2014, a group of noteworthy economists—Dennis Egger, Johannes Haushofer, Edward Miguel, Paul Niehaus, and Michael W. Walker—sought to answer these questions with a field experiment in a poverty-stricken area of rural Kenya. They provided randomized, one-time cash transfers of $1,000 apiece to some ten thousand thatched-roof households spread across 653 villages of the Siaya region near Lake Victoria. That's right—a total of $10 million! As the researchers noted, "The cash transfers amounted to over 15 percent of local GDP during the peak 12 months of the program."

Over the next two and a half years, they collected all manner of economic data and found no evidence of negative spillovers. For example, inflation didn't spike, as they had feared. But several positive spillovers had occurred. It turned out that the cash infusions significantly increased consumption not only among families that received the money—this was a given—but also among households that *weren't* part of the experiment. Naturally, the rise in consumption among recipients of the cash meant more profits for local businesses, which in turn meant the owners of those businesses now could afford to employ more local workers—the result being that both business owners and the workers they employed all had more money to spend themselves. The overarching result of such a large cash infusion into the economy created a proverbial rising tide that lifted all boats; a family didn't have to receive a cash payment to benefit from the payments' effect on the region's economy as a whole. This was thanks to a general-equilibrium spillover.

In the world of business, you can think of the buzzword "disruption" as another way of describing general-equilibrium spillovers. Our digital age has brought several waves of disruption, and will continue to do so. The rapid pace of innovation has upset the equilibrium in seismic ways, sending many companies and even whole industries, like travel agencies and print magazines, sliding toward the dustbin of history. Yet, like any system that desires equilibrium, the business landscape continues to self-adjust, with new companies and industries constantly emerging in the place of those that have been lost.

At a macro level, spillovers can make headlines. How many cases have there been of a factory that creates jobs but also produces pollution runoff that harms the health of a nearby community? Or a new highway that benefits a city's transportation infrastructure but also depresses the value of adjacent homes that now face elevated levels of noise and air pollution? There are countless examples like these—economists call them *externalities*—since the generation of unintentional reactions to intentional actions is both widespread and common.

At scale, these unintended reactions can create ripples across the globe, but it's important to remember that spillovers bubble up out of a vast web of individual choices that eventually hit a critical mass. Understanding how this occurs on a macro level is essential for designing and sustaining a scalable enterprise; however, focusing entirely on the macro is a mistake.

On a more micro level, spillover effects can have just as much impact, though they often manifest in indirect or even undetectable ways. This hit home for me firsthand when I tried to do a good deed and raise money for our local youth baseball organization, the Flossmoor Firebirds, in Flossmoor, Illinois.

The Social Side of Spillovers

In the summer of 2010, I hired more than two hundred solicitors (or canvassers) to go door-to-door asking for donations for a team of young underprivileged ballplayers called the Firebirds. I was unsure of how much to pay them for their time, but then it dawned on me that I had serendipitously stumbled into an opportunity for a field experiment. Would $10 an hour be enough to incentivize the solicitors to successfully amass the desired donations? And would raising the cash incentive raise their motivation levels, resulting in even more donations? So I did a bit of experimentation: after splitting them into two groups (at random), I hired half the solicitors at $15 per hour and the other half at $10 per hour. Naturally, this was done in private, so only they knew their hourly pay. Then they all piled into vans that took them to different neighborhoods to canvass. For ease of transportation logistics, the two groups were mixed together in the vans. I figured they wouldn't talk too much about pay, but if they asked me, I had a stock response that pay differences were possible (no one asked).

In reviewing the data, it became clear that the canvassers earning $15 per hour had worked much harder. They approached more houses per hour and raised more money from each house compared to those who were paid $10 per hour. The extra $5 was well worth it.

So when fundraising season came around again the following summer, I hired hundreds of solicitors once again and this time paid them all $15 per hour, thinking that I was going to leverage my scientific findings from the previous summer for the good of the underprivileged ballplayers. All was going well until one weekend late in the summer when we began running short on cash. Realizing we needed to pinch our pennies to reach our fundraising goal, we paid a new vanload of solicitors just $10 per hour. I expected that they wouldn't secure quite as many donations as the $15-per-hour canvassers, but that the $10-per-hour investment would still be worth it. Yet much to my surprise, these low-wage solicitors worked just as hard and raised just as much money as their higher-wage peers.

This plot twist was puzzling. Could it be that the size of the cash incentive really had no demonstrable effect on the canvassers' motivation or performance? Clearly, I would have to run another field experiment to get to the bottom of these wage effects.

So the following summer we designed an experiment with three van configurations. The first set of vans had some solicitors who were paid $15 per hour and others who earned $10 per hour. This was the design from the first summer, which mixed the low- and high-wage workers. The second set of vans included only solicitors earning $15 per hour. Meanwhile, the third set of vans shuttled only solicitors who were paid $10 per hour. Importantly, the solicitors in the second and third groups had no idea about each other or that other solicitors were making a different amount than they were.

What happened next was fascinating. I found no differences in performance when comparing solicitors in vans two and three. Each group canvassed with the same effectiveness, their differing pay having no impact on how well they did out there knocking on doors and asking for donations. But in the mixed group (the set in the first van), we again found differences in how much money they raised and how hard they worked: the higher-paid solicitors considerably outperformed the lower-paid solicitors on every dimension.

As it turned out, it wasn't the extra $5 that incentivized the higher-paid solicitors to work harder. It was the $5 *less* that *dis*incentivized the lower-paid workers when they knew others were making more than them. The fact was, at odds with my original belief in the very first summer, the solicitors did talk about pay and this served to *dis*incentivize the lower wage earners. This group shirked their duties by visiting fewer houses, and even engaged in more theft, pocketing donations at a much higher rate than the higher-paid solicitors.

This is an example of the psychological phenomenon called *resentful demoralization*. It's the flip side of the famous John Henry effect, which is the bias introduced into experiments when members of the control group are aware that they are being compared to the experimental group and react by trying harder than they typically would. In my field experiment, the solicitors did the opposite. The feelings of resentment resulting from the knowledge of the wage disparity (i.e., that they were being underpaid compared to their peers) created an unintended effect that undercut our fundraising.

It might make sense intuitively that if you pay someone more money you'll get more effort from them. But inside the tapestry of events, people, and circumstances, this seeming truth can break down in an unexpected manner. I should have just paid everyone $10 per hour, and we would have raised more money for the underprivileged ballplayers.

The results of this field experiment have broader implications beyond just fundraising. It is relevant to a new push in many sectors of the economy for companies and organizations to be more transparent about employee compensation. The idea is that salary data should be made publicly available—at least inside the company—so that everyone knows how much everyone else is making, from the bottom all the way up to the top. Based on my experience with the baseball fundraising, one would expect that making salaries transparent could drive resentful demoralization if people saw peers making more. But that is not the full story.

In 2017, two crafty economists, Zoë Cullen and Ricardo Perez-Truglia, ran an ingenious field experiment with 2,060 employees of a multibillion-dollar commercial bank in Asia to explore how employees' misperceptions about the salaries of their managers and peers might impact their motivation and behavior. At the bank Cullen and Perez-Truglia studied, managers on average made between 114 percent and 634 percent more than other employees. Meanwhile, salaries for non-managerial employees varied between 16 percent more than and 16 percent less than the average salary of their peers with the same title from the same unit. When given a survey designed to elicit employees' perceptions of their colleagues' salaries, employees underestimated the salaries of their managers by 14.1 percent but were slightly better at guessing how much their peers made. This is significant because it suggests that if employees were to learn that their managers made even *more* than they thought, they might experience even more resentment, and thus be even less motivated.

Then came the fun part. The researchers provided the employees information about managers' and peers' salaries and observed their behavior for the next several months. After analyzing the results, they found that employees who were told their manager made 10 percent more than they originally thought actually worked slightly *harder;* the average number of hours they worked increased by 1.5 percent over the next ninety days. Conversely, when employees learned that peers made 10 percent more than they did, they worked 9.4 percent *less* over the next ninety days. It even demoralized employees to the extent that they were more likely to leave the company.

It turns out that when people find out their managers earn more than they thought, it can have a motivating effect. This is because they become more optimistic about their future salaries—and this effect on the whole is stronger than any resentful demoralization about a superior receiving a much higher salary than them. In contrast, when it comes to peers earning more, the resentment over what is perceived (perhaps rightly) as an unfair discrepancy eclipses any possible optimism about the future.

So what are the possible spillover effects of this type of salary transparency at scale? First, it's important to recognize that as organizations grow, they tend to add fewer managerial positions than non-managerial ones; for each manager a company hires, they generally hire several lower-level employees, so as the company grows, the ratio of managers to employees shrinks. In a large company, then, one is likely to have many more peers than managers. Accordingly, if companies wish to share managers' salaries, the value proposition of that choice improves as the organization scales. Which is to say you could expect a voltage gain. Sharing salaries of lower-level employees, however, would likely produce a voltage drop as you scale (assuming those employees are not all compensated equally) since there are more employees who may experience resentful demoralization, leading to lower effort and inducing some to seek jobs elsewhere.

More broadly, leaders should recognize that people don't make choices in a vacuum. Individual behavior is also a function of the information we have available, particularly when we compare our situation with that of others. As these wage examples drive home, hidden spillover effects like these are crucial to watch out for, and it requires great agility to respond to them effectively. There is much we can learn from surprises that unleash unexpected results and reveal new insights.

High-Voltage Social Spillovers

Whether we're aware of it or not, our peers can influence our behavior in powerful and unexpected ways. And while understanding these dynamics in the workplace is invaluable, the workplace does not have a monopoly on peer-to-peer spillovers. Being a parent has led me to think hard about the impact of my children's peers on their human capital formation (that is economese for their education). Indeed, peer effects in education have recently received a great deal of attention from researchers and teachers, many of whom argue that peer composition is as important a determinant of student outcomes as other widely cited factors including teacher quality, class size, and parental involvement. The wonderful work of economist Bruce Sacerdote reveals that in elementary, secondary, and postsecondary education, within certain contexts and for certain outcomes, peer effects are indeed a powerful determinant of why students turn out the way they do. This research, combined with my personal experiences as a parent, played into my expectations as my team prepared to launch the Chicago Heights Early Childhood Center.

From the day we opened our school's doors, I believed that early childhood learning was fundamentally a social activity. So spillovers had the potential to spring up, and I hoped they would be the good kind. Previous research had shown that in experiments like ours, ef-

fects on the *treatment group* (the participants who were randomly selected to receive the intervention, which in our case was our special
preschool curriculum) could, through sheer proximity, have an inad-
vertent influence on the *control group* (the participants who don't receive the intervention but who are measured as a comparison sample).

A "treatment effect" spilling over in this fashion seemed highly
likely in the context of CHECC because kids and parents from both
groups lived in the same neighborhoods and belonged to the same
communities. Of course, the big question was how these effects
might manifest if we scaled the CHECC program to other schools
and to more children. But first we would have to be sure the spillovers
helped rather than hurt, and my clever colleagues Fatemeh Momeni
and Yves Zenou joined me to examine how this might play out.

Months passed, then a couple of years. Meanwhile, day after day,
the adorable kiddos filed into our classrooms, where our hardworking teachers faithfully followed our curriculum. Our main curriculum for the treatment group involved special techniques designed
to strengthen both the children's cognitive skills (activities involving
intellectual effort, like reasoning and remembering) and their noncognitive skills (interpersonal skills like teamwork and sharing). At
the end of each day, the kids from both groups would go home, and
many would spend time together. They would play tag and sports,
invent imaginative games, have fun, and of course have conflicts to
resolve. In short, they were kids being kids, and to do all these things
together they communicated constantly. Which is how the *direct spillover* occurred—from the treatment group to the control group.

Essentially, kids who were in our treatment program were im-
parting their rapidly developing cognitive and noncognitive skills to
the control group children *simply by their proximity and daily interactions*. When the kids spent time together, the way the treatment
kids talked, shared, and played subtly and unconsciously registered
among the kids in the control group, who eventually began to emu-
late the behaviors, choices, and skills their peers had been taught in
our program. This effect was even highly localized, increasing as spa-

tial distance decreased (i.e., among kids who were neighbors). We see yet again the rising-tide-lifts-all-boats principle, where the benefits to some members of a group spilled over to benefit the group as a whole. This spillover all but guarantees that, when scaled, the program will generate a voltage gain for most children in a community.

We saw a similar effect within the treatment groups as well, in that the kids in our program who shot ahead in cognitive and noncognitive skills created a self-reinforcing cycle that caused the group as a whole to accelerate. Put simply, the children spurred each other to develop faster. The treatment group gains spilled over right back into the treatment group, unlocking an exponential voltage gain—benefits squared! This effect is built to scale because the advantages that accrue are magnified with more participants.

Meanwhile, there was also another spillover at work in Chicago Heights. While kids in the community played together, their parents inevitably talked. The adults in the treatment group actively discussed their kids' participation in our program, and their own participation in our Parent Academy, perhaps even mentioning some of the new techniques they were learning. In other words, the news was getting around about CHECC, and parents' motivation about their kids' futures spreads like wildfire! Naturally, the parents in the control group (who had signed up for the program but lost the lottery, so their child didn't get randomly assigned to our treatment program) cared as much about their children's futures as the other parents did, so just hearing about the program from those parents motivated them to get creative and look for ways to independently support their children's cognitive and noncognitive development—perhaps through after-school programs or other supplementary support, or by implementing techniques they heard about from adults who participated in Parent Academy.

In a way, this effect is similar to the employees who worked harder when they knew their managers were paid more. Instead of resenting the fact that they hadn't been (randomly) selected for the program, the parents in the control group worked harder to get involved in their kids' education because the CHECC parents gave them a model to aspire to, and instilled optimism that their kids could realize the same gains as the program kids. It was as if the CHECC parents had opened their eyes to a new horizon of possibilities, and they wanted to make sure their kids didn't fall behind. This unplanned effect of the CHECC program represented a massive positive spillover. All told, when we included the spillover effects alongside the original measurement of program efficacy, the overall impact of the program expanded at least tenfold. High voltage in action!

Yet there was also one negative spillover that should be recognized. The extra time those CHECC parents were investing in the education of the child in the program had to come from somewhere, and our data showed that often it came from time spent with the child's sibling(s). So one unintended consequence was that siblings received much less parental attention. While this effect was small compared to the direct spillover discussed earlier, a failure to account for this effect would make the intervention seem more beneficial than it actually was. To obtain the complete picture, we had to look at the entire ecosystem and account for the program's impact on *all* of the kids within it.

The positive spillovers we observed with CHECC are a type of spillover known as the *network effect,* or a *network externality,* and it is potently relevant to business in the digitized twenty-first century. Take the examples of Facebook and LinkedIn (or pretty much any social networking platform). If only ten other people use these platforms, the benefits they provide are small because the network is small. In Facebook's case, you want to stay connected to the lives of many people you know, and in LinkedIn's case you won't have much new terrain to explore for professional contacts if there are few users. But if lots of people are on these services, then benefits are far greater. This type of voltage gain is called *parabolic growth.* And as a network scales, the benefits to its members get bigger and bigger and bigger—often to the point of what is known as "lock-in," which means members are almost shackled to using these platforms.

Or think about Lyft Pink from Chapter 2. As more riders join the marketplace, more drivers will join, too. This allows wait times and prices to drop because there are many more readily available driver-rider matches. And when wait time and prices are low, more riders join, starting the cycle all over again. This is very good news at scale.

Network externalities also play out in other areas of society. Take vaccinations, for instance. Whether we're talking about polio, measles, the flu, or Covid-19, the aim of administering a vaccine to someone is to reduce the likelihood of that person getting sick or dying. This is the primary benefit, but at scale—that is, when a critical portion of the population receives a vaccine—there is a spillover benefit as well: herd immunity. If herd immunity is reached, the people who were not vaccinated still benefit indirectly from the vaccine since everyone around them is immune. The flip side of this, of course, is that the greater the number of people who refuse the vaccination, the greater the risk to the population as a whole. This is one reason modern societies might use social messaging intended to shame the anti-vaxxers: to curb the negative spillovers.

*   *   *

THE LESSON OF spillovers in all their surprising manifestations is that the moment you begin to scale up your enterprise, you need to keep a very close eye out not just for the effects that you intended but also for the unexpected and sometimes hidden ones you didn't intend. Everything is interconnected, and the web you weave will only become more tangled and complex at scale.

As a quick recap of what to look for, you should consider and measure spillovers in three basic categories:

1. *General equilibrium effects.* These tend to occur at scale and lead to unintended consequences that can have large positive or negative market-wide effects. This type of spillover emerges as a tipping point.
2. *Social-side behavioral spillovers.* These occur when others affect your behavior, either through observation or through direct

impact. Observing others causes people (consciously or unconsciously) to change their own behavior in ways that can be either positive or negative.

3. *Network effect spillovers.* These occur when the use of some product or adoption of some policy amplifies the benefits or costs for all users / adopters. These may be built in intentionally or emerge organically as you scale.

If you find negative spillovers, address them right away. And if you see positive spillovers, exploit them, as they contain the key to unlocking the true promise that your idea holds at scale. Once you have done so, you have cleared the fourth hurdle to scaling. But the fifth and final pitfall of the Five Vital Signs can still kill your voltage: unsustainable costs at scale.

THE COST TRAP

A rivale was going to revolutionize the health of millions of people. Founded in 2014 and open for business the following year, the company was the brainchild of Leroy Hood, a pioneering scientist working at the intersection of biology and medicine. For decades Hood had led the way on groundbreaking innovations in DNA sequencing, which fueled scientists' ability to understand the human genome and connect the dots between genetic predispositions and their impact on human experience. With Arivale, Leroy and his cofounder and CEO, Clayton Lewis, aimed to bring the potentially transformative advances of the emerging field of "scientific wellness"—a quantitative, personalized approach to health and lifestyle design—directly into people's lives.

The services Arivale provided were simple, even if the scientific processes undergirding them were not. After signing up, customers underwent a genetic workup that provided a valuable snapshot of their biological vulnerabilities, followed by periodic blood tests, gut microbiome evaluations, and one-on-one sessions with a health coach who used the lab results to offer tailored advice about diet, exercise, and other choices. Not only would customers receive personalized recommendations based on genetic biomarkers revealed by the battery of tests; they would also receive evolving, real-time feedback on how their bodies were responding to Arivale's program.

The great promise of this innovative approach was better health both in the present and in the future. If you had a genetic predisposition toward a certain disease that hadn't manifested yet but might later in life, Arivale's targeted guidance would help you make smart choices now that could lessen the likelihood of that illness or others damaging your future health. Or if you had developed unhealthy habits in the past, your coach would help you learn how to correct them before it was too late. In other words, Arivale sold a service akin to a doctor, accountability coach, and crystal ball all rolled into one new model for health and longevity—a true promise to increase your quality of life in future years. No wonder they had no trouble raising $50 million in investment capital and were named Start-up of the Year by GeekWire in 2016. The excitement surrounding the Seattle-based Arivale wasn't just about the future of the health of its clients. It also seemed to suggest a new promise for the future of health itself. This was clearly an idea worth scaling.

Lest it sound like Arivale was more hype than substance, let's pause here to note that the optimism about the company's potential wasn't based merely on a sexy, of-the-moment sales pitch in a world in which personal wellness is both a cultural obsession and a multibillion-dollar industry. Hood and Lewis's vision for rocketing health into the twenty-first century checked the four boxes necessary for scaling that we have examined so far. What they offered customers hinged on evidence-based science—the breakthroughs in genetic analysis that Hood and others had pioneered, as well as a peer-reviewed observational study (published in 2019) of over 2,500 Arivale clients demonstrating clinical improvements in their health thanks to the combination of biomarkers and coaching. In short, the company's game-changing technique did not appear to be a false positive. Moreover, the sky was the limit for the number of people their service would appeal to—after all, who doesn't want to be healthier and avoid future maladies?—and because it was customizable and tailored to each individual, it could meet the needs of a broad and diverse population. Likewise, they knew their non-negotiables (lab testing and lifestyle coaching) and understood they needed to remain faithful to them. And no spillovers had bubbled up. Arivale's success seemed guaranteed.

And yet the company still wouldn't scale.

The Cost Side of Scaling

In 1776, Adam Smith published his landmark study of classic economics, *The Wealth of Nations*. The book is most famous for laying out Smith's elegant idea of the "invisible hand"—the unseen forces in a free market that keep the supply and demand of goods in a state of shifting but healthy equilibrium. As Smith examined the implications of this natural give-and-take between what consumers buy and what sellers provide, he identified a facet of the invisible hand's mechanics that affects the scalability of any endeavor: *economies of scale*.

Just about every person on earth has enjoyed the benefits of economies of scale in some way, even if the term is unfamiliar. If you own a cellphone, watch movies, use electricity, or take prescription medication, you've been on the winning end of economies of scale. Bringing any of these products to market demands the investment of an enormous amount of money: the design and development of the cellphone (the engineering process, metals and plastics, and factory assemblage), the production of the movie (actors and crew, sets, publicity), the infrastructure for distributing the electricity (power lines, the technology controlling the grid), the years' worth of research and development to conceive and test breakthrough pharmaceutical drugs (lab costs, clinical trials). You can think of this up-front investment as a *fixed cost*. There is no getting around it.

But after these companies' initial up-front investments in their products, their average cost to produce the goods drops dramatically as a function of scale. This is because their costs are now spread across hundreds of thousands or millions of units, which means that each one gets cheaper to make as more are produced.

As Apple orders more iPhones to be made at its factories, the cost of making each phone goes down, allowing the company to make the device available at an accessible price point for customers while still turning a profit. When movie studios scale a film by opening it across the country or even the entire world, they can charge a low ticket price and still push their ledger on the film into the black. Once utility companies have the infrastructure to move electricity around in a city, the average cost to provide service to one more neighborhood keeps decreasing as more homes are added. And once a breakthrough drug is developed, the more people who take the medication, the lower the cost of producing each dose. These are all examples of economies of scale, which occur when the average total cost per unit of output decreases as output increases. In other words, the more phones and movie tickets and electricity they sell, the less companies have to charge customers to consume those goods and services. And since consumers tend to like low prices, the invisible hand ensures that the companies that achieve economies of scale are the ones that end up winning.

Inversely, when the average cost of producing something *increases* as you produce more or as your operation grows, what you have is *dis*economies of scale. This can happen, for example, when a key resource necessary for production is scarce or becomes increasingly difficult to obtain. Think of oil and gas extraction. For the first few hundred barrels, oil might readily flow from the well with the use of very low-cost pumping equipment, but as the well is drawn down, expensive specialty equipment might be necessary to reach the last barrels. Likewise, consider a school district that has the goal of hiring only teachers who have impeccable credentials. Hiring the first few dozen might be easy, but it might cost a pretty penny to hire the last few dozen because you're competing with other employers for talent that is now in short supply. Obviously, your idea can quickly lose voltage if scaling up means a spike in cost.

In *The Wealth of Nations,* Smith mainly focused on the idea of division and specialization of labor to achieve economies of scale. It is a commonsense argument: not only would workers be more productive by concentrating on a single task that they are good at, but they would also get better at it over time. In other words, specialization would lead to more efficient and thus more cost-effective production, and the more a company scaled, the more these advantages would multiply. For instance, as factory workers making iPhones become more efficient at assembling them, the resulting productivity gains would lower the cost of making each phone, and in theory lower the prices for consumers, too.

This matters because no matter how good an idea is, if the returns on your product don't surpass the cost, or if the results achieved by your nonprofit don't justify the expenditures, then you lose voltage and your idea isn't scalable. It doesn't matter if you have cleared the hurdles we've established in the previous four chapters; you could have a proven idea, a large and captive audience, fidelity to your non-negotiables, and no detectable negative spillovers (or even lots of positive spillovers), but if costs grow out of control, the idea simply won't scale. End of story.

Economies of scale (firmly rooted in the supply side of economics) is a concept that may ring a bell from the Reaganomics era back in the 1980s. Supply-siders argued that the optimal method of spurring economic growth was to roll back taxes and government regulation in order to lower operational costs—and, by extension, the prices consumers pay for goods and services. While supply-side economic theory takes us into macroeconomic territory that isn't directly related to the science of scaling, it nevertheless reinforces the inescapable truth that operational costs have a powerful impact on everything from a nation's economic prosperity down to the success or failure of individual businesses.

That was certainly the case for Arivale, whose revolutionary approach was ultimately undone by cost problems.

Until That Time Arrives

When Arivale first launched, it charged customers approximately $3,500 per year for its state-of-the-art wellness program. The lab costs for the battery of genetic and physiological tests, plus the salaries of the health coaches and other employees, created high overhead, so making the company's innovative services any cheaper threatened profitability. But considering the improved quality of life and decreased healthcare costs the coaching-and-biometric program would likely provide in the long term, $3,500 annually was arguably a decent price. After all, you can't put a price on a longer, healthier life, right?

Actually, in this case, you could—and it was far less than $3,500 for most people.

As a result of the high starting price point, Arivale didn't generate the demand the company and its investors were hoping for. At first blush, this wasn't alarming. Many companies take years to become profitable. After all, it's not just the price point that influences demand but also marketing, competition, and other factors that may delay a product or service from finding its customer base. Even Amazon took ten years to become profitable (though part of founder Jeff Bezos's trick was building an infrastructure that opened up huge cost advantages thanks to economies of scale). Sometimes it's a matter of simply staying the course, tweaking offerings, and trying out new promotional strategies while simultaneously trying to slow the burn rate of capital. But for Arivale, the passage of time didn't translate into a meaningful enough bump in clients. In spite of the overwhelmingly positive experience of enrolled participants, new customers just weren't flocking to sign up for the company's one-of-a-kind services. Adam Smith's invisible hand, it seemed, was *too* invisible. It wasn't tapping enough people on the shoulder to say, *Hey, check this out.*

But despite the fact that new customers weren't joining up at the rate Arivale needed, its leaders didn't want to lower the price. If they wanted to eventually be financially viable, they couldn't. The cost of supplying their product was just too high. Moreover, there were not significant economies of scale to suggest that their margins would improve once they acquired a critical mass of customers. Health coaches couldn't be mass-produced at a low marginal cost the way, say, a smart thermostat or similar technology can (remember, humans are nearly impossible to scale), and the volume of tests and bloodwork wasn't nearly high enough to meaningfully capitalize on the kinds of economics of scale hospitals or doctors' offices enjoy. As CEO Clayton Lewis later put it, the genetic tests, bloodwork, gut microbiome analysis, and coaching added up to costs that were "wickedly expensive." In short, Arivale couldn't grow itself out of an entry price that was too high; after all, groundbreaking science-based wellness wasn't cheap to produce! The company would start hemorrhaging money if they charged clients too little, so for three years they kept the price of services where it was, while at the same time investing their remaining capital in marketing in an attempt to attract new customers. But the new customers didn't come.

In 2018, three years after Arivale opened for business, the company threw a Hail Mary pass by significantly lowering the price for its services—from $3,500 annually to $1,200 (or from $290 per month to $99 per month). Even with this new, more affordable rate, by the following year the company still had only 2,500 enrollees. Instead of jump-starting the engine, the more affordable price point became like a hole in a jet's fuel tank, causing the craft to leak fuel (that is, the money needed to operate) at a terminal rate. Through a bit of learning by doing, they had managed to decrease testing costs slightly, but not enough to save the company from a crash. In April 2019, with no warning to the public of how dire things had turned, Arivale proclaimed its death in a public message:

> We founded Arivale with the vision of making personalized, data-driven, preventive coaching a new wellness paradigm in the United States. . . .
>
> Regrettably, effective today, we are terminating our consumer program. Our decision to terminate the program today comes despite the fact that customer engagement and satisfaction with the program is high and the clinical health markers of many customers have improved significantly. Our decision to cease operations is attributable to the simple fact that the

cost of providing the program exceeds what our customers can pay for it. We believe the costs of collecting the genetic, blood and microbiome assays that form the foundation of the program will eventually decline to a point where the program can be delivered to consumers cost-effectively. Regrettably, we are unable to continue to operate at a loss until that time arrives.

That month Arivale let go of its 120 employees and closed up shop, leaving all of its customers—many of whom felt devastated by the loss of their personalized health program—in the lurch. It was a painful moment for everyone involved. Executives at the company believed that if they had been able to sustain the lower entry price, Arivale would have found a big enough base to hit profitability. But the costs of keeping things running had been too high. In a postmortem interview reflecting on his company's demise, Lewis said, "Instead of launching with lower-cost, simpler programs, we stayed laser-focused on our flagship offering and we clearly did that to our peril." The promising experiment in scientific wellness had failed to scale.

From Economies of Scale to Fixed Costs

It might be tempting to attribute Arivale's fatal voltage drop, at least in part, to a miscalculation of the degree to which their early users were representative of the general population, which is to say they were overestimating their potential audience. After all, the company ultimately failed because its offerings didn't generate enough demand even after it significantly lowered its price tag. Did Arivale take a wrongheaded build-it-and-they-will-come approach from the very start? Were Americans still not mentally ready for a forward-looking healthcare strategy that focused as much on long-term, less visible preventative measures as on short-term, easily detectable improvements? Put simply, was there no scalable audience to begin with?

On the one hand, there is some merit to this argument. On

the other hand, there were plenty of people who desired Arivale's services—early demand suggested that a large population would be attracted to the wellness product. They just didn't like it at a price of thousands of dollars. There *was* demand, just not at the level and price point that the company's dwindling bank account needed, and it wasn't increasing rapidly enough. Because Arivale's burn rate on the supply side was so high, it ran out of runway before it could distinguish itself from its competitors to capture more customers—and before it could reap economies of scale.

The lesson here is that in order to successfully scale an enterprise, you need to figure out not only how many people like your idea but also what they are willing to pay for it and, importantly, how much it will cost to provide.

The cost-side misfortune that befell Arivale is a common hazard for start-ups, especially ones whose early success seems to demand rapid scaling. Take the case of Wise Acre Frozen Treats. In 2006, Jim Picariello started making organic ice pops with unrefined sugars out of a schoolhouse in a small town on the coast of Maine. He was way ahead of the curve in recognizing the demand for health-conscious ice pops, and two years later he had over a dozen employees, a real manufacturing facility, and contracts with supermarket chains across the East Coast. Then came his biggest break yet—a West Coast distribution deal. Wise Acre Frozen Treats was poised to scale and explode. But then disaster struck. As Picariello would later recall, "We never got the chance to fill all the orders. By the end of the year, we'd gone bankrupt and I was unemployed."

What went wrong? Well, first of all, making and distributing these ice pops wasn't cheap. Factoring in everything from equipment to high-quality ingredients to insurance and marketing, his costs totaled about $30,000 per month. And gains from small economies of scale didn't offset these operating costs, which ate up the company's capital reserves. There might have still been hope had the Great Recession not hit in 2008, all but eliminating any possibility that angel investors might come to the rescue by buying the company more time so that it could keep scaling until it reached profitability. With hindsight, Picariello said he thought he should have raised more money before scaling. But even so, with costs as high as they were, it's likely that an infusion of capital would have only delayed the inevitable unhappy ending for Wise Acre Frozen Treats. The company had fallen into the cost trap that threatens every business, and economies of scale would not be there to dig them out.

When we think about economies of scale, we tend to envision low-cost, mass-produced products: something off a factory assembly line. But economies of scale can be found in unlikely endeavors—even high-end products or services that seem utterly unscalable. The emerging space-tourism industry offers an intriguing case study. Today, there are at least a dozen companies around the world that hope to soon sell tickets for round-trip flights to outer space and back. The most well-known are perhaps Richard Branson's Virgin Galactic, Jeff Bezos's Blue Origin, and Elon Musk's SpaceX (though SpaceX's grander, long-term goal goes beyond mere tourism, as the company aims to fly humans across our solar system to colonize Mars as an alternative to the earth; Blue Origin's ultimate objectives are similarly oriented toward humanity's far-off survival).

All three companies have invested many years and many billions of dollars in the technology required to (safely) take passengers out for a jaunt around our planet, but the extreme cost-side considerations involved in pioneering space travel obviously make it a wildly dicey business proposition.

Initially, tickets to outer space will be extremely expensive—as of this writing, Virgin Galactic is planning to charge $250,000 per passenger—making its potential customer base infinitesimally small and the chances of recouping its invested capital almost implausibly low if the companies were to focus solely on commercial passenger space flight. This is why each is exploring parallel revenue channels that rely on their existing (read: already paid for) research and technology. Virgin Galactic, Blue Origin, and SpaceX, for example, are all acting as cargo transporters for researchers with space-based projects or work at the International Space Station. SpaceX also created a public-private partnership with NASA, for which it receives enormous subsidies. These revenue streams will help to offset the tremendous investments needed for their bigger goals.

Yet those parallel revenue channels aren't likely to be enough. The key to scaling space exploration will revolve around the cost side—that is, finding economies of scale.

Perhaps nothing sets Elon Musk apart as a businessperson more than his obsession with economies of scale. Ever since he transformed the world of online banking long ago, each major innovation he has undertaken thrives on scale economies. Consider Tesla, his electric car start-up. A stock market darling that is worth more than half a trillion dollars, its massive success can be traced to economies of scale of its two most important components: batteries and solar power generation cells, both of which can be manufactured significantly cheaper in higher numbers. In addition, everything at Tesla is geared toward increasing the efficiency of "the machine that makes the machines," or what Musk affectionately calls his "Alien Dreadnought"—that is, a highly advanced, fully automated production facility.

Even SpaceX has found a way to capitalize on the idea of scale economies. This can be seen vividly in a remarkable video in which two of its rockets land at the same time at the Kennedy Space Center. This is where the real brilliance begins: a manufacturing strategy based on reusable components. Manufacturing in a completely automated way and reusing as much as possible is the basis for SpaceX to build more than one rocket per week. This strategy has already allowed the company to put a network of satellites, Starlink, into orbit at a fraction of the usual cost (much to the chagrin of the telecommunications companies). Indeed, using reusable rockets to exploit the benefits of economies of scale, SpaceX cut cost-to-orbit by a factor of eighteen.

It is possible that space travel will one day be scaled to the point of allowing humans to settle other planets, but it is a long way off and would cost astronomical (ha!) amounts of money. But in the meantime, these companies are shrewdly leveraging economies of scale to reduce their average mission costs, and this at least gives them a better shot at one day scaling up.

The investment capital required for moonshots speaks more broadly to a challenge that many scalable innovations face in their infancy: the up-front cost to create the innovation. For start-ups, this often requires attracting funders willing to put in the capital necessary to get past this initial cost obstacle. For researchers with a big idea that will take time to produce reliable data, it means landing big grants, finding deep-pocketed donors, or establishing corporate partnerships (each of which, as we have learned, comes with a risk of mission drift). In many industries, these up-front costs are prohibitively expensive for outsiders with little financial backing, acting as a barrier to entry. I may have a game-changing idea for a new social media platform that filters out fake news and hate speech, but I'm just John List, an economist and professor with no computer-engineering skills to build my great new platform, no relevant experience that would convince investors I know what I'm doing, and no pilot data showing that my idea isn't just a misguided daydream. And in the absence of the capital to hire engineers, lure more experienced partners, and test a prototype, my idea will never get off the ground.

The wonderful thing about fixed costs is that once you have the technology, prototype, data proof, or whatever innovation is the foundation of your enterprise, you never have to spend that money again. Unlike ongoing operating costs like ingredients and employee salaries, or biometric tests and health coaching, a big up-front investment pays its dividends by not needing further big investment. (This is why patents and copyright laws exist—to allow the entity that put the sweat, blood, and money into creating something new to benefit exclusively from their up-front efforts for a while.) If what you are supplying generates demand in the marketplace, ideally you will then move on to the gratifying part of scaling: taking advantage of economies of scale.

Look at ride-sharing. Lyft and Uber required significant up-front fixed costs in order to launch their innovative transportation model, the most expensive part being the computer engineering to create the digital infrastructure that does so much: connecting drivers and passengers with real-time data through the vendor and customer interfaces, determining the ride price, facilitating financial transactions, updating a rating system for drivers and passengers, providing a venue for complaints, and a million other small but essential functions. This wasn't cheap to build! But once all of it was up and running, economies of scale kicked in—every extra rider that comes on the platform allows Lyft to spread out more of their fixed cost, so the average cost of each ride decreases.

The lesson here is to take stock of what your fixed costs are likely to be right from the outset. Then make sure you have sufficient funding, and even if you do, look for ways to reduce the up-front costs involved in launching your idea. This is largely an unattainable goal for costly endeavors like space travel, but more doable when it comes to software and other start-up ventures. For instance, you may be able to balance lower salaries for employees by offering equity in the company, which in some cases can lead to a big future payday. The less you spend on up-front costs, the less you will have to charge customers to recover it later, which will undoubtedly increase demand. You can also look for ways to offset an up-front cost by reusing some materials, or even creating and selling a byproduct of the main production process. For example, it is not a coincidence that many companies that produce crude oil also produce natural gas. This happens because natural gas is a byproduct of the oil drilling process, in the same way that molasses is a byproduct of sugar refining, sawdust is a byproduct of the lumber industry, and feathers are a byproduct of poultry processing.

And wherever you can, try to build in the potential for economies of scale as you grow in the future. In many cases, there might be important trade-offs to fixed and variable cost. As some of the preceding examples suggest, high costs up front can mean significantly lower marginal costs later on. In this way, a high up-front cost can actually be preferable, if the necessary capital is available. Ideally, operating costs will get cheaper as you scale up.

Once you're ready to launch, calculate what your ongoing operating costs will be, and then assume they will be at least 10 percent higher than expected. Then look at your estimated revenues versus those operating costs and try to figure out how much you need to scale before your idea will be profitable (or, conversely, how much time you have before your coffers run dry). Keep an eye on how fast you're burning through money. You may want to take Jim Picariello's advice and secure more investment early to lengthen your runway.

Lastly, if you have built substantial scale economies into your model, it makes sense to offer a low price point in order to get customers in the door. You may be absorbing a loss at first, but if you know that your costs will go down as you acquire more and more customers, your margins will ultimately improve, so you can still make a profit without raising the price. This is why many software products and apps have a "freemium" strategy: they offer you a simple service for free to get you hooked, then dangle more cool services for a fee. Finally, do your due diligence on your "choke price"—the price at which demand drops to zero—and run some tests to figure out how different prices influence demand. Selling something at a loss can be painful, but remember that smaller profits are better than zero customers.

These principles will help you design strategies to reduce up-front and operating costs, which will give you a better chance of scaling.

The Costs of Social Change at Scale

So far we have been focusing mostly on business, but cost problems inherent to scaling are just as common outside the moneymaking world, and maybe even more so. Indeed, cost obstacles are endemic to public policy, nonprofits, and philanthropy precisely because programs and interventions in these realms are designed not to make money but to have a positive impact on society and people's lives.

That being said, some metric must be applied to determine their utility. And cost-effectiveness at scale is essential for positive social impact.

Take the polio vaccine. In the 1950s, the poliovirus afflicted tens of thousands of young children in the United States each year. The disease was highly infectious, spreading through bodily fluids (saliva and sneezes, for example) and contaminated liquids. Parents, understandably, were terrified. It was a serious public health crisis. Thankfully, virologist Jonas Salk came along and developed the first polio vaccine. He used hundreds of thousands of kids (including his own) as test subjects, dispelling any doubts about its efficacy. His testing showed that the vaccine worked on children no matter who they were or where they lived (representativeness of population and situation). And the only spillover it had was of the positive variety: the more children who were vaccinated, the less the virus spread because it had fewer hosts to jump from—a herd immunity property.

But for the polio vaccine to be truly successful at scale, it needed to be manufactured and distributed cost-effectively. Fortunately, the vaccine was cheap to produce, thanks in large part to economies of scale, and easy to deliver (at least in the United States, where the shot could be administered by medical centers and outreach workers in urban centers and rural areas). It was these qualities that enabled the United States to fully eliminate polio by 1979.

Contrast this to an example that has become a public policy urban legend of sorts. As the story goes, there was an effort to deliver the polio vaccine to a remote community of some fifty thousand people scattered among the wetlands of northern Zambia. In a pilot program, an organization supposedly purchased hovercrafts to navigate the complex terrain and reach people in need of the vaccine. The pilot program was a success, but when aid workers attempted to expand the strategy to reach all fifty thousand people, they quickly discovered that it wouldn't scale. A fleet of hovercrafts was just too expensive! Tragically, they were forced to abandon their plans to achieve complete vaccination in this region.

In theory, the social benefits of any program must always outweigh its financial costs in order to justify funding it. So organizations and governments that finance and adopt social interventions will naturally favor the ones that yield more for less. This is basic math. If a city decides to invest in a drug rehabilitation program, it will choose the one that helps the most people per dollar spent. Even if a program has a 100 percent success rate, if it costs $50,000 per person it won't scale. (Unless perhaps it is used or funded by celebrities or tech billionaires who can pony up the cash.)

Moreover, even in cases of successful and scalable interventions, continued financial support isn't guaranteed since there are so many competing and urgent causes that also need scalable solutions. If the drug rehab program isn't benefiting the community to the extent that is required to justify the cost, the city might shift its budget and divert the rehabilitation funds to a new nutrition program in schools. Additionally, there are always competing solutions for any problem. For instance, the international aid sector is full of organizations using different technologies to bring low-cost renewable energy to people in underdeveloped rural locales. With everything from solar panels to small wind turbines and even pig-manure methane conversion systems vying for funding, the low-voltage programs are those most likely to lose support. And the low voltage is often due to high costs that don't produce good enough results.

Now we know what we're up against when it comes to the cost side of scaling. Governments don't want to spend too much money, start-ups struggle with high up-front costs, and companies can't compete on price if overhead is too high. While the circumstances may differ, the strategies discussed in this chapter are just as relevant whether you're trying to scale a new technological breakthrough, expand a research-backed education program, or deliver vaccine doses to remote villages. But even if you follow these principles to the letter, there's one more factor that may cause your costs to balloon as your idea grows: human beings.

Perfection Is the Enemy of Scale

When my team and I were first designing the educational model at the Chicago Heights Early Childhood Center, we had a clear goal: to create a program that would not only improve life outcomes for the kids in our program but also be scalable to thousands of communities all over the world.

As every parent knows, teachers are the bedrock of children's development during school hours. So early on, one of our non-negotiables was to employ only the absolute best teachers—to search high and low for those one-in-a-million educators with a true gift for bringing a classroom to life. On the surface, this seemed logical—hire the best teachers, and the kids will get the best educations.

There was just one problem: the best teachers are also very expensive to retain.

As we saw in Chapter 3, people with specialized skills—in this case, teachers—are very difficult to scale. And not only because it's hard to find a large number of "chefs," but also because highly skilled workers don't become cheaper as you "buy" more of them at scale the way, say, the wholesale price of lettuce goes down for Costco when they buy thousands of heads for their locations every week. Indeed, the opposite happens: they become more expensive. This is because to attract more high-quality people into the teaching profession, you must raise teachers' salaries in order to compete with employers that might pay them more, such as a Wall Street bank or a Silicon Valley tech company. And at CHECC, this wasn't something we could just ignore.

Our team designing the CHECC curriculum was trying to avoid the same fate as others who had come before us. For instance, in the 1990s, California reduced class sizes statewide in an attempt to improve student achievement. The problem was, scaling this approach required many more teachers, and those available often lacked necessary skills or experience. More recently, the same thing occurred with a similarly hopeful initiative to reduce class size in Tennessee. In both cases, initial small-scale results were promising, but at scale the benefits turned into vapor. The schools simply couldn't hire the teachers they needed.

To solve our scaling problem, we turned to the work of the German mathematician Ernst Zermelo. Born in Berlin in 1871, Zermelo grew up to be a caricature of a brilliant European logician: wire-rimmed spectacles, a penetrating stare, and a goatee perfect for stroking while contemplating mathematical puzzles. One of the puzzles he devoted himself to ended up playing an important role in early game theory and bears its creator's name: Zermelo's theorem.

Game theory uses math to model the different strategic and strictly rational decisions available to players in a game. In other words, game theory is not a simulation of real life, because in life no one is always fully rational, but its insights are useful to apply to real life. Zermelo posited that in a two-person game like chess the player in the stronger position at any given moment always has a series of moves that will lead to victory. Not every player can figure it out, of course, but it is logically built into the structure of the game. All of which is to say that in the theoretical mathematical universe of game theory and Zermelo's theorem, perfect strategic decisions do verifiably exist.

Some four decades after Zermelo published his theorem in 1913, mathematicians in the 1950s combined his work with the concept of *backward induction*. This fancy-sounding term simply means to reason backward in time from the best outcome possible of your current problem—whether that's winning the game of chess you're playing or creating a new educational curriculum that remains cost-effective at scale—and design your strategy accordingly. To put it another way, to get from here to there I have to walk my mind backward from there to here. By using logic to carefully imagine what victory or success at scale realistically looks like, you can then uncover all the necessary steps you would have to take. Once you have thoroughly imagined these necessary future steps, you can implement them in the present. The best chess players use backward induction, as do people whose ideas maintain high voltage at scale.

To solve our human capital dilemma, the CHECC planning team used backward induction. We began from the reality that, once scaled to thousands of schools, our program wouldn't have its dream budget or a dream applicant pool of teachers to choose from. So we had to do something very unidealistic but very practical: design the curriculum under the assumption that teachers with only average abilities would be teaching it.

If we could design a model that still produced improvements for students in spite of not having the very best 1 percent of teachers on the market, we could avoid the risk of being hamstrung by the high costs of obtaining top-notch human capital at scale. This meant resisting the temptation to rig the pilot program with the best teachers. We knew the results of the pilot would be less dazzling, which might cost us publicity and grants in the short term, but we also knew it was essential to the program's long-term success.

As we prepared to open CHECC, we hired our thirty teachers and administrators the same way the Chicago Heights public schools would, from the same candidate pool and with the same salary caps. They weren't master chefs, so to speak, but they could cook pretty decent food. And if we needed thirty thousand of them, we would be able to find and pay them. That was the most important part. We were avoiding the fate of the restaurant owner who opens one restaurant serving only the very highest-grade ingredients, then opens two more restaurants and can no longer afford those ingredients and so is forced either to downgrade or to skimp elsewhere. Much like with the teachers, the restaurant owner would have been better off if she'd used less expensive ingredients from the beginning. We took a similar tack to ensure that high teacher quality at the beginning wouldn't lead to voltage drops in other places later on.

People often cite Voltaire's quote "Perfection is the enemy of good." We might rephrase this as "Perfection is the enemy of scale." When it comes to replicating non-negotiables in a variety of contexts at scale, you sacrifice perfection but gain real-world viability. In Chicago Heights, by engineering our program with real-world cost limitations in mind, we could concentrate on testing the efficacy of a program that could eventually scale.

It may sound counterintuitive, or even idiotic, not to search out the best talent in the early stages of your endeavor. When it comes to, say, designing new, innovative hardware that will be scaled, I'm not saying to choose mediocre computer engineers. After all, the hardware or digital interface must be of high quality; that's a non-negotiable. But if maintaining that hardware at scale will require forty thousand technicians, the reality is that not all of them will be five-star workers, so those in the development phase shouldn't be, either. Hiring less-excellent technicians is admittedly not ideal, but it is a negotiable. Most important of all, it allows you to maintain fidelity even with hyperspeed growth.

Ideal conditions are not realistic in most cases, so you must ask yourself a question infused with a rude dose of reality: will you actually be able to hire the best people at scale, or will either budget restrictions or the finite pool of talented candidates make this impracticable? Most likely it will be impracticable, so when thinking ahead, you need to remember the costs of human capital, and make sure yours are sustainable as you scale.

*   *   *

WE HAVE SPENT the last five chapters on the Five Vital Signs, the hurdles you must clear in order to ensure the vitality of your idea: false positives, representativeness of population and situation, spillovers, and costs. But now that you've learned how to recognize the critical features of a scalable idea, you might be wondering: *How do I take a good, scalable idea and make it truly great?*

The next several chapters move from avoiding voltage drops to engineering voltage gains. I have developed four key strategies, which constitute the second half of this book: using behavioral-economic incentives to maximize your results, exploiting easily missed opportunities on the margins of your operation, knowing when to quit in the short term in order to win in the long term, and designing a winning and sustainable culture.

So let's crank up the voltage.

Part Two

FOUR SECRETS TO

HIGH-VOLTAGE SCALING

INCENTIVES THAT SCALE

everal years ago, a company that provided loans to small business owners approached me and my friend and colleague Steven Levitt to help them try to do something intriguing: accurately evaluate the character of people who had applied for loans. The company's rationale was fairly intuitive. If the potential borrower appeared to have integrity, it stood to follow that the person would do their best to honor their commitment to the lender. Moreover, such a person would likely be a strong leader, run their business competently, and represent a smart investment. So our task was to design a field experiment to try to predict these qualities in loan applicants. Never ones to think inside the box, we adopted an innovative idea from academia and applied it here: the "dropped wallet" experiment.

Over the course of several weeks, a research assistant walked by each establishment whose owner had applied for a loan and "accidentally" dropped his wallet on the sidewalk out front. Seconds later, a different member of my research team would pick up the wallet (in which we had placed a slip of paper with a name and phone number), walk into the establishment, and turn in the wallet to the owner, saying that they had found it outside on the sidewalk and weren't sure what to do.

Then we waited.

Our first metric coded how long it took for the loan applicant to call to tell us that they had our wallet—that is, *if* they called at all, which several in fact didn't, and which naturally left a dent in their score. Next, after those people who returned the wallet had done so, we looked at how much money remained inside: the original $60 we'd left in the wallet (in the form of three $20 bills), $40, $20, or no money at all. In the cases where the person had pocketed some or all of the cash, we were invariably treated to a declaration to the effect of "This is how I found it." I thanked each person who called; then, once we had the data we needed, my team and I generated character/integrity scores for each business owner and sent our reports to the company that had hired us.

I never learned which applicants the company decided to lend to, or how well our metrics predicted whether they paid back their loans. But that is incidental to the more critical issue that was implicitly at play in the experiment. Beneath the surface question of wanting to assess the integrity of loan applicants, the loan company was probing a much deeper, more urgent question: how can we predict whether a business organization will be run successfully? Since success almost always requires increased scale in one form or another, it's natural to think that the loan applicants who scored high on integrity might also have a high success rate at scaling. In other words, could character be a hidden pathway to high-voltage scaling?

Well, not exactly.

In our individualistic culture, which elevates CEOs and founders to rock star or celebrity status, when trying to predict the success of an enterprise we tend to focus on the behaviors, personalities, and philosophies of the individuals leading it, rather than on the organization as a whole. This is true not just of CEOs but also of everyone else in a leadership position, from career government bureaucrats to top-level politicians to directors of research centers. Inevitably, most of us believe that looking at who leaders are and what they do yields important insights. As one extreme example, I know an owner of a private investment firm with over $2 billion in capital who hires a former CIA agent with a proprietary methodology to assess candidates for executive positions! He is certain that this technique contributes to the success of his company, and it probably does. The character of our leaders matters, as does the culture they foster within their organizations (we will do a deep dive on scaling up culture in Chapter 9). But just as much does not.

The widespread focus on individuals makes sense intuitively. Our human fallibilities lead us to be "fast thinkers" and seek the easy explanation for any given phenomenon. It's much easier to conclude that a company succeeded because it had a great leader than it is to consider the complex interaction between multiple factors. Yet when we overestimate the influence of personal characteristics and underestimate the influence of situational factors, we are falling into the trap of something called *correspondence bias* (also known as a *fundamental attribution error*). To succeed at scale, it's not always the *who* that matters. It's the *what* and the *how*—what decisions you make, and how you carry them out.

An overemphasis on leadership style and personality also ignores an element key to the success of any enterprise, which is fueling motivation among the people within it. And motivating people in the service of a common goal hinges on one thing only: you have to get the incentives right. This essential ingredient has more to do with *how* people work than with *who* works.

If we get incentives right, character becomes largely irrelevant. This is a relief on several fronts. First, given that humans don't scale well, from a quality or cost perspective, it's encouraging that success doesn't hinge entirely on specific individuals. While we should always strive to hire well, of course, every once in a while a rotten apple gets hired, so it's good news that even those apples can behave with integrity and work hard with the right incentives. Second is the fact that incentives, if designed well, are almost infinitely scalable and can have an enormously positive impact on shaping behaviors and outcomes. Moreover, incentives are something we all have the power to influence, regardless of whether or not we occupy a formal leadership position.

No matter if an enterprise involves three people or 333,000, incentivizing these people is often the difference between triumph and defeat at scale. When most people hear an economist mention incentives, they roll their eyes and think, *Here we go again. They are going to tell us that paying someone more will make them work harder.* While this is usually true to a degree, it isn't the whole story. In fact, incentivizing high performance at scale doesn't have to come with a hefty price tag. To begin unpacking why this is the case, we can look to an unlikely source: the moment we decide how much money we want to part with when leaving a tip.

The Uber Tip Cup

When Uber first launched, customers loved lots of things about it: the short wait times, the geolocation tracking that effortlessly connected passengers and drivers, and the fares that were cheaper than taxis. People also loved that they didn't have to tip. The drivers were paid the ride fare, based on Uber's algorithm. Passengers didn't have to spend time thinking about how much they should tip, if they had tipped too much or too little, or what the driver might think of them. From the passenger's point of view, it was a frictionless transaction.

Until it wasn't.

Early on in my time at Uber, we began getting more and more reports that drivers were putting out tip cups for passengers or even directly asking for tips. This may have been because Uber's main competitor and my future employer, Lyft, had tipping built into their platform from the outset, or it may have been because drivers felt they should be earning more; it was likely a combination of both. At any rate, Uber drivers wanted to receive tips, and passengers were feeling the pressure to give them, as they were accustomed to doing in taxis. Travis Kalanick might have ignored what was going on if it hadn't been for a much larger problem: the #DeleteUber campaign, which started in January 2017 in response to accusations that the company had tried to opportunistically profit from people needing rides from a protest in New York City against Donald Trump's recent travel ban. The fury only grew when the hundreds of thousands of customers deleting the Uber app discovered that Uber didn't have a fast automated system to handle the high volume of requests for the deactivation of user accounts.

All of this crescendoed into a viral uproar that didn't just damage Uber's reputation among customers but also sparked outrage among drivers, fueling their distrust in the company. Yet drivers were and are the sine qua non of Uber's model, its most basic non-negotiable, given that a large fleet of drivers is essential (until self-driving vehicles are scalable, at least) to the product and premise of Uber: a cheap, convenient ride. It was clear we needed to do something to win back their trust—and fast.

I believed that tipping was the answer. Travis was resistant to the idea at first; it seemed at odds with his mission of keeping prices as low as possible for our riders. Moreover, there was the worry that Uber's unique rating system (where both drivers and passengers can rate the other) would place undue pressure on customers to overtip, for fear of being rated poorly by their driver. But I made my case with the help of two other executives, Daniel Graf (at the time a leader in Uber Marketplace) and Aaron Schildkrout (at the time Uber's head of Growth, Driver, and Data), and Travis eventually gave in. Retaining drivers was an existential issue, so if tipping helped do this, it was worth it—even if some customers would miss the good ol' non-tipping days. Plus, we figured that the prospect of tips would motivate drivers to deliver an even higher level of service, and when have customers ever complained about great service?

In the summer of 2017, Uber instituted a suite of new perks for drivers, including giving passengers the option to tip. But unlike taxi-cab tipping, it wasn't done face-to-face, or even necessarily on the spot as the ride ended. And the driver had to rate passengers *before* finding out how much they tipped. So the practice generated less emotional and mental friction than tipping in the pre-ride-sharing world, factors that were key to nudging Travis over the line to support it. Nonetheless, I still got emails and texts from friends and acquaintances who were angry about the advent of tipping in the app.

At first drivers were grateful. But their gratitude soon gave way to disappointment, as it turned out that while their total take per ride went up thanks to tipping, their overall wages didn't. Why? When we crunched the data, we discovered that by instituting tipping on the platform we had created a problematic spillover: so many new drivers signed up with Uber after we implemented tipping that each driver was getting fewer rides—and thus fewer fares.

On top of this, judging from customer ratings of drivers, tipping didn't lead to higher-quality service, as we had anticipated. We weren't sure exactly why this was the case, but it did fly in the face of years of hospitality management research. In other words, the advent of tipping incentivized more drivers to put in hours on the Uber platform, but it didn't sufficiently incentivize them to up their game on customer service.

But these surprises seemed insignificant compared to the big surprise that came next.

When we looked at the data on how often passengers tipped—or didn't tip—we found that *only 1 percent of Uber passengers tipped on every trip they took.* That's right, only one in every hundred people was sure to tip their driver! Meanwhile, 60 percent of people *never* tipped, and 39 percent sometimes did.

This revelation was startling, to say the least. When I thought more about it, though, it made perfect sense. Sure, from a purely economic standpoint, tipping isn't rational—why pay more than you absolutely have to? But there was more at play here than classical economics would suggest.

Thirty-nine percent of Uber passengers tipped only some of the time, and 60 percent tipped none of the time, for one simple reason: *no one was there to observe them.*

They had nothing to lose.

Loss Aversion

In Chapter 1, we touched on Daniel Kahneman and Amos Tversky's groundbreaking work on cognitive biases, in particular the way confirmation bias can play into false positives. Their most famous and influential work, however, centers on another bias in the human mind: *loss aversion*.

For a long time—a scandalously long time, in retrospect—social scientists saw economics and psychology as separate domains. Economists relied on the "rational agent" theory of choice—that humans consistently make rational choices in the service of their own self-interest—to analyze the logic of economic patterns, while psychologists looked for logic in all the seemingly irrational thought and behavior patterns of people. It didn't seem like these two disciplines had too much to say to each other until Kahneman and Tversky came along and demonstrated how all the illogical quirks of human psychology play into our economic decisions. It was through their research—and the explosive body of work that followed—that the field of behavioral economics coalesced.

Loss aversion is one of the pillars of behavioral economics. The basic idea is that humans hate losses of any kind, to the point that we avoid losses more than we pursue equivalent gains. Another way of framing this notion is that the pain of loss is more psychologically powerful than a gain of the same intensity. Which is why avoiding loss—and the psychological pain that accompanies it—is a potent incentive.

Kahneman and Tversky demonstrated that as a result of this human tendency, we make all sorts of harebrained decisions. For instance, when housing prices fall after a boom, sellers attempt to avoid the inevitable loss by setting a higher asking price—often higher than their home's current value—and in turn the property sits on the market for a longer period of time than it otherwise might. Similarly, investors in the stock market tend to hold losing stocks too long, because they don't want to face the realization of losses, and to sell winning stocks too soon, for fear of losing their gains if the stock price should fall, a phenomenon known as the disposition effect.

The reason we humans developed this asymmetry in our intuitive decision-making is fairly straightforward, evolutionarily speaking. When our species was struggling to survive in the wilderness, say, a hundred thousand years ago, obtaining some extra food would make tomorrow easier. But losing our only food meant there might not be a tomorrow. In this context, the possible stakes of loss were higher than those of gains, so we evolved to become very sensitive to loss and thus to try to avoid it at all costs.

This is true beyond just the loss of material resources, like money or food. It applies to losses of any kind, including *social* losses.

Humans are inherently social creatures, another trait that reaches back into our species's long-ago evolution. In order to survive we needed to get along and work together with other members of our tribe. This allowed us to ward off threats, hunt as a group, share resources, build sturdy shelters, and face the other challenges that required us to cooperate with one another. As a result, we evolved to be highly sensitive to how others treat and react to us. We perceive that others perceive us.

This is called *self-monitoring,* and one of the things we consciously and unconsciously monitor is our social standing in the eyes of others. For our ancestors, the loss of social capital meant a risk of being cast out of the tribe, which lowered their chances of survival. Naturally, then, humans evolved to be highly incentivized by the desire to stay in the good graces of others.

This is where tipping—or *not* tipping—Uber drivers comes back in.

While the stakes are usually lower today than they were for our ancestors, we generally attempt to avoid being perceived negatively by others. This is why social norms and cultural expectations exert such power in human life—because violating one in public has the potential to harm our image. One of the social norms in American culture, of course, is tipping for a variety of service providers, from restaurant servers to haircutters, massage therapists to hotel porters. This tipping is public in varying degrees. In some cases, your companions—say, the friends with whom you split the dinner check—can see exactly how much you've tipped the server. And in most cases, the recipient of the tip learns the amount you have chosen to give as soon as you give it (admit it: you notice your server's reaction if they pick up the check and see how much you tipped while you're still seated). In other words, when in public, we are incentivized to adhere to social norms and protect our reputation, and how much we tip—if at all—has the potential to affect how other people view us, as well as how we see ourselves.

But Uber's method for tipping drivers removed this immediate social and reputational pressure. And once this was gone, the fear of violating an established norm disappeared. This undoubtedly felt really good for passengers, but it also eliminated the powerful incentive: to avoid the potential loss of social esteem in the eyes of others.

The significance of this story isn't that Uber should have made tipping more public. (That being said, if tipping is a non-negotiable part of your business model, you may think differently about whether it is done in public or in private, especially at scale.) It's that how we are perceived in public incentivizes certain behaviors over others.

Indeed, this technique is so powerful it can even increase the wealth of nations.

The $100 Million Nudge and the Power of Social Norms

The Dominican Republic had a problem. Millions of citizens weren't paying the taxes they owed.

Contrary to Benjamin Franklin's famous assertion that nothing is certain in life except death and taxes, most countries struggle at least to some extent with tax evasion. This is particularly true in the developing world, and in fact the level of tax evasion in the sunny Caribbean country was higher than in other countries in the region. In 2017, for instance, nearly 62 percent of Dominican companies failed to pay their corporate income tax, while roughly 57 percent of people failed to pay their individual income tax. That's a whole lot of uncollected money!

Unpaid taxes, of course, mean less money for infrastructure projects, social welfare, and other important public programs, so getting more people to pay their taxes was a priority for the Dominican government. In 2018, the country's equivalent of the IRS put into action a campaign to increase tax compliance, and when they came calling for help, several colleagues and I offered to join the fray—with the caveat, of course, that we could run a natural field experiment.

The main thrust of the campaign was a series of messages the government sent to citizens and companies. Almost every person or entity that decides not to pay their taxes is essentially weighing the benefits versus the costs of that decision and concluding that the possible gains (more take-home profits) outweigh the possible losses (financial penalty or incarceration, punishments that are oftentimes challenging to enforce). The goal of the messaging campaign was to tip the scales so that the potential costs became more salient in people's minds than the potential benefits.

One of our messages sought to do this by informing/reminding people of the jail sentences for tax evasion. The other message informed/reminded people about a new law that made any punishments levied for tax evasion a part of the public record. In other words, the names of those who got caught not paying their taxes would be made available to anyone in the Dominican Republic. This emphasis on public disclosure aimed to harness the same relationship between reputational pressure and loss aversion at play in public tipping. We wanted to incentivize people to avoid perceived damage to their social standing.

So as tax season rolled around, out went messages to 28,000 self-employed Dominicans and over 56,000 Dominican companies. Half received the message about jail time, and half received the message about tax offenders' names being made publicly available. With this nudge, the benefit-cost analysis for those deciding whether or not to pay their taxes suddenly looked very different.

Cha-ching: our intervention worked.

In 2018, our messages increased tax revenue by more than $100 million (more than 0.12 percent of the Dominican Republic's GDP that year), income that the government would *not* have received without our nudges. Unsurprisingly, we found that of the two messages, the reminder about jail time was the more effective; after all, the loss of one's freedom is a loss that all humans have a severe aversion to. However, while the *threat* of jail time could be scaled quite easily— we'd simply have to send the same letter to more people—actually incarcerating a huge portion of the population for tax evasion is neither practical, ethical, nor scalable. Fortunately, the message about public disclosure was also quite effective; simply threatening the loss of social standing resulted in millions of dollars in additional revenue for the Dominican government. And keep in mind that we only targeted a tiny fraction of the taxpaying population. At scale nationwide, the messaging strategy would generate much more money and cost the government very little compared to what it would gain.

Of course, this is not an advisable strategy in every context. I'm not here to suggest that someone trying to scale their business, for example, should make public shaming and threats against people's reputations a part of their incentive structure for scaling. That sounds like a recipe for a toxic workplace culture, and would likely have a *dis*incentivizing effect.

What I am suggesting, however, is that an aversion to the loss of social standing is part of human nature—and incentivizing people to preserve their reputation by adhering to certain norms can clearly have an acute influence on behavior, often in positive ways. Furthermore, this type of incentive scales well because the more widespread someone believes the norm to be—or in other words, the more that violating that norm becomes stigmatized—the more incentivized they are to comply with it.

But this is only one way in which loss aversion and social norms intertwine in curious (and curiously scalable) ways.

Keeping Up with the (Eco-Friendly) Joneses

In 2013, Virgin Atlantic contacted my brilliant colleagues Greer Gosnell and Robert Metcalfe about an ambitious objective. The airline wanted to significantly reduce its carbon emissions through greater fuel efficiency. Attaining this would clearly be good for the environment while also saving Virgin a lot of money. The only question was how to go about it.

The company knew that the key to increasing fuel efficiency lay largely in the hands of their airline captains, since tiny choices made by pilots can affect consumption in several different ways. Before takeoff, for example, captains have to plan the fuel load of the airplane, taking into account the craft's weight and the weather they will encounter. In the air, the altitudes at which they choose to fly and the shortcuts they request and execute from air traffic control, along with the flap settings they choose for the wings as well as other aerodynamic decisions, can burn more or less fuel. And upon landing, they can turn off at least one engine to taxi to the gate, but don't have to.

Since captains ultimately maintain authority over these decisions, airlines generally encourage but don't mandate a set of required practices around fuel usage. Yet Virgin saw potential benefits in gently nudging their pilots in a carbon-reducing direction. The challenge was how exactly to tweak habits their captains had formed long ago.

This is where my fellow economists and I came in. We had an idea that leveraged social norms, but less publicly than in the Dominican Republic tax payment experiment, and in a way that wouldn't create an unpleasant atmosphere that could damage Virgin's famously cheerful work culture.

Airline captains train meticulously to earn their seat in the cockpit and invest great effort at excelling in their profession, so we knew we had a population predisposed, at least in theory, to taking pride in their work. They were likely to want to be responsible stewards of the planet, or at least of their employer's bottom line; unlike the tax evaders in the Dominican Republic, they received no financial gain from engaging in the unwanted behavior (in this case, wasting fuel). Yet consciously or unconsciously they also might be resistant to modifying their established operational styles. With all this in mind, the strategy we designed relied neither on punitive measures nor on personal rewards. The key was simply collecting and sharing information privately, a subtle nudge we hoped would act as its own kind of social incentive.

From February through September 2014, we sent three different reports to three groups of Virgin pilots. The first group received reports on their fuel efficiency from the previous month; the second received the same type of reports, with the addition of a message encouraging them to reach the personal targets of fuel conservation that we created for them; and the third group received the same reports and encouragement as the second group, and were also informed that a small donation to a charity of their choice would be made in their name for each of three targets met (this is called a "prosocial incentive"). The fourth group, the control group, received a letter merely notifying them that their fuel usage would be measured. So for seven months, the pilots did their jobs flying around the world as usual, only with a little voice in their ears talking to them through the monthly letters we sent.

Our field experiment didn't dangle the possibility of social shame (and certainly nothing resembling jail time) the way the tax experiment in the Dominican Republic did. None of the letters threatened to make this fuel efficiency data public or suggested that it might impact their yearly earnings or performance evaluations. Yet our experimental design did implicitly communicate that Virgin aimed to establish a *norm* inside the company aimed at reducing carbon emissions, though it wouldn't damage, say, the pilots' yearly earnings or performance evaluations. Their individual choices wouldn't have any negative repercussions, but the pilots knew that the data resulting from those choices would be available to executives (and us economists). In other words, the implications of their choices were reflected back to the pilots in an organizational context that was inherently social, so there was a faint whiff of social loss if they didn't adhere to the new norm.

As it turned out, it wasn't the fear of looking bad in front of other pilots and coworkers that incentivized them to adopt more fuel-efficient practices; it was their desire to view *themselves* as someone who met social expectations (or the company-wide norm) of reducing carbon emissions. Would our nudge scale across 335 pilots, some 40,000 flights, and over 100,000 pilot decisions? Human beings' finely tuned neural hardware for constructing self-image made us optimistic that it would.

We turned out to be right. After analyzing the data, we found that *all three* treatment groups implemented more fuel-efficient behaviors. Even better, so did the control group, who knew they were in an experiment but didn't receive the same sort of nudge. This was likely thanks to the Hawthorne effect, a phenomenon in which people act differently either because of a change in their environment (like different lighting in the original Hawthorne plant experiments in the 1920s, which gave the effect its name) or because they are aware that they're being observed (which can trigger a desire to please). In this case, the mere knowledge that their fuel usage was being measured and would be included in our data was enough to incentivize them to alter their habits. In industrial psychology, the Hawthorne effect is used as a technique to improve worker performance, and this is what we saw with the pilots.

Among the three nudge groups, those who received the letter with the report along with clear targets and words of encouragement produced the biggest gains—by up to 28 percent above the group that received solely a report. It was as if the mere possibility of not meeting their targets motivated pilots to save fuel and save face—that is, the self-image of themselves as people who met expectations and fulfilled norms. Interestingly, the added incentive of the donation didn't seem to have an effect; on average, the pilots who received the message about the donation didn't conserve any more fuel than those who received the targets-and-encouragement letter. The incentive had already maxed out.

All told, we estimated that Virgin saved 7,700 tons of fuel, saved $5.37 million in fuel costs, and reduced emissions by more than 21,500 metric tons of carbon dioxide as a result of this experiment—a high-voltage gain for the airline and the planet. As an added bonus, a survey indicated the captains liked the experiment, so much so that 79 percent of them said they desired more such initiatives (and only 6 percent didn't). Lastly, the experience appeared to positively affect captains' reported job satisfaction relative to the control group.

Initiatives like these are easily scalable once you have the mechanisms in place for efficient data collection. This is because the Five Vital Signs are naturally met with this type of nudge. This is good news given that energy conservation, of course, is a concern not just for the airline industry but for pretty much every industry in the twenty-first century. For proof, we need to look no further than Opower, the engagement platform for utilities whose "smart" thermostat technology lost voltage at scale because its users had a hard time using it properly, as we saw in Chapter 2.

On the heels of the smart thermostat debacle, it became clear that Opower (along with consumers and the planet) could benefit from an initiative that, rather than promoting any one product, simply encouraged consumers to adopt energy-saving techniques. So the company implemented a program called the Home Energy Report (HER), a social nudge that involves sending out periodic mailers comparing a household's energy use to that of its neighbors. Like the Virgin experiment, this is a strategy that leverages self-perception and social norms, only with the addition of one powerful incentive: social comparison. The idea was to nudge people to conserve more energy by tapping into the fundamentally human desire to "keep up with the Joneses," akin to if we had shared the fuel-efficiency reports among all the pilots. What is at stake is your self-image as a person in your community who responsibly consumes energy—a self-image that is difficult to preserve once you discover that your household is guzzling more fossil fuels than your "greener" neighbors. It doesn't matter that the data are anonymized and no one will know if you're the neighbor with the Tesla or the one who keeps the living room lights on all night. The psychology of social loss aversion gets triggered either way. When we analyzed thirty-eight distinct field experiments that sent HER behavioral interventions to some 250,000 homes, we found that on average consumers reduced their electricity consumption by 2.4 percent when they received information comparing their usage to that of the other households in the area.

Amazingly, as we dug deeper into the data, we discovered that the effect of the Home Energy Reports was longer-lasting than we expected: 35 to 55 percent of that reduction persisted *after* Opower stopped sending out the report, often even years after the experiments had ended. It was as if an energy-conservation angel remained on consumers' shoulders reminding them to save at least as much energy as their neighbors, and their desire to preserve that self-image outlasted the messages about the neighbors.

This represents a huge boon for scaling purposes. Not only is it far easier to scale incentives that only need to be implemented once, but also one-time messages hold greater promise than continuous ones, which tend to produce diminishing returns when they are received over and over again. In short, constant messaging becomes stale, and people become immune to it.

Other field experiments I've conducted have shown this type of incentive works in all types of situations and for all types of people. For example, in Chicago, I ran an experiment using similar social comparison messaging that successfully prodded many households to increase their use of energy-saving compact fluorescent lightbulbs, something Americans have shown a tremendous resistance to in spite of their many benefits. This suggests that we can tap into the power of self-image and social norms not only to reshape people's behaviors in ways that benefit the environment and society but also to drive the adoption of important new technological innovations that people might resist at first.

Such incentives even reach the voting booth. It turns out that many people go to the ballot box at least in part because they know others will ask whether they voted, and that they will feel pride telling others that they voted, or shame from admitting that they did not. Admitting that they didn't bother to take time out of their day to go cast a vote, in other words, threatens their self-image as an engaged citizen who participates in the democratic process. As a voting study I conducted revealed, simply requiring people to *report* on their behavior (even when they could lie) incentivizes them to make more prosocial choices.

This has profound implications for scaling in a variety of contexts. For companies, as the cost of monitoring employees becomes more and more taxing at scale (not to mention all the other issues around trust and engagement), this insight opens up the possibility of using questionnaires and surveys, which are easily deployed, to incentivize positive behavior (like attending training and development workshops, for example) and *dis*incentivize misbehavior (such as theft).

Similarly, when a company provides information on the toxic emissions from their plant or factory to the Toxics Release Inventory, a publicly available database, managers have a strong incentive to reduce their use of toxic chemicals. And when organizations announce that they will begin to provide annual data on workplace diversity, managers naturally begin to take diversity more seriously in their hiring and promotion decisions. In fact, if a multilayered organization takes the further bold step to publish their data by division (such as the publisher of this book did in 2018), managers not only are incentivized to improve the company's reputation by making progress on this issue but also are incentivized to be seen as making progress relative to the other divisions. Otherwise, a *loss* in both social capital and self-image might result.

Unlike other popular incentives—such as paying employees more or providing free lunch or some other perk, which can get prohibitively expensive as an enterprise scales—social incentives can be much more cheaply implemented on a large scale. Moreover, the fact that human psychology doesn't vary much across groups (most people experience loss aversion to a similar degree, and nearly everyone cares about their social image) makes this type of incentive strategy highly scalable. In contrast, the level of financial rewards necessary to incentivize one's employees will vary widely from person to person, and for some might be unduly high. Whether you're scaling for profit, social impact, better health or educational outcomes, or anything else, the goal should be to engineer incentives that tap into our highly social and loss-averse brains to nudge people toward the behaviors that will benefit everyone involved.

These principles hold true outside the world of business as well. For example, doctors could incentivize patients to comply with their treatment plan by having them keep a daily log in which they record each time they took their prescription medication, did their recommended exercises, et cetera. And educators could have students track their study time, completion of homework assignments, and so on. Yet these types of incentives aren't the only pathway to voltage gains. Money works, too (as an economist, I couldn't leave this out!). But financial incentives used at scale can be more creatively employed than the tired old "pay more to get more."

The Clawback Approach

Just as humans are more sensitive to social losses than to gains, and more averse to pain than we are appreciative of pleasure, we also hate losing something we already possess more than we like acquiring something we don't. This is especially true when it comes to money, yet most financial incentives are actually structured the opposite way: we receive some sort of compensation when we meet a certain performance target. While the logic of this approach may appear solid, research reveals that it is in fact *not* the most effective way to leverage financial incentives at scale. What if we flipped the order of things and gave the reward first, and the work and performance came after?

Humans' extreme aversion to losing something we possess is known as the endowment effect, and it was starkly revealed in a now famous laboratory experiment Daniel Kahneman conducted with Jack Knetsch and Richard Thaler. The experiment is a simple one: they gave participants a mug. Not an especially fancy or expensive one—just a run-of-the-mill mug. Then they gave participants a chance to either sell the mug for money or trade it for another object they deemed equally valuable (in this case, a candy bar). They discovered that as soon as subjects felt ownership of the mug—as soon as it became *theirs*—they valued it at literally double what they would have paid to acquire it. Once the mug was *endowed* to the participants, their mental relationship to it changed radically.

This seemingly irrational effect has been replicated in other experiments, including one by Dan Ariely and Ziv Carmon that showed the astronomical amount people would charge for NCAA Final Four tickets they possessed versus how much they would pay to buy the same tickets from someone else. Because humans evolved to really hate losing things—be it social status, money, or kitchenware—we are highly motivated to hold on to what is ours. But how can this effect be useful outside of the laboratory?

I had the opportunity to explore that very question in 2008 when an electronics manufacturer in China wanted help upping productivity at one of their factories. The Wanlida Group is one of the top hundred electronics enterprises in China, with centers located in Nanjing, Zhangzhou, and Shenzhen and over twenty thousand employees. When executives from the company approached Tanjim Hossain and me about a low-cost incentive to increase the effort of their workers, we proposed a field experiment using another loss/

gain cognitive bias known as the *framing effect*. The idea of a framing effect is fairly straightforward: whether a task or a situation is framed or presented to you as a loss or gain will affect your attitude and behavior toward it.

The Wanlida Group makes and distributes an assortment of consumer electronics, from notebooks and PCs to GPS devices and home appliances. Tanjim and I carried out our experiment at the Nanjing factory, which manufactures DVD players and digital photo frames, among other things. Our experiment involved using different bonus schemes with a subset of Wanlida employees to learn whether the framing of simple incentives influenced productivity, both in teams and for individual workers. So we gave employees a mug.

Well, not an actual mug, but a small bonus that had the same function as the mug in Kahneman's experiment. Instead of having to hit a production milestone to earn the money, we gave it to one group of employees *before* they had actually earned it. The catch was, we told them, it was provisionally allocated, to be disbursed not immediately but at the end of the week, provided they met their production goal. This was a polite way of saying that they would have to say adiós to the bonus before payday if they *didn't* meet their goal. The money was theirs to lose. I call this the "clawback" approach.

As you can see, it was all about the framing of the motivation. The "loss treatment" group *felt* as if they already had the money—though it actually wasn't in their bank account—that was now at risk of slipping away. Meanwhile, the "reward treatment" group received a different framing. They were presented with the bonus as the conventional incentive—that is, *first you hit the goal, then you get the money*. This second group didn't feel like the money was yet theirs.

For over six months, the Wanlida factory workers went about their regular tasks and continued with their standard work schedules. But each week the people in the loss group either kept or lost their bonus, while the reward group either did or didn't win theirs. Of course, in reality they were chasing the same benchmark for the same money received on the same day, yet they experienced the incentive very differently. And that simple fact had a significant impact on their productivity.

As it turned out, the clawback approach outperformed the classic bonus approach, with total team productivity increasing by over 1 percent in the loss treatment group—an effect that didn't diminish over the course of the six-month experiment. This might not seem like a lot, but at scale, a persistent increase in productivity of 1 percent has a large impact over the long run. For a company like Wanlida this could mean tens of millions of dollars more in profit within a few years.

The clawback experiment highlights the power of loss aversion to motivate employees, and it appears to be perfectly scalable. Importantly, even the sum of the bonus is negligible to the participants' overall financial picture, and therefore not enough to incentivize them if offered using the standard incentive structure. The desire (conscious or not) to avoid the mental discomfort of loss was powerful enough to produce a change in behavior.

I have implemented the clawback approach in several other field experiments and in several countries in order to test whether it worked across different people, cultures, and situations—and indeed, it did. For example, in the suburbs of Kampala, Uganda, we had 1,200 workers who sort beans participate, and we saw an increase in productivity that blew Wanlida away—a staggering 20 percent! Like any behavioral effect of this sort, there are boundary conditions. One such boundary condition is documented in a series of papers I produced in the early 2000s. One key finding is that people with vast experience in trading assets showed very little, if any, sign of loss aversion. This makes sense, given that in our research we find that people who have extensive experience in giving up a good over time will begin to encode losses in a different part of their brain. The fact that repeated exposure to loss can desensitize us to it represents an important boundary condition for how far we can push this type of incentive, but one that I have yet to reach within organizations.

In this sense, framing incentives in this way is an invaluable approach to produce high-voltage gains for businesses at scale. Best of all, this isn't a lopsided strategy that only benefits executives and shareholders. The clawback approach helps workers earn bonuses. Moreover, as both our research and the work of Alex Imas, Sally Sadoff, and Anya Samek have shown, many employees enjoy and value the commitment aspect of the clawback bonus scheme. It feels good to own something and to work harder to hold on to it. However, companies that scale the clawback effect must make a commitment of their own: not to dangle bonuses for impossible or unrealistic benchmarks that could lead to toxic stress for employees. Also, they must be prepared to follow through on the payout no matter how many employees meet their target and earn it. Upholding organizational ethics when using incentive nudges is more important than any voltage gain.

Cash and Trophies

While the clawback approach might seem particularly well suited to business, it can also have a positive impact in nonprofit arenas as well, especially education. Outside the business world, we tend to feel a bit uncomfortable about paying people to change their behavior, but the fact is, this practice works, and there is no reason to steer clear of it. Many college scholarships are contingent upon students maintaining a certain GPA, for example, and as we saw in the case of the Chicago Heights Early Childhood Center, cash incentives increased participation in our Parent Academy. And given that even small sums have been proven effective, such incentives can potentially have a place in cash-strapped initiatives aimed at fostering social change at scale. They may even be particularly well suited to spur certain behaviors that have the potential to narrow socioeconomic gaps, as I observed firsthand in an experiment I conducted with economists Roland Fryer, Steve Levitt, and Sally Sadoff in Chicago Heights—not at CHECC, but in primary and secondary schools within the same district.

Chicago Heights contains nine K-8 schools with a total of approximately 3,200 students. Like many other larger urban school districts, it is made up primarily of low-income students of color who are often at a disadvantage when it comes to conventional measures of achievement. In the year prior to our intervention, for instance, only 64 percent of students met the minimum standard on the Illinois State Achievement Test, in contrast to 81 percent of students statewide. To give the students in our sample group opportunities that could help pull them—and others like them elsewhere—out of cycles of systemic disadvantage is a challenging and urgent task. But these young people weren't the subjects of our experiment. It was their teachers.

At the start of the 2010–11 school year, we worked with school officials in Chicago Heights to explain to teachers that we would be doing an experiment for which they would stand to take home a bonus if they opted in. It turned out they liked this idea: 150 of the teachers elected to participate—nearly 95 percent! I was excited because the experiment had the potential to be a win-win: the teachers (who, like most public school teachers in America, were notoriously underpaid) might earn some extra cash, I would get to examine the clawback's effects on teaching quality to determine if our intervention might be scalable, and the children might reap the benefits in the classroom.

Here is how it worked. One group of teachers—the reward group—would receive a bonus at the end of the school year based on the improvement (from September to June) in their students' overall percentile scores on a standardized test—$80 per percentile, with a maximum possible reward of $8,000. (While standardized tests aren't the only, or always the most accurate, measure of how much a student has learned, from an experimental design perspective they are an attractive way of ensuring that the students, and therefore the teachers, were being graded according to the same metrics.) In contrast, the teachers in the second group—the loss group—received $4,000 at the *beginning* of the school year, and signed a contract stating that if their students' overall performance on that same standardized test was below average, they would return the difference between $4,000 and their final reward. If, however, their students' performance was above average, we would issue the teachers an additional bonus of up to $4,000 for a total of up to $8,000. So, "gain" and "loss" teachers could receive identical net payments for the same performance. The only differences were the timing and framing.

It was like the Wanlida experiment all over again, except instead of manufacturing DVD players, our subjects were producing educations and better futures for children to benefit. And this time, instead of allocating them the money provisionally, we actually gave the teachers in the clawback treatment $4,000 in cash when the program started.

Fall came and went, then winter announced itself with snow carried in by bone-chilling winds off Lake Michigan. The new year arrived, followed by spring as the temperatures began to rise and living things (humans included) reemerged out of the gray, icy landscape. All the while, the children and teachers in Chicago Heights dutifully engaged in the slow and complex dance of learning. There were lots of bumps along the way, but also plenty of triumphs—and, hopefully, more triumphs than other years, thanks to our incentive. When the end of the school year came around, we administered the standardized test. Little did the students know that their scores would affect their teachers' bank statements!

What did we find? The teachers in the loss group saw tremendous gains in their students' test scores. Their desire not to lose the bonus they had already been given had indeed incentivized teachers to work harder—even harder than the teachers who were promised a bonus of equal value later. On top of all of this, the teachers in the clawback group seemed to have developed some good habits: in looking at teacher quality for the next five years after our experiment ended, we found evidence that their improved performance in the classroom lasted, even in the absence of the incentives—which meant that students who had one of these teachers up to five years later experienced considerable gains above other students. Like a good holiday gift, this incentive kept on giving, making it a cherished one indeed at scale.

The success of our experiment when conducted with teachers raises the question of whether a similar strategy could also work for students. To find out, we ran a new field experiment with over six thousand elementary and high school students in the Chicago area, using both financial rewards ($10 or $20) and nonfinancial rewards (a trophy) for improved educational performance. The results were encouraging. First, we found that the traditional incentives work, but the clawback works a bit better. Second, we found that the reward didn't even need to be cash to be effective; giving money *or* a trophy up front led to an improvement in test scores. Yet, given that one of the biggest puzzles in education is why many students invest so little effort given the high returns they stand to gain over the course of their lifetimes, we decided to explore the timing of rewards further.

This time we took it in the opposite direction of the clawback, and told some students that if they performed well on the test, they would receive their reward one month *after* the test. Suddenly the incentives didn't matter. That is, rewards—even large ones—delivered with a delay didn't impact students' performance at all. This finding suggests that one explanation for students' low investment in their own education, and their high dropout rate, is that the current returns (get into college, get a higher-paying job, et cetera) are delivered with too long a delay to sufficiently motivate some students. After all, if delaying an incentive by just one month can tank motivation, the abstract prospect of better opportunities in the far-off future clearly won't be very persuasive. So when you think about incentives to combat climate change, encourage healthy eating, curb smoking, promote regular doctor and dental visits, and affect the many other behaviors for which people incur the costs now but receive the benefits later (sometimes much later), you can quickly understand why there is so much underinvestment in these areas. When it comes to incentives, timing is everything.

Some experts argue that incentives of any type in education have negative downstream effects on students because the driver of better performance is extrinsic rather than intrinsic motivation, and ultimately personal satisfaction is limitless whereas external rewards are not. In other words, the worry is that if you rely on outside incentives, you may learn to wait for others to motivate you rather than build your own ability to motivate yourself. While these points are valid, in situations in which intrinsic motivation is already very low, as is the case in communities like the South Side of Chicago, where a lack of opportunities can make children feel like there is no point to putting in effort at school, some research shows that rewards have a large positive impact without long-term downsides. And in fact, extrinsic motivation in the form of money or trophies can *build* intrinsic motivation. The students learn because they want the reward, only to realize that learning is its own reward.

Learning to take satisfaction in the fruits of hard work is a skill that always scales.

·   ·   ·

OUR EXPERIMENT IN Chicago Heights makes a forceful case for leveraging the endowment effect in domains far afield from the business world. In theory, this approach should be scalable not just in education but in other domains of the public and nonprofit sector, such as social work and policing. Of course, because cash bonuses cost money, there is always the risk of running into the final obstacle in the Five Vital Signs: the cost trap. But if your organization is able to raise or find the funds for clawback bonuses, you might find it a worthwhile investment.

It's important, however, to recognize that when we scale either type of incentive—whether with our employees, the people we aim to serve, or other stakeholders—we must do so responsibly. This means that the rewards these nudges promise must always be implemented fairly and equally to benefit companies, communities, and organizations as a whole. Moreover, judiciously choosing an approach that is not overly paternalistic and is in harmony with a positive orga-nizational culture is vital. Meaning you should not—and do not need to—constantly make people feel vulnerable by showing them what they are at risk of losing. The goal should be to engineer situations that generate more than enough gains to go around.

Finding these gains is often a matter of maximizing the positive impacts of limited time and resources. And in order to do so, we have to learn how to think differently.

We have to think along the margins.

REVOLUTION ON THE MARGINS

There I was, sitting at my desk in the Eisenhower Executive Office Building, a stately, six-story block of granite that stood just a two-minute walk from the West Wing of the White House. My office was on the first floor of the historic nineteenth-century building, with no windows to speak of. Not that I would have had time to gaze outside even if I'd had the option. It was the summer of 2002, a few months into my tenure as a senior economist in the administration of President George W. Bush, and I was so busy that arriving at 6:30 A.M. and making it back home around 9:00 P.M. was my typical schedule Monday through Saturday. Sundays I was afforded a chance to enjoy my four kids, all under the age of four, including a newborn, Greta, who arrived that summer.

A few months earlier, I had received a call out of the blue inquiring whether I would be interested in joining the White House team. This seemed too good an opportunity to dismiss out of hand, which is how, soon after, I found myself arriving bright and early at 1600 Pennsylvania Avenue to an opening interview question unlike one I'd ever received in academia: "Which way do you lean?"

"Socially liberal, fiscally conservative, making me straight as an arrow," I stated confidently. The interviewer sat expressionless, only remarking, "That is what we thought from your writings." By the time I made it to my afternoon interviews with the economists from the Council of Economic Advisers, I figured the job was all but gone;

surely this White House would demand a card-carrying right-wing economist. But I was met with an entirely different tone.

"What questions did they ask you this morning?" wondered Glenn Hubbard, the chair of the Council. I mentioned the query about my political leanings, and he stopped me at once. "We don't care—you are here as an economist, to do work as an economic thinker. We need your brain, not your politics." I was back in business—or, rather, in government.

The next day they offered me the position, subject to my passing the myriad of background checks (someone even visited my kindergarten teacher and questioned her about what kind of boy I'd been when I was five!). I had never had a chance to serve my country in such a capacity, and with no way of knowing that the weapons-of-mass-destruction debacle and the invasion of Iraq were nine months down the road, the notion of working in the White House filled me with pride. In the end I couldn't say no—beyond just serving the country, this offer (like the one I would receive from Uber nearly fifteen years later) was an opportunity to study economics and human behavior in the real world, and on a national scale.

Policymaking is, in a very real sense, one gigantic field experiment—a method for scaling ideas and tracking the effects they produce. When implemented with care, government policies have the potential to improve countless lives, both in the present and in the future. Plus my role would be scientific, and frankly, politics is always in need of more science.

Now that I was in D.C., I had more work to do than hours in the day. My office looked like a vacation resort for messy piles of paper: they sprawled across my desk, accumulated atop office chairs, and were quickly taking over every available inch of space on my floor. And almost every single page related in some way to one part of the job I'd been brought in to do: benefit-cost analysis of implementing policies on a large scale. This chore is an important one because the more than one hundred federal agencies issue approximately 4,500 new rulemaking notices each year. Of those, about fifty to a hundred per year meet the necessary condition of being "economically signifi-cant" (more than $100 million yearly in *either* benefits or costs). Every economically significant proposal, then, receives a formal analysis of the benefits and costs.

All decision-making, at its core, involves this type of analysis: weighing what we gain against what we lose. We do this practically every moment of our lives without thinking about it. If the benefits of buying an apple (it's a healthy snack) exceed the costs (which could be either the price or the likelihood that we won't enjoy it as much as we would a candy bar), we drop it into our grocery basket. If the benefits of renting an apartment (lots of space, great location) exceed the costs (high rent, loud neighbors), we sign the lease. If the ben-efits of joining a gym (physical fitness, socializing) exceed the costs (monthly fees, added pressure), we fork over the membership fee. We do a similar calculus when deciding how to spend our time as well as our money. If the benefits of a friendship exceed the costs, we regu-larly carve out time to spend with that person.

Of course, much of the time we determine that the costs *do* out-weigh the benefits. We don't buy pricey filet mignons every week. We pass on the apartment that would eat up 70 percent of our in-come even if we love it. We cancel our gym membership if we find ourselves going only twice a month. And we stop making time for that friend who takes passive-aggressive jabs at us. This benefit-cost framework extends to the choices we make about education, jobs, marriage, having kids, and even committing a crime or adultery. Of course, sometimes we make miscalculations, in which case we store the mistake away in our minds to inform future decisions. It's an in-nate, highly adaptive form of economic thinking that has served our species well over eons.

The calculus involved in government policymaking is no different—that is, when it works the way it should.

The year before he became a U.S. Supreme Court justice in 1994, Judge Stephen Breyer published a book called *Breaking the Vicious Circle*. By this time, benefit-cost analysis had become part and parcel of the government policymaking machinery. This approach actually began with the Flood Control Act of 1936, but it wasn't standard practice until Nixon, Ford, and Carter. Then Ronald Reagan came along and it became formally codified with Executive Order 12291, which increased regulatory oversight and required federal agencies to prove that their actions led to more benefits than costs. (This order was a crucial tool in Reagan's aggressive campaign of deregulation and cutting spending on the social programs he disliked.)

This was the context Breyer waded into with his book, though unlike Reagan he didn't believe rolling back spending was the solution to all of our problems. He contended that government needed to more effectively prioritize the programs and policies it implemented. Every country has a (theoretically) finite pot of money that it collects from taxation, Breyer argued, so it is the obligation of government to use that money to scale initiatives that improve as many lives as possible. In other words, Breyer believed government needed to get better at measuring benefits against costs.

This line of reasoning is bulletproof in theory. In practice, it's trickier. As Breyer pointed out, figuring out how to get the most benefits for every dollar spent isn't so straightforward. In fact, it's downright maddening, even for economists like me trained to study such things. For example, after cleaning up 90 percent of a toxic dump site, should the government spend more money to scrub the last 10 percent clean, or divert those funds to some other urgent public-health issue that is also costly to fix?

To put it more simply, where should the money go? And more broadly, how do we properly measure the benefits and costs of attacking big national problems the government needs to address on a massive scale, like the obesity epidemic or the educational achievement gap? Vexing questions like these were responsible for all of those piles of paper lounging around my office. I had to analyze benefit-cost reports and provide policy recommendations based on a single goal: to help get the most for every dollar we spent.

I was tasked with environmental (and later homeland security) issues, which meant I worked with the Environmental Protection Agency (EPA), the Food and Drug Administration (FDA), and the Departments of Labor, Energy, Transportation, and Housing and Urban Development. The Bush administration was committed to rigorous benefit-cost exercises, so no domain was off-limits. A key colleague was John D. Graham, the regulatory czar at the White House Office of Management and Budget, who pushed the provocative idea of examining benefit-cost based on *years* of lives saved rather than *number of* lives saved, which weighted policies in favor of benefiting young people. As heartless as it may sound, scaling a solution that saves or improves the lives of eight-year-olds instead of eighty-year-olds has a bigger cumulative impact over time and thus arguably calls for a larger slice of the budget.

Naturally, there were many critics who argued that a life is a life and each has the same value, period. I sympathized with this moral approach, yet I was stuck with an economic one. When used in the proper fashion, benefit-cost analysis isn't a political strategy, as it often was under Reagan. It is a tool for doing the most good with limited means. If money wasn't a limitation, policymakers wouldn't have to frame spending in such seemingly cold and cerebral terms. But government funds *are* limited, which is why benefits need to be maximized and costs minimized. And once I dug into the data, I began to notice a lot of poorly spent money.

Sitting in my office looking through benefit-cost reports from several federal agencies one afternoon (or maybe it was evening; due to the aforementioned lack of windows, it was often hard to tell), I had an epiphany—what I like to jokingly refer to as my "John Nash policy moment," an homage to the brilliant and psychologically tormented mathematician and Nobel laureate who inspired the film *A Beautiful Mind*. The insight, in a nutshell, was simple: The data that policymakers were making decisions with represented averages. If a new clean-air policy that costs $100 million would save two hundred lives, they would calculate that it costs $500,000 per life—and this would be the new gospel. But in cases where I could break the data apart, I saw that the reality was not quite so simple. Specifically, I noticed that not every dollar spent on a single policy had equal value; for example, the first $50 million spent on a clean-energy plan might reduce emissions by much more than the second $50 million spent.

Within the EPA, for example, there were dramatic and problematic discrepancies in how much the *last few dollars* affected outcomes. While removing tailings dams (a type of human-made embankment that stores byproducts of mining) cost tens of millions to save one human life, implementing compliance standards to reduce pollution that had the same life-saving impact only cost tens of thousands per life saved. And—staying true to my economics training—once I looked at all the charts and graphs and figures across the various agencies, I knew that if we wanted to identify and prioritize the policies that got the most out of taxpayer money, just as Justice Breyer had suggested, we needed to look not at the positive impact per dollar spent on average but the positive impact of the *last* dollar spent.

That's because the benefit-cost averages that lumped all the dollars together were obscuring more specific figures revealing that *certain policies became much less impactful the more they were scaled.*

For instance, a $30 million intervention aimed at reducing student absenteeism nationwide might be quite effective for the first $20 million spent, but there might be diminishing returns for the last $10 million. But shouldn't every policy be held accountable beyond just demonstrating that overall benefits outweighed overall costs? It was the government's responsibility to prioritize the policies that made the most out of every *last* dollar spent; if not, we weren't allocating taxpayers' money in the most scalable way. But how do you fix a problem like this?

I knew the answer: scale from the margins.

The Marginal Revolution

In the late nineteenth century, the field of economics took an intellectual leap forward that came to be known as the Marginal Revolution.

Yet, in spite of its name, it wasn't at all marginal. Indeed, it became a central insight in economics. The breakthrough in thinking that it represented would take center stage in economic theory and forever change the way economists measured the value of things.

The Marginal Revolution came about thanks largely to three men from three different countries: Englishman William Stanley Jevons, Austrian Carl Menger, and Frenchman Léon Walras (who also pioneered general equilibrium theory, which we touched on in Chapter 4 in relation to spillovers). A focus in economics throughout the eighteenth century was understanding why goods and services fetched the prices they did on the market. For example, why was gold so much more costly than food, when we can live without precious metals but not without nutrition? Why do diamonds command a much higher price than water, which we need to survive? The diamond-water paradox is now taught in classrooms around the globe.

This is called value theory. Going beyond the limited concept of supply versus demand, Jevons, Menger, and Walras introduced the *utility function,* or the theory of utility, into the discussion of value. (They were building on the work of English economist Jeremy Bentham.) Their idea was fairly simple yet radically new. Everything we spend money on provides a certain amount of satisfaction, or utility, whether we are paying to own an object, use a service, or have an experience. And this level of satisfaction determines the value we receive from goods and services.

But there is another layer. Jevons, Menger, and Walras posited that utility isn't static: that goods and services—broken into "units"—have different value to consumers depending on if they are the first or last unit consumed, or somewhere in between. The value of that final, most recent unit is referred to as the *marginal utility,* and it is rarely the same as the value averaged across all units. So back in the Eisenhower Executive Office Building when I was attempting to estimate the value of the last dollar spent by each agency on each program, in order to figure out which last dollar had the most positive impact, I was in effect trying to calculate marginal utility (though, of course, that related not to consumption but rather to spending money on policies).

As a general rule, for consumers, there exists a law of *diminishing* marginal utility, which means that the last unit has less value than the first unit. For a simple example of this, look no further than . . . donuts.

I like donuts. Let's imagine I've already had two donuts today (which, to be honest, is quite possible if I'm not careful) and am trying to decide if I should have a third. If I make my decision based on how much I enjoyed the first donut, or how much I enjoy a donut on average, then I would probably reach for the next donut. However, if I make my decision thinking about that third donut specifically, I will realize that it will likely make me feel sick. In other words, the satisfaction I receive from that donut—its marginal utility—is about to drop precipitously. This is exactly what happens with many government programs, which begin to deliver diminishing returns on the dollar as the level of investment in them increases.

For another policy example, take the United States' War on Drugs. Much more money has been invested in the law enforcement and military side of the drug war even though the marginal benefits are much greater from the last dollar spent on prevention and substance abuse recovery. Naturally, when you miscalculate marginal benefits at scale, the amount of money that gets squandered increases exponentially. This is why benefit-cost analysis for government needs to focus not just on average utility but on utility at the margins, too.

The marginal analysis pioneered by Jevons, Menger, and Walras can even apply to helping your kids get the most out of the time they spend studying. If you want to know how they can best spend three hours on the night before a test, for example, you don't want to look at the average number of hours spent studying with a tutor versus studying online versus rereading a textbook to determine which has the biggest payoff in terms of performance. You want to compare the returns on the third and *last* hour of tutoring, online studying, and book studying, and see which has the strongest yield. Once you know which has greater marginal benefits, you can reallocate more resources there. The same calculus applies to time spent studying. Experts have taught us that learning/mastery of skills is like picking apples: early on it is pretty easy, but that last 5 to 10 percent is very difficult. In such cases, if that last hour of studying for the math test is only going to raise their grade by a percentage point or two, why not shift gears and have them work on other homework, or maybe even get an extra hour of sleep?

The thing about marginalism, as economists call it, is that it's really hard to think this way. It doesn't come naturally to our bias-laden brains, which are programmed to always simplify things for the sake of efficiency. The human mind tends to apply heuristics ("fast thinking"), since most of the time those work well enough and are less effortful ("cheaper") than "slow thinking," which is quite costly in terms of the neurons required and metabolic costs. Unfortunately, this tendency often distorts our benefit-cost analysis, making it harder to allocate our time and resources most efficiently.

Think about how we perceive our utility bill. While you might not even know it, when we consume electricity we are typically charged a tiered price that increases with the amount of electricity we use. For example, for the first 100 kilowatt-hours (kWh) we might pay 10 cents per kWh, whereas for the next 100 we might pay 15 cents per kWh. Researchers have looked at how consumers respond to changes in these price tiers and have found strong evidence that people are affected almost entirely by average prices rather than marginal ones. Consumers are thinking fast, and it's much easier to calculate the average price per kWh consumed—in this case, 12.5 cents—than the price of the *last* kWh consumed when deciding where to set the thermostat.

Economists Richard J. Zeckhauser and Jeffrey B. Liebman (who worked in the Office of Management and Budget for Barack Obama), who have studied this in the real world, jokingly refer to the phenomenon of consumers "ironing" out the differences in price schedules (a company or organization's explanation of different rates or charges) into one flat rate as "schmeduling." The more consumers make decisions based on averages rather than by thinking on the margins, the more they lose opportunities to save money.

This isn't only true for consumers. For example, a small business or start-up that is growing will probably have higher bills over time, so when making decisions about expenditures and budgeting, the owner or founder should look at the most recent month, not the average. Similarly, because the return on advertising dollars often diminishes at scale, marketers and entrepreneurs should compare the return on the last dollar spent on various strategies when deciding where to invest more money. The goal is to shed light on which margins are successfully scaling and which are not.

At this point, it should be clear what I had to do from my windowless and paper-strewn office in Washington, D.C.: put the marginal analysis of each program from each agency I was tasked with studying under a microscope to locate exactly where the law of diminishing marginal benefits kicked in. Once I did this, I would know at exactly what dollar value the program began to lose voltage, so that the government agencies could efficiently redistribute the remaining funds toward policies that would produce a more positive impact per dollar. Then we all would sit back and watch the marginal gains explode at scale.

Is this what happened?

Of course not!

This was not because marginal thinking is wrong in any way. Rather, it was because reallocating large sums of money takes time and energy—and in this case political consensus, which is not easy to achieve when you are in effect taking money away from one constituency and giving it to another. This was, after all, the federal government, and by this point I understood full well that government bureaucracies aren't just sluggish—they are irrational and insatiable.

By its very nature, each agency is concerned only with its own sur-vival, and that survival depends on the level of its funding. The re-sult is a culture where efficiency (i.e., how effectively funds are being spent) is secondary to political self-preservation. This isn't to say that the bureaucrats at the top of agencies or running the programs are rapacious thugs (though certainly every once in a while they are); rather, they are simply players in the inescapable drama, wherein competing departments try to amass as many resources as possible, gobbling up money like the biblical whale that swallowed Jonah. Worse, funding for agencies is determined by how much they spent in the previous years, which actually *disincentivizes* those agencies from saving money.

The problem in the American government—and in most govern-ments, for that matter—is that marginal gains are short-circuited by the slow-moving, highly politicized mechanisms of bureaucracy. Thankfully, I still was able to be useful to the administration (and in turn American citizens) in other domains, like running field ex-periments that used scientific evidence—not politics!—to inform en-vironmental, homeland security, immigration, and trade policies. Then, in 2003, I left my government post.

Fifteen years later, however, I would have a second chance at bringing marginal thinking to bear when scaling ideas. Not in govern-ment, which doesn't have the profit-driven incentives to save money on the margins, but in the dog-eat-dog world of business, which does.

At Lyft, I would get to unleash the Marginal Revolution to crank up the voltage at scale.

The Adam Smith Memo

Soon after I started working for Lyft, I was sitting in an executive meeting led by CEO Logan Green in the company's San Francisco headquarters. Everyone in the room was looking at a jam-packed spreadsheet of different expenditures and the returns they generated.

Lyft has to focus its marketing on both sides of the business model—supply (recruiting drivers) and demand (capturing riders)—so one of the areas the company was spending a lot of money on was, unsurprisingly, advertising: Facebook, Instagram, and Google ads, TV commercials, radio spots, and other media. We needed to find cost-effective pathways to get the word out, and this was what we were discussing.

As I gazed at the grid of numbers on my computer screen, some seemed to start flashing and pulsating at me. It felt almost like my John Nash moment in my office at the Eisenhower Executive Office Building—data points unexpectedly coalescing into meaning. Something wasn't right. It wasn't that the numbers weren't accurate. It was that they didn't make economic sense. This feeling was by now familiar. Between my White House days and becoming the chief economist at Lyft, I had worked with dozens and dozens of organizations, and a fundamental error that I once thought was an exception had now become a rule in my mind.

Like so many of the others, at Lyft we weren't thinking on the margins.

After the meeting, my superb deputy, Ian Muir, the rest of my team, and I dug deeper into the data. It turned out my impressions were right. Diminishing marginal benefits were all over the ledgers. The last bucket of dollars we spent on Facebook ads, for instance, yielded a *fiftieth* of the business than from the last bucket of dollars going to Google ads. In this case, there was a simple solution: just move some of the Facebook ad spending to Google, where we got a bigger bang for our marginal buck. But I couldn't help but wonder if similarly misguided allocations of money were occurring in other parts of Lyft's business operations beyond merely marketing—and, most concerning of all, if such miscalculations were occurring at scale.

Sure enough, they were. Extending from our investments to money spent recruiting drivers to refer-a-friend offers, Lyft was not scaling from the margins. Some strategies produced higher returns than others, but overall, Lyft was looking only at the average returns on its entire investment in advertising and other facets of business, which masked the real truth about which were performing well and which were performing poorly on the margins. Which is to say, the company had no idea whether every last dollar spent was generating the highest possible voltage.

While I had had little luck applying marginal thinking to optimize how money was spent by the federal government, I was more optimistic that change could be achieved at Lyft. After all, in business, unlike in politics, leviathans that get too big without making a profit meet their demise sooner rather than later. The economic inefficiency, irrationality, and misaligned incentives that allow the poor allocation of money to persist in government bureaucracies simply don't fly in the private sector. In part, this is because companies are designed to be lean, nimble, and adaptive to stay competitive in an ever-shifting marketplace. But really, it's simpler than that: it's a question of survival. If companies waste too much money, they'll cease to exist. This is what makes business both so efficient and so ruthless.

Soon after the meeting where the numbers jumped out at me, my team and I wrote a company-wide memo outlining what I had uncovered in the spending ledger and how marginal thinking could help the company. We called it "Adam Smith Visits Lyft: Making Use of the Invisible Hand to Allocate Resources Efficiently." The memo became one of the most-read memos in the company's history, and ended up morphing into a key part of our cost-savings playbook after the onset of Covid-19, when ride-sharing ground almost to a standstill for several months in the spring of 2020. We later renamed it "Adam Smith Visits the Mandalorians," after Logan (a *Star Wars* fan) declared a "bounty hunter" approach to saving every possible dollar in cost-cutting. Here is how it began:

> When dollars are left strewn on the ground, economists get angry, especially Chicago economists. One important way to avoid this was first alluded to by Adam Smith in 1776, and econ-

omists now refer to a main application of Smith (1776) as the "Invisible Hand." . . .

The principle is simple: economic theory teaches us that a firm is operating efficiently only when the marginal benefits of the last dollar spent on all inputs are equalized across the firm. This gives us a decision rule on how to spend our next dollar on inputs. We should allocate the investment to the input where the marginal benefit per additional dollar spent is the highest.

This is common sense, and everyone at Lyft would agree. Put in a simple manner: if Logan finds a dollar lying on the ground, where should he invest? He should spend the dollar where it will make the biggest impact—in other words, he should spend it on the input that gives us the highest marginal benefit for that dollar. We all know that.

In particular, this principle suggests that Lyft should compare marginal benefits across all of its spending avenues in an apples-to-apples manner—say, driver or passenger acquisition or driver or passenger engagement. When marginal benefits for the last dollar spent are equal across teams, regions, and projects, then resources are efficiently allocated and growth is maximized—we are getting the most out of our investment spend.

The memo was well received, I think, because it was as if the marginal benefits had been hiding in plain sight. Logan called upon managers in every group to look at the impact of the last dollar spent and make decisions accordingly. Nothing was off-limits, from insurance and marketing to driver and rider incentive spending. It is worth noting that the positive culture that Logan and cofounder John Zimmer built at Lyft also played a role in people's positive reactions. Employees weren't punished or pilloried for previous spending choices with diminishing marginal returns. Certain allocations might now find themselves on the chopping block, but no one's proverbial head did. And the best part was that the company was actually motivated to adopt marginal thinking, unlike government agencies.

As of this writing, we remain in "high efficiency" mode at Lyft; even after mass vaccinations began and the economy opened back up, marginal thinking did not die. It was simply repurposed. Now, instead of simply stemming unnecessary expenses and keeping us afloat, marginal thinking dictated where to increase spending as the company began to scale again. What was the best way to get drivers back online? Google ads? "Refer a friend to drive" programs? Making cars available for potential drivers? And on the demand side, how could we convince consumers that Lyft was their best option for getting from point A to point B as they began returning to work and resuming their pre-Covid lives? Safety measures? Fare discounts? All these choices have benefits (and associated diminishing returns), and all have costs, which we navigated on the margins.

You might be thinking that this approach is possible only in Silicon Valley, where companies tend to be more nimble and more data-driven, and often have billions to throw around. Not so. Marginal thinking can ensure high voltage at scale anywhere and everywhere, though in some cases it may take a bit more experimentation than others.

Experimenting on the Margins

When I was in high school in the mid-1980s, I spent two summers working at the Wisconsin Cheeseman, a food gift company that specialized in—you guessed it—cheese (of which I consumed quite a lot on my breaks). My job was driving a forklift, so I spent my days delivering skids of cheese from the basement warehouse to the lines where workers would assemble them in gift baskets to ship all over the world.

I noticed an interesting phenomenon emerge that first summer. The season started with the assembly lines filling about half of the floor space in the building. To my amazement, each line could take several skids of cheese every hour. About a quarter of the way through that first summer, a large number of new assembly workers were hired to fill out the other half of the floor space. As a forklift driver, my job would get a bit more hectic during this time, but despite the fact that I was now delivering to twice as many assembly lines, I never had to deliver twice as many skids of cheese.

This irked the plant manager, and I vividly recall getting called onto the carpet late one summer afternoon. "Mr. List," my boss said, "our logs show that you are delivering about one-half the product to the new lines compared to the old lines."

"Yes, sir, that sounds about right," I responded.

"This is unacceptable. We need more product going to those lines."

I shrugged and looked at the line managers, who could only muster, "The forklift drivers are delivering the right amounts. Those lines are just not producing at a high rate."

The plant manager by now couldn't conceal his exasperation—understandable, given that for months he'd been paying twice as many workers who were producing nowhere near twice as many gift baskets. "We have not budgeted it out this way and now we are doomed!" he blurted out.

How had this state of affairs come to pass? Very simple: he had budgeted based on averages rather than marginal thinking. The plant manager's fixed budget assumed that the original batch of workers and the newly hired batch of workers would be equally productive—failing to account for the fact that as the company hired more and more workers, diminishing marginal productivity set in. This is the same phenomenon that happens when hiring teachers, as we discussed in Chapter 5: the most productive workers tend to be hired first, and if you want to continue to scale once that "superstar" pool is exhausted, you must hire less productive people. Yet in this case the diminishing returns were compounded because the line only moved as fast as the slowest worker (i.e., the "weakest link") could work. In short, the company had been budgeting based on average productivity, rather than the productivity of the last worker to be hired. Somehow, the business was able to plod along until 2011, when they closed the plant. If only the Wisconsin Cheeseman had employed marginal thinking.

The lesson here is that almost every enterprise, whether nonprofit or for-profit, has areas of spending or production where marginal thinking is not holding strong. Yet we're not always aware of them because they are aggregated in a way that makes them impossible to detect. If you don't address these weak spots, you put yourself at risk of stumbling into the cost trap at scale, which will inevitably lead to voltage drops.

The first place to start looking for the weak spots is anywhere you have a lot of levers in either investment or production. For instance, at Lyft, there is a variety of different ways to increase profitability: there are numerous marketing strategies used to recruit new drivers and new customers, and there are a host of investments made to lower insurance costs, lower litigation expenses, and so on. Thus, there is a variety of ways to improve the value of the last dollar spent.

At the Wisconsin Cheeseman, the primary lever was productivity, but there were vast productivity differences across the factory. Periodically measuring the amount of time it took to produce the last gift basket off each of the assembly lines rather than the average time for the entire factory would have offered a more accurate picture and yielded insight into how to best allocate workers.

Ultimately, the key is not just to collect data but to collect it in a more granular way: over time and across all the distinct strategies and investments. You have to look under every rock to find marginal discrepancies. Inevitably, you'll find that some investments will naturally scale, and some won't. Certain investments will deliver the desired outcome, whereas others will be a complete bust. Of course, you have to incentivize this type of detective work inside your business or organization.

Thinking on the margins also means experimenting more. You have to pull as many levers—and different combinations of levers—as you can to figure out what the most beneficial ones are for your enterprise. At the Cheeseman, for example, having a different number of workers on various lines and comparing subsequent productivity rates would have yielded insights into how many workers to put in each line as the operation continued to scale. This discovery process is useful before scaling up, or even if you never scale up, but it will shift and become even more important at scale. Recall the earlier chapters in which we discussed the representativeness of population and of situation. Often, voltage drops occur when the group of people you hope to reach or the conditions in which you reach them become more diverse or complex as your company or organization grows. This likely will produce weak spots that are specific to a certain place or group of employees. To locate where you're losing voltage on the margins, you will have to do multisite trials and then compare the data.

These types of explorations are equally valuable on the customer side. For instance, when you release a new product, examine how many units are being sold per day in different regions, rather than the national daily average. The resulting data offer insights into the allocation of marginal resources. For example, you might halt shipping of a new product to a region where sales are lower until economies of scale can be leveraged—that is, until sales revenue in those areas begins to exceed all the costs involved in getting the product on shelves. Looking under multiple hoods in this fashion will require a significant investment of time and resources, yes, but if every last dollar spent is equalized across a broad group of people, regions, and situations at scale, you will have attained high voltage.

Lest you think, however, that harnessing marginal thinking is always about comparing the numbers on a balance sheet, here's something to remember. Some marginal benefits are intangible and hard to gather data about, but this doesn't mean they are not important or valuable. I learned this firsthand when, at the urging of some of their donors, the Make-A-Wish Foundation asked me to do a benefit-cost analysis of sorts to better understand the value of the gifts the organization gave to terminally ill children.

Did kids live longer after having their wish come true? Did their many smiles have a quantifiable value? This was trickier than any task I ever encountered in my messy, windowless office across the way from the White House. But in the end my answer was simple: some things worth doing—and scaling—transcend monetization and conventional measurements.

You never know where the pot of gold lies, which is why curiosity and experimentation—rather than defensiveness—must be part of your cultural DNA. But once you find weak spots, correcting your course by reallocating your spending or restructuring your job functions may not be the only challenge you face. Quite frequently, there is another obstacle to confront first: mentally leaving your past mistakes in the past, where they belong.

Let Bygones Be Bygones

Soon after I began teaching at the University of Chicago, the school's fundraising department reached out to me for help. Naturally, their goal was to raise more money, and since I had spent several years earlier in my career studying the behavioral economics of fundraising, I eagerly said yes.

One of the first things I learned was that the fundraising department had a fully equipped call center that they no longer used. When I asked why they had stopped using it, someone explained to me that even though phone calls generated more donations than mailers, the cost of mailing a letter was cheaper, so they had phased out telephone fundraising. When I pushed to understand how they had arrived at these conclusions, it turned out they had calculated the average total cost of each phone call by adding the cumulative cost of the computer-networked phone-banking system to the cost of employing students to make calls, then divided that amount by the total number of calls.

Whoa, I thought.

The fundraising department was ignoring what economists often refer to as the *bygones principle* or *marginal principle*—the rule that money spent in the past should have no influence over rational decisions made in the present. The dollars already spent are long gone, a *sunk cost*. Now it's only the return on the *next* dollar spent that matters.

For the fundraising department, that included the initial investment in the phone-banking system: an up-front, one-time fixed cost. The money was already used and thus was impossible to get back. I explained to the fundraising staff that this past expenditure was no longer relevant. Because the call center's system wasn't part of the regular operating costs anymore, it should have been discounted from their current calculations toward the future.

Their mistake hadn't been investing in the call center; rather, it was in not leaving that investment in the past. When we recalculated the operating costs, it drove down the cost of each call to the point that the margin was less than for the mailers! Moreover, we found that it was not only less costly but also more effective in securing donations. As a result, the department rebooted the phone-banking system, hired student callers, and raised a whole lot more money.

When we factor investments or mistakes from the past into our decision-making about the future, it is almost guaranteed that we will fall into what is known as the *sunk cost fallacy*—an irrational commitment to money, time, or other resources already spent. Often, this faulty commitment comes at a price, as happened with the University of Chicago fundraisers, who sank more time and resources into what they later discovered to be a less than optimal strategy.

Avoiding the sunk cost fallacy is easier said than done, however. This is because our emotions often get in the way of rational decision-making—and, as we've learned, the emotions we hate the most and will therefore go to the greatest lengths to escape feeling include loss and regret.

We fall into the sunk cost fallacy all too often in our personal lives, too. Say you bought tickets for your family to go to an outdoor concert to take place early in the fall. While you were hopeful that it wouldn't be too cold, on the day of the concert a merciless cold front rolls in and the temperature drops below freezing. You have two choices: go to the concert anyway or skip it. Because you have already bought the tickets and don't want to later regret spending the money on a concert you didn't attend, you tell your spouse and kids, "Cold weather be damned, we're going to the concert!" Then what happens? You're all cold and have a miserable time. You allowed a sunk cost from the past to determine your future; the money for the tickets was gone either way and going to the concert wouldn't bring it back. And so you paid an extra price—lost time that could have been better spent another way, like watching a movie together in your warm home.

One thought experiment that might help you avoid such situations is to reverse the events and ask: *If we did not have tickets yet, would we now buy them?* If the answer is no, ignore what your past self did and curb your losses while you can. You might suffer some discomfort from doing so, but in the end you will be better off. (And you won't end up wet and cold.)

This aversion to cutting our losses and leaving sunk costs in the past manifests in practically every area of our lives, and oftentimes with much higher stakes than a crappy Saturday night shivering to music we're too chilly to enjoy. We stay in bad romantic relationships because we hate the idea of "losing" the time we've already put in—a sunk cost. We don't sell off a disastrous investment we lost money on—a sunk cost. We plod to the end of a graduate degree in a field that we've realized we don't want to pursue rather than just dropping out—a sunk cost. We don't leave a job that makes us unhappy because we've already spent years building a career inside the company—a sunk cost. And we see this on the global stage, too, as when a world leader refuses to pull out of a conflict abroad that has already cost so many lives and resources. Again and again, people let irrecoverable past losses taint both the present and the future.

This tendency to succumb to the sunk cost fallacy is urgently relevant for applying marginal thinking. When you bring marginal analysis to bear on your enterprise, as we did at Lyft, you are liable to uncover past mistakes. In our case, we realized we had been making suboptimal decisions about spending and resource allocation. It's painful to discover a poor allocation of finite resources that has now become a sunk cost. Your reputation or even job might be on the line if it's revealed you spearheaded or green-lit a bad allocation of funds. It is here that the temptation emerges to double down on the mistake and invest still more in the hope of recouping the sunk cost, much like a hopeless gambler trying to win back the money he has already lost. But throwing good money after bad will almost never work out, especially at scale.

The political and reputational obstacles to rooting out sunk cost fallacies in your enterprise often depend on the organizational culture (more on this in Chapter 9). Do people feel psychologically safe enough to admit mistakes? Do they see the successes and failures as the result of individual or collective efforts? Are they properly incentivized to put the interests of the organization or company over their personal ones? The answers to these questions will define how prudent your operation will be in responding to discoveries in the margins and overcoming the sunk costs that inevitably come to light.

Beyond culture, there are also organizational mechanics you can institute to avoid getting mired in the mistakes of the past. Some money-management firms, for instance, rotate portfolios between employees every six months, allowing a fresh set of eyes to determine which investments haven't performed well and sell them off—with no feelings of shame or regret clouding the right decision. Whether it's in your business, your career, or your personal life, an objective third-party perspective can often provide the nudge you need to let bygones be bygones.

* * *

CUT YOUR LOSSES. Let sunk costs sink into the past. When you recognize things your past self did wrong, a voice in your head might tell you to stay the course even in the face of marginal costs. Remind yourself that that's just loss aversion and anticipatory regret talking. Ignore that voice. You have to be willing to upset your past self, and your future self will be grateful that you did.

Even if that means doing the unthinkable: quitting.

8

QUITTING IS FOR WINNERS

was a very good high school golfer. I wasn't Tiger Woods–caliber good, but good enough to earn myself a spot on the University of Wisconsin–Stevens Point golf team, where I went on to become a two-time Academic All-American athlete. I loved golf with a deep passion.

When I was growing up, all of the men in my family were truck drivers (my grandfather August Sr., my father, August Jr., and my older brother, August III!), and I had been told that I would be one, too. Yet I dreamed of a different life, even if I didn't know exactly what that life might look like or where to find it. Golf, however, was a door that opened a whole new horizon of possibilities to me, since I very well might not have gone to college at all had it not been for the sport.

By attaining a four-year degree, I would hop up a rung on the socioeconomic ladder and gain access to opportunities withheld from my parents and grandparents. Golf had gotten me this far, so the best way I could imagine prospering was by making it my future career. If I stuck it out and gave the sport my all, was there a chance I could make it as a professional? I believed the answer was yes, though in retrospect I was a victim of my own confirmation bias, conveniently focusing on the tournaments I won while ignoring the empirical evidence of the ones I lost. I had no trouble remembering the good rounds—shooting 32 on the front nine of a prestigious tournament, for instance—but conveniently blocked out the 41 on the back nine that cost me first place. As I packed up my belongings and left my childhood home for Stevens Point, playing on the PGA tour was the dream I clung to. And why shouldn't I? I believed I could scale my past successes as a golfer into future ones on the PGA tour.

But then something surprising happened during my very first year in college that changed the trajectory of my life. About midway through our fall golf season, I had an off weekend, so I returned home to visit my family. When I went out to Cherokee Country Club in Madison, Wisconsin, to hone my game that Friday morning, there happened to be a bunch of college golfers at Cherokee, including some of the older players I used to compete against in high school—golfers like Steve Stricker from the University of Illinois and Jerry Kelly from the University of Hartford, both of whom have subsequently had long and successful PGA careers. I had not seen them for a few years, so I welcomed the chance to find out how my skills compared.

Back in high school, I'd managed to stay competitive, even though I was a few years younger than them. Now, however, something had dramatically changed. As we all worked on the practice range, something felt amiss. Incredibly, they had become Jack Nicklauses, while I was stuck as John List. Yet rather than accept the reality of this fact, I brushed off the initial episode. *They were always better ball-strikers than me,* I told myself, *but I always got them back around the greens. Plus,* I reminded myself, *this is just practice. It's the score of the actual game that matters, so let's see how their scores match up against mine.*

After they had all teed off, I followed by playing my round with a few friends. Same tees, same course, same weather conditions. The crushing outcome was that both Steve and Jerry scored in the high 60s, as did many of the dozen or so other golfers out with them (including a high schooler named Mario Tiziani, now also a professional golfer), and while I thought I played pretty well, I shot a 75. For those not familiar with golf scoring, at this level that difference was akin to an A+ versus a D.

That night, rather than sleep, I did what any data guy would do: I researched all of their golf scores for the past several years, comparing them to what I had scored on the same courses. I did the same all day Saturday and Sunday. This was not easy work; since there was no internet back then, it took two solid days in the library digging through old local newspapers for data. By the end of that weekend, as I drove back to Stevens Point, sleepless, I came to terms with the fact that no matter how much I cared about golf and practiced it—and no matter what it symbolized for me—I was never going to be good enough to make it onto the PGA Tour, or even come close. I was playing fine for a collegiate golfer, but figuring out how to shave those last several strokes off my score necessary to compete at the highest levels was unfathomable. Suddenly I was unable to delude myself further. Reality had intervened and revealed my pro-golfer aspirations for what they were: a false positive.

My talent had gotten me this far, but as a career, it just didn't scale. Pursuing it past this point would only lead to a crushing voltage drop and perhaps even more crushing disappointment. So I decided it was time to quit on my dream.

Making this decision wasn't easy. It went against the values I had learned as a child growing up in small-town Wisconsin, the kingdom of the legendary Green Bay Packers coach Vince Lombardi, who famously said, "Winners never quit and quitters never win." This was the local culture I was steeped in. I was a product of it, as were my supportive parents, who believed in my golf career and told me to stay resilient and never give up.

This wasn't a uniquely midwestern phenomenon. American culture as a whole tells us that if we refuse to quit, if we just hang on a little longer and give a little more, then all our dreams will come true. This is buttressed by the proliferation of success stories on social media that all seem to inevitably hit the same note: "Thankfully I didn't quit and persevered through all of the setbacks." This success should be applauded, but for every one of these feel-good stories, there are likely a hundred thousand people who toil away and never get to the finish line, never get to do the victory lap. Where are the tweets from these people? Who is talking about how they could have accomplished something really great if they'd quit something else twenty years ago and tried an entirely different path? How many life-saving drugs, innovative new products, and bold policy interventions has our society lost because people refused to quit pursuing unscalable dreams? These are tragic and unwritten stories—unwritten because they have not had the chance to play out in reality, since from birth we are told we shouldn't quit.

But what if I told you that achieving something great often means quitting—that is, giving up a dream, pursuit, or career path that is going nowhere, in exchange for one where you can make a greater contribution?

In my case, once I gave up my dream of professional golfing, I turned my attention to the one thing that I had come to believe I did have a true talent—and passion—for: economics. In 1992, I graduated with an economics degree from UW–Stevens Point and received my doctorate four years later from the University of Wyoming.

After completing my PhD, I applied for 150 tenure-track jobs. I got turned down by 149 of them, yet I wasn't shaken by this less than enthusiastic embrace from my chosen field. Because unlike golf, economics was an area where I knew I was good enough to make a mark. While I didn't have a fancy Ivy League degree, the response to my research suggested I had the right kind of mind. So this time I heeded Lombardi's advice and persisted. I threw myself into the field-work that has since defined my career at the one school that wanted me, the University of Central Florida.

It paid off. In some alternate corner of the multiverse, John A. List is a golf "teaching pro" at a second-rate country club quoting Vince Lombardi to the clients he gives lessons to. Not the worst existence, but not the best, either. Thankfully, in *this* universe I'm me, constantly feeding my own curiosity with new field experiments and new science. I've done a few things I'm proud of, and maybe even helped some people. As a golfer, I simply wouldn't have made much of an impact—*not* because economists are inherently more valuable to society than golfers (lots of professional golfers inspire children and contribute to social causes, and club pros do wonderful things as well) but simply because I am better at economics than at golf, which made me more likely to successfully contribute things of social value. Put another way, my skills as an economist were more scalable than my skills as a golfer.

In cases like these, the best thing you can do is quit. It may be a wrenching decision, but I would argue that getting good at quitting is one of the secrets for scaling successfully. Indeed, I believe that not only do people, companies, and organizations *not quit enough,* they also don't quit *soon enough.*

Which raises an inescapable question: how do you know when to quit?

Time Is Money

It's perhaps no coincidence that the field I turned to after giving up on my golf career was a discipline that could scientifically explain why I had made the right choice. That explanation can be found in one of the bedrock concepts of economics: *opportunity cost,* or the gains you miss out on when you choose one option over another. We can think of opportunity cost as an attempt to quantify the path not taken, which often means the path we would have taken if only we'd quit the path we were on. In my case, pursuing a golf career would have cost me the chance to teach economics to eager young minds, publish lots of scientific studies and books, and advise various leaders.

I saw a useful example of the dynamics of opportunity cost at work one day when my son Mason, then eight years old and a precociously competitive baseball player, was shopping for a new bat. Mason had saved up $325 and wanted to buy a top-of-the-line baseball bat that he hoped would help him raise his batting average. (Yes, his data scientist dad tracked his stats from his very first at-bat as a five-year-old!) He quickly found two very good options—one for $200, the other for $325. He couldn't decide between them, so I did what any economist father would do and said, "Mason, think about it like this. If you buy the $200 bat, then that leaves you $125 to also buy a good new Rawlings baseball glove." He took this suggestion in. Within a minute we were at the cash register with the cheaper bat and a new Rawlings glove.

Mason had factored opportunity cost into his decision-making. Because he had a finite amount of money to spend, had he opted for the more expensive bat, not only would he have had to shell out $325, but he also would have had to forgo buying the new glove as well.

Sometimes we do such calculations instinctively. But often we don't stop to consider opportunity cost until both options come into our field of vision, a phenomenon demonstrated by a body of influential psychological research showing that our judgments and preferences tend to be based primarily on information that is explicitly presented. As discussed in Chapter 7, when we make decisions we tend to apply mental shortcuts, or heuristics, that allow us to think fast, which means there is no time for careful opportunity-cost thinking. Relatedly, research on affective forecasting—our ability to predict the emotions we will feel in the future—reveals that judgments about our future well-being are excessively sensitive to current mood, causing us to neglect other relevant factors. In other words, we magnify the importance of the emotions sitting in front of us, which can lead to more impulsive decision-making.

When I was a sports card dealer I saw this all the time. Too many times to remember, a buyer would have a hard time choosing between two cards—buying, say, a $250 Ken Griffey rookie card or a $200 A-Rod card—so I would frame the choice as follows: "Would you rather have the Griffey, or the A-Rod card and five packs of Upper Deck cards?" Remarkably, the decision that had seemed so difficult just moments before was suddenly no longer difficult at all: A-Rod and the five packs.

Experimental research suggests that policymakers are also vulnerable to the same bias, known as *opportunity cost neglect,* when evaluating the best programs to fund, causing decision-makers to commit to one program without fully considering others. I have often heard "What benefits can $10 million produce if invested in this policy?" But rarely have I heard "Alternatively, what benefits could the $10 million reap if invested elsewhere?" The business world is subject to this phenomenon, too, though it has more built-in practices to guard against it, since understanding opportunity cost is crucial in a competitive environment. This takes us back to the concept of marginal thinking from Chapter 7, which is inseparable from opportunity cost. When resources are limited, if you're not getting the most out of every last dollar spent, the opportunity cost includes the additional impact your dollars could have had if allocated more effectively.

All of this is to say that evaluating opportunity costs requires consideration of alternative options that are not explicit components of a decision, like the five packs of Upper Deck cards and Mason's new baseball glove. But the opportunity cost isn't always about what money can buy. When we ignore opportunity cost, we often squander that most precious limited resource of all: time.

In the same way that when we spend our money on one thing we can't spend it on another, when we spend our *time* on one thing we can't spend it on another. When a company focuses all of their resources on scaling one product, they can't scale another. When a government scales one public program, they don't scale another. To implement such endeavors means investing not just money but also thousands of hours of time by the people involved. In this manner, as an organization scales, opportunity costs grow—more money is spent, but so is more time. And time, economically speaking, *is* money.

Ever since Gary Becker, the famous Chicago economist, began working on determining the actual value of time, economists have explored various ways to measure this slippery economic entity. At present, economists have managed to estimate the value of our time across different settings, places, and populations. For instance, what is the value of the time a transportation program will give back to citizens if, say, it funds a new rail line that will shorten riders' commutes? There are numerical estimates that can be made by looking at the value of the productive things people will do with the time they recoup. But the opportunity cost of time isn't just about money made or lost—it's about how we spend the tick-tocking of hours endowed to us during our limited time on earth.

We want to get the most out of our lives, which is why we don't like requesting Lyft rides whose wait times feel too long (and why we hate waiting more generally) and are always on the lookout for productivity hacks. We want to maximize what we accomplish with our time and minimize the opportunity costs of time wasted deleting spam emails or standing on a corner waiting for a Lyft to show up.

For people and organizations with big, bold ideas they hope to take to scale, opportunity costs are especially important to consider. The more an idea scales, the more time, money, and opportunity can be lost. Moreover, for most people who dream of scaling something they are passionate about, there is also an emotional cost: the fear of disappointment and heartbreak that comes with investing their time—which is to say, *their life*—in something that doesn't work out. Think about the scientist who chooses one line of research in the hope of discovering a cure to a disease, or the start-up founder with an idea for a new technology that might revolutionize an industry. Pursuing such objectives requires tremendous sacrifices, the most significant of which is the opportunity costs of paths not taken. This is why it is so devastating when an idea you pour your heart and soul and time into fails to scale. It's not just voltage you lose. It's all the other promising opportunities you turned down in the process. The more time you sink into the wrong idea, the more you are misspending life's most precious resource. But if you quit at the right time (and ignore that sunk cost), then you can move on to scale something else—something with a better shot at success.

This is what I call *optimal quitting*.

Sometimes you have to leave behind that professional golf career you've been dreaming of—by which I mean that idea you dreamed of scaling and changing the world with but which just isn't performing how you want—in order to shift gears and find a better one. And the sooner you do this, the lower the opportunity cost you'll pay. Yet giving up at the right moment—before we sacrifice overmuch—doesn't come naturally to us for the same reason that accurately calculating opportunity cost doesn't come naturally to baseball card collectors or eight-year-old Little Leaguers. It requires an effort that runs counter to our deep-rooted heuristics and fast way of thinking. We have to battle our own default mental complacency.

An experiment conducted in the 1990s captures this challenge well. Participants were permitted to ask questions about an exciting opportunity, such as going to see a film in a foreign city, before deciding whether to do it. The best strategy for making this decision would have been to weigh the appeal of the proposed activity against the appeal of other options for how to spend that time. But instead, they thought very narrowly. Their inquiries pertained almost exclusively to the focal event rather than to possible alternatives available in the city, such as visiting a museum or attending a concert.

You can see the dangers of this tunnel-vision type of thinking when aiming to scale. Rather than imagine what other ideas they could spend their time pursuing, people often zero in on various aspects of the idea they have already invested time and resources into. But far better to do both things: scale one idea while simultaneously considering other possibly worthy ideas. To develop this practice, you must, as a famous study of consumer opportunity cost neglect put it, "actively generate the alternatives."

When you have lots of alternatives, quitting will be much less painful, both emotionally and practically. Perhaps the best example of this is Google's moonshot factory, X Development. With a mandate of making a 10X impact on the most urgent challenges facing humanity—a high-voltage goal if there ever was one—the employees of X are empowered to explore the most creative and ambitious pursuits imaginable. This had led Google's moonshot group to pour time, collective brainpower, and money into seemingly crazy ideas such as teleportation and space elevators—which they ultimately chose to abandon, given that teleportation required surmounting the laws of physics, and the physical materials needed for space elevators don't exist yet or can't be made cost-effectively.

But having to constantly quit on ideas like these isn't a byproduct of X's process—it is its foundation. As the research lab's chief, Astro Teller, put it in a TED talk, "We've got this interesting balance going where we allow our unchecked optimism to fuel our visions. But then we also harness enthusiastic skepticism to breathe life, breathe reality into those visions." This means lots of discarded ideas, approaches, and prototypes, some of which are eventually reengineered all over again from scratch, as with the disappointing first version of Google Glass. Yet this gospel of optimal quitting is how Google X aims to discover and scale some of the most innovative endeavors in human history.

Despite the pain of having expended effort on something that doesn't come to fruition, there is beauty and freedom (not to mention savviness) in pulling the plug. In 2011, when Netflix made the blunder of splitting its streaming and DVD-by-mail services and rebranding the latter as Qwikster, for example, CEO Reed Hastings listened to peeved customers and canned the already-scaled idea immediately. The opportunity cost was simply too high to let things ride and see if the DVD-by-mail business could survive. This was the right move. Netflix recovered from this momentary voltage drop and kept its meteoric pace of scale going. Of course, the list of businesses that didn't quit soon enough is much longer than the list of those that did. But no one remembers them, because we never will know what they could have created or scaled had they used their time and resources differently.

Yet while Netflix furnishes an example of bold and wise quitting, it's debatable whether it was an optimal quitter. The company squandered a great deal of time, money, and effort. Cutting their losses was much better than not doing so, but no person or organization wants to be the one who drives up to the edge of the cliff and then swerves to safety at the last moment. You shouldn't have been close to the cliff in the first place! Far better to quit early, when the opportunity cost is still low. Doing so doesn't mean you don't have the much-celebrated quality of "grit," made famous by my friend Angela Duckworth, the wonderful behavioral psychologist. Grit isn't about persisting with something that's hopeless. It's actually about having the emotional resilience to quit early in order to start again—to lose battles in order to win the war.

Scale What You Do Best

When an idea yields considerably diminishing returns (profits and/or impact) as you scale, that's often a clear sign that it's time to call it quits or pivot to a different approach that has a better scaling profile. But when deciding whether or not to throw in the towel, we have to consider not only whether our idea is scalable but also whether *we* are the right person to scale it.

Take wine and cloth. These were the two commercial goods that the British economist David Ricardo offered as examples in a now historic paper he published in the spring of 1817. The topic was international trade, and in particular, a theory that would soon establish the influential concept of *comparative advantage*. The idea was very intuitive: whether due to natural resources, infrastructure, or any number of other factors, certain countries are able to produce certain goods more efficiently—that is, at a lower opportunity cost—than other countries, so those are the things they should focus on, rather than wasting resources on goods they don't make as well as their trading partners do.

Portugal, Ricardo pointed out, was excellent at making wine. They had the right grapes and the right weather, as well as a long tradition of vintners who gave the country both the human expertise and the logistical know-how to produce good wine that was exportable at a competitive price. England, meanwhile, was excellent at producing cloth. The country had a storied textile tradition that, like the

Portuguese with wine, had given the English the skills and machinery to produce and peddle cloth with an efficiency that gave them an edge in the global economy. Ricardo's argument was simple: do—and by extension *scale*—what you're good at!

The implications of comparative advantage, however, didn't just pertain to the side producing the specialized good. All parties involved would benefit, including the buyer, who would get the best product at the best price. Thus every country should buy wine from Portugal (or other countries with mature and efficient winemaking industries) and cloth from England (or other countries with mature and efficient textile industries). Here again we find ourselves in the presence of Adam Smith's "invisible hand" as the elegant dance of supply and demand coaxes an orderly equilibrium out of the seeming chaos of the marketplace.

In practice, things end up more complicated than in theory (as they usually do in economics), since tariffs, taxes, and occasional trade wars can inflate the cost of exports. But on the whole, Ricardo's law of comparative advantage is as relevant today as it was in the early nineteenth century. Japan efficiently makes good cars, and its top export is cars. Saudi Arabia sits on tons of oil it knows how to produce, and its top export is oil. The U.S. tech industry is the best in the world, and its top export is hardware, including computers. We choose to scale the things most likely to generate high voltage.

Or do we?

Looking beyond international trade, we discover that we can apply David Ricardo's insight to nearly every endeavor we pour our time and resources into. In theory, this would mean we build careers doing the things we excel at, champion causes where we can make the most impact, launch businesses we are uniquely suited to lead, and so on. But again, the reality is a bit more complicated. Sometimes we dedicate ourselves to goals that we are less likely to succeed at, as if the English had decided to drop textiles and switch to wine in the nineteenth century. This miscalculation dogs both our collective pursuits and our individual ones. The epiphany I experienced during my first season of college golf—namely, that I wasn't good enough to ever play professionally—was nothing more or less than the realization that I didn't have a comparative advantage in the sport, whereas in the field of economics I did. Not only would the opportunity cost have been extremely high for me if I had continued pursuing golf professionally, but worst of all, the sacrifices that choice entailed wouldn't have been worth it because I would almost certainly have failed in the end.

While most start-ups, nonprofits, and other enterprises rarely fly as blindly as an eighteen-year-old American male—especially one from Vince Lombardi country—many start losing altitude almost as soon as they have taken off, often because they have launched before understanding their comparative advantage or because they have not developed a comparative advantage at all. And to avoid a fatal crash landing, they must be willing to give up on an idea that is going nowhere, thereby freeing time and resources to invest in other directions where a breakthrough edge might emerge. In other words, trading in a comparative disadvantage for possible future advantage underlies an all-too-familiar business buzzword: *pivot*.

One example from the start-up world is Twitter, which was actually an idea born inside a podcasting platform called Odeo. Odeo wasn't a bad venture, but not the best, either; a number of tech start-ups had already opened up the frontier of podcast publishing and aggregation, making it an increasingly crowded space. Odeo, like other similar platforms, allowed users to make, store, and share audio files, but it had no game-changing innovation to give it a leg up against its competitors. So after executives created and spun off a new company with a new name—Twitter—Odeo made a sharp turn midflight away from "audioblogging" and toward "microblogging." And from their ubiquitous platform for public 140-character messages (now 280 characters), a novel form of social media emerged. In other words, Twitter created a whole new sport in which it was the best player in the league: the definition of a comparative advantage. The takeaway here is that failure isn't always failure; by cutting losses at the right time and discovering your comparative advantage, a broken egg can turn into a golden one. That is, with one caveat, as PayPal's founders learned back in the early days of the consumer internet.

In 1998, the company started under a different name, Confinity, and hoped to scale programs for secure payments between Palm-Pilots, but there was no comparative advantage here because there was no market—in the late 1990s people just weren't moving money around the way Confinity prophesied, at least not yet. (Sending money between PalmPilots . . . say *what*?) But from their home computers, netizens were transferring more money online than ever before, so the company pivoted to exploit its edge in this new domain. They realized that their secure financial technology represented a comparative advantage at that time because there were few other ways for ordinary consumers to quickly transfer money to one another without intermediaries like banks or credit card companies. Seeing this opportunity and constantly iterating its business model for its first few years, PayPal finally reached scale as eBay's preferred peer-to-peer payment system.

The lesson here is that sometimes it's not enough to be the best at something. You have to be the best at something that people need and want. And to scale, it has to be something lots of people need and want.

So the question of how to know when to quit on your idea and pivot to something else is, on the surface, quite straightforward: when you don't have a comparative advantage, or when you have figured out that there is no substantial market to serve with your comparative advantage. Yet, as we have seen, often your competitive edge—or what to do with it—isn't immediately obvious or apparent. Confinity had minted a groundbreaking technology, but the way in which it was employing it didn't scale at the time. Luckily, the company quit and pivoted on this early incarnation before it was too late, as did Odeo. Could they have quit even earlier and scaled sooner? In theory, yes, they could have—but better late than never!

In the first half of this book, we unpacked the Five Vital Signs, or the five causes of voltage drops that sabotage scalability and prevent your idea from taking off: false positives, overgeneralizing across people and situations, spillovers, and unsustainable costs. Together, they demonstrate that scaling is a fragile endeavor, as any one of those traits can doom you. To avoid that fate, you must quit in order to give yourself another chance at winning.

Knowing When to Quit

The thing about optimal quitting is that it's really, really, hard. There's the rational, economist side of our mind with which, if we slow down enough, we can estimate our opportunity cost (of time and dollars) and make a clear-eyed determination about our comparative advantage (or disadvantage). In other words, we have the mental tool kit for optimal quitting. Yet we don't always quit when we know we should. And once again, this doesn't just apply to ideas we dream of scaling. Marriages, unfulfilling jobs, bad investments, crappy friendships . . . the list could go on forever. Although I likely made a good call about quitting golf, I've made countless mistakes by not quitting something soon enough in other areas of my life. Why?

Quite simply, we are reluctant to quit things because we want to avoid the resulting heartbreak. The pain of failure is magnified by the sunk costs: all the time and effort and emotion you have already invested. The opportunity cost of paths not taken is easy to bear when our sacrifices lead to success, but when we fail, we tend to experience deep regret.

In such situations, it's important to recall what we learned about sunk costs in Chapter 7: you should avoid factoring previous costs into decisions about the future. Those losses—whether in the form of time, money, or both—have already been incurred, so it's far better to ignore them than to keep investing in them in the hopes that they will someday pay off. (Hint: they won't.) In other words, you must learn from the past but scale for the future.

Another reason many of us cling to the status quo when we

shouldn't is that we fear the unknown, as an experiment I helped design demonstrates. Back in 2013, Steve Levitt and I asked participants who were on the fence about some decision in their life to flip a virtual coin on Freakonomics.com. Some people wanted to quit their jobs, others were considering selling their house, and some wanted to leave a romantic relationship. If someone flipped heads, they got a message advising them to go ahead and make a change: quit the job, sell the house, leave the relationship. If they got tails, they were advised to keep the status quo. Over the course of a year, subjects flipped more than twenty thousand virtual coins. To see how their decisions had panned out, we emailed twice with each person two months after they tossed the coin, and then six months after. It turned out that those who had made a major change, like filing for divorce or leaving their jobs or buying a new house, were more likely to report being happier two months later, and even happier still six months later, compared to those who had stuck with the status quo.

The lesson here is that while change can be scary, when people push past the fear and make the change anyway, they are usually happier, and tend not to feel the big regret they dreaded in the first place. Ultimately, whether you're pulling the plug on a business venture or leaving a marriage (or anything in between), quitting involves the same type of courage required to take that leap in the first place: the ability to cope with uncertainty.

Quitting on something means not knowing exactly what will come next. This is so challenging for us because of a cognitive bias that behavioral economists call *ambiguity aversion*. This quirk in our thinking causes us to overly favor the known over the unknown, even if the known leads you or your enterprise to a disastrous voltage drop. This is why tolerance for uncertainty is important not just when throwing your time and resources into something—it's also necessary for pulling the plug.

Most of the time we never learn what we would have produced or achieved if we had quit at the right time (commonly called the "counterfactual"). This is what makes quitting so hard: you often don't know what you have missed, so you never learn the true cost of not quitting.

Of course, risk and ambiguity cannot be avoided, no matter how averse to them we are. The best we can do is to use all the information at our disposal to determine (1) if an idea is scalable and (2) if this scalable idea can generate higher voltage than other ideas you might have a comparative advantage in doing.

Even though you can never observe the counterfactual—or what might have been—directly, there are a few exercises you can do to learn from your decision. For example, as an entrepreneur, you might decide not to pursue some opportunity, such as expanding into a new region or a new product category. Afterward, you would be well served to closely watch how it works out for the competitor who *does* grab that opportunity; if it turns out you were wrong, explore any biases you might have had. More generally, try making a list of all the things you could have been doing over the past six months, other than what you actually spent your time on. This reminds us that our scarcest resource (time) is precious and not to be wasted, even if the emotions produced by uncertainty can be vexing.

*   *   *

THOMAS EDISON ONCE said, "I haven't failed 10,000 times. I have successfully found 10,000 ways that will not work." Edison stands as a poster boy for the power of giving up. He discarded low-voltage idea after low-voltage idea; if he had toiled away on unscalable ideas forever, he might never have produced some of history's greatest inventions, like the lightbulb (a high-voltage idea if I ever heard one—literally!). He demonstrates that our greatest potential to make a real impact lies not in persisting against all the odds. It lies in quitting early so that we can try, try again. And that is a scalable mindset.

Optimal quitting should become part of our strategy as we scale, rather than a panic button we hit as a last resort. As tech entrepreneur, investor, and author Reid Hoffman writes, "It's easy to kill a product that's failing; it's much harder—and more strategic—to kill one that lacks the potential to truly scale."

Choosing the intense but brief pain of quitting now over the prolonged pain of failure later is a skill that both individuals and organizations must cultivate. As we'll learn in Chapter 9, this is why a meritocratic, cooperative culture is so important. By bringing diverse points of view and perspectives together, teams and organizations have a better chance of identifying initiatives that should be abandoned, while also supporting people who may feel vulnerable if it is their idea that is optimally shelved. So while optimal quitting represents our third key secret to high-voltage success, it is only one piece of a larger organizational puzzle that must be built to scale: culture.

SCALING CULTURE

On the edge of the Bay of All Saints, on the Atlantic coast of Brazil's lush northeastern state of Bahia, lies a small fishing community named Cabuçu. There are virtually no other jobs in the region except for fishing, so each morning the men there wake early and take to the sea together in search of the day's catch. The fishermen work in groups of varying size, most commonly in teams of three to eight. This collaborative approach is no random happenstance, but rather a strategy honed through time and experience. The choppy waves and strong currents of the bay necessitate boats that have multiple crewmembers, and the large fish they pull in from the blue depths require heavy fishing poles and other instruments that demand the hands and strength of several people. Setting the large nets is tricky work, while hauling them in full of flopping fish is physically strenuous. For a single fisherman to go it alone out on the sparkling waters would be pointless, not to mention dangerous. For the community to eat together, they must first fish together.

Some fifty or so kilometers inland from Cabuçu along the Paraguaçu River sits another small fishing society: Santo Estêvão. In contrast to their seaside counterparts, however, the people of this village pull smaller, lighter fish from the placid waters of a lake. Thus their crafts are smaller, as are their poles and nets. As a result, these fishermen largely work solo; fishing as a team is neither necessary nor efficient. The men start the workday alone and end it alone (unless you count their bounty of fish).

The fishing villages Cabuçu and Santo Estêvão, in effect, represent two different workplace cultures—not the typical workplace that comes to mind in the twenty-first century, but a real one nonetheless. One is highly collectivist and relies on cooperative labor; the other is individualist, with little collaboration. They share an identical goal—to catch enough fish to feed and sustain their community—but each village has developed methods of working best suited to their distinct environments. But do the differences end there? Or do these two communities differ culturally in other fundamental ways, beyond the confines of just the "workplace"?

This was the question my friend, and clever economist, Andreas Leibbrandt hoped to answer when he visited Cabuçu and Santo Estêvão and conducted a set of field experiments with help from me and my esteemed longtime collaborator and friend Uri Gneezy (Andreas's wife is Brazilian, and she was the one who told us about the unique research opportunity the two communities offered).

The reason we were curious about cultural differences between the lakeside and seaside fishing societies was that one of the key elements that distinguish organizational cultures is the extent to which the labor is done in groups. And research suggests that the degree of teamwork involved in this labor may promote stronger (or weaker) norms of cooperation among its members. Cabuçu and Santo Estêvão, then, seemed like the perfect laboratory for investigating just how far-reaching the impact of teamwork could be. Would the way the people in each community fished affect the way they lived and related to one another? Would the lakeside society be more individualistic overall than the seaside one? And then there was the question of whether one community was more productive, in economic terms, than the other. Would Cabuçu be a cooperative utopia where collective action ensured that public goods readily flowed and benefited everyone? Or would Santo Estêvão's culture foster healthy competition and a well-functioning free market?

To compare the two communities, we ran a series of game-based field experiments with fishermen from both villages. As odd as this may sound, games like these are a staple of behavioral economics research, even in far-flung, remote places, because they quickly reveal patterns in how people think, why they make the choices they make, and the values that guide their behavior. I myself have run such games with CEOs of coffee mills in Costa Rica, professional traders on the Chicago Board of Trade, members of the Masai ethnic group in Tanzania beneath the towering peak of Kilimanjaro, and members of the Khasi community in the verdant and mountainous Meghalaya region of northeast India.

One of the most popular tools among behavioral economists is called the "trust game." In this exercise, one player is given an amount of money, say, $10. She then decides how much of that $10 (if any) to give to a second, anonymous player. The first player is also informed that whatever she gives will be tripled by the experimenter. So let's say the first player sends $8. The second participant then gets $24 and must decide how much of this sum she should send back to the first player. In this game, the first player is said to "trust" the second player if she sends a large portion of the $10, and the second player is said to be "trustworthy" if she returns a large portion of the received money back to the first player. As is clear, there could be a lot more going on behaviorally here, such as reciprocity, fairness, altruism, and the like, but the general principle is that the person will give the second player more money if they trust that player to respond in kind. In addition to the trust game, we also ran games with the fishermen involving donations, lotteries, bargaining (aka ultimatum games), coordination, competition, and public goods (things that benefit everyone and are usually paid for by everyone, like roads). After Andreas collected all the data, Uri and I analyzed it with him.

Just as we had expected, we found sharp behavioral differences between the two communities, and sure enough, these differences were consistent with the ways they fished. The fishermen of Cabuçu trusted others significantly more than those from Santo Estêvão did, and they were also much more trustworthy. The Cabuçu fishermen also proposed more equal offers in the ultimatum game, contributed more to collective interests in the public goods game, and donated more to a charity outside their own society. In other words, they prioritized inclusivity and care for the well-being of others, while also exhibiting a higher degree of trust and cooperation. It wasn't that they were better people than the participants from Santo Estêvão; it was simply that their fishing habits of daily teamwork and collaboration had instilled in them more prosocial behaviors. They had experienced firsthand the benefits of working together, and this lived appreciation for cooperation carried over into other important areas of decision-making.

In other words, their culture scaled.

This chapter is about how to scale up positive workplace cultures. And as this "tale of two fishing cities" demonstrates, workplace culture isn't just about the work itself. The ways in which people work impact whether they prize certain behaviors and norms over others, like trust or distrust, cooperation or individualism, fear or security, workaholism or work-life balance. Our results fit nicely with the body of research showing that similar spillovers exist in settings such as the modern workplace. Which behaviors take root defines an organization: not just how effectively and innovatively work gets done but also what human values underlie that work. And these different values can produce drastically different results at scale.

Some workplace cultures thrive as they scale. Others, self-destruct. More often than not, the latter occurs because a culture that served you well in certain ways early on ceases to do so at scale.

Just ask Travis Kalanick.

Meritocracy at Its Worst

On my first official day of work at Uber in the summer of 2016, I walked into the company's headquarters and, just as I had on the day of my interview, appreciatively noted the credo posted on pillars in the central common area: *Data is our DNA.*

But then I noticed something else.

As I glanced around the open-plan communal space, I noticed a worker at one of the work carrels doing her best to hold back tears. An employee was openly distraught, yet no one approached her or even acknowledged her; it was as if seeing an upset employee was the most commonplace thing in the world. That was when I got my first inkling that certain things might be amiss at Uber. Sure, the business side of the culture was flourishing at scale, but what about the human side? Would Uber's culture hold up as the company continued to expand?

The answer, of course, was no.

During the first few months of 2017, the culture Travis Kalanick had fostered at Uber unraveled spectacularly in a series of widely reported scandals. First, a twenty-five-year-old engineer who had formerly worked for the company, Susan Fowler, published a viral blog post that blew the whistle about Uber's toxic workplace culture, in which sexism and sexual harassment were tolerated. A week later, Waymo, a subsidiary of Google developing self-driving cars, filed a suit against Uber that alleged the stealing of trade secrets. The week after that, a dashboard-cam video of Travis laying into an Uber driver who challenged him about driver compensation was leaked. "Some people don't like to take responsibility for their own shit!" Travis berated the recently bankrupted driver. And finally, like the proverbial cherry on top, the *New York Times* exposed a software innovation called Greyball, which Uber had designed and used to evade law enforcement and government regulators (a fact Uber later acknowledged). It was a very bad few months for Travis Kalanick, and the company as a whole.

My personal experience of this tumultuous period was, in contrast to the public version, oddly uneventful. My arrangement with Uber only required me to be at its San Francisco headquarters a few days per month; the rest of the time I was in Chicago teaching and conducting research, though my former student Ian Muir acted as my eyes on the ground at the company, spearheading the day-to-day efforts of our Ubernomics team. Plus, I entered the company's hierarchy at a fairly high level, so even when I did show up to headquarters I wasn't in the bullpen with the coders and data analysts. Additionally, as someone who isn't a woman, queer person, or person of color, I wasn't acutely aware of the power imbalances that many employees faced. As a result, I missed a lot of what went on at Uber. The distraught employee I'd noticed on day one notwithstanding, on most days things at Uber seemed tranquil: people beavering away at their tasks with focus and dedication, doing the work that needed to be done.

While this might sound surprising in light of all that would occur, during the time I spent at Uber's headquarters in San Francisco Travis had seemed like a decent enough leader to me in many ways. His dedication was second to none. He liked to joke about Uber being his wife, and it was clear he really did put the company before everything else—not exactly a good work-life balance, but he never asked anyone to give more than he did. In this way, he led by example. Anytime I saw him walking around and checking in with employees, he was solicitous and genuine; he listened to their ideas and engaged with them. Moreover, his skill as a salesperson was unmatched, and he was a business visionary made for the twenty-first century who foresaw how peer-to-peer digital technologies would change the transportation industry forever. Yet in spite of Travis's strengths, the culture that had been established at Uber was in for a crushing voltage drop.

It turned out that the combative job interview with Travis I described in the Introduction was a perfect preview of how ideas were exchanged at Uber. While the mood out on the floor might have been quietly industrious, meetings were fast, fierce, and gladiatorial. Stepping on toes was not discouraged, and even encouraged, if it could lead to innovation or an edge in the marketplace. Ideas and results were the currency at Uber, rather than people's experiences of how those ideas were utilized and those results were achieved. Meetings were jousting matches, and I eventually realized that my first encounter with Travis had actually been relatively tame compared to interactions I later witnessed. You didn't go into meetings with the right to be heard; you had to fight to prove you were worth listening to. And if you could talk louder or faster or more persuasively, your idea usually won. It was this atmosphere, among other cultural mores, that left the occasional employee on the brink of tears. And many people at Uber seemed desensitized to it.

Travis's rationale for this approach to driving performance, innovation, and profits was logical on the surface. He believed in meritocracy in its purest form: only the best ideas should win, and determining what the best ideas were required rigorous, even antagonistic clashing. This cultural ethos had served him and the company well during Uber's explosively successful early years, when the company was a scrappy and ambitious disruptor. It had scaled because it created a competitive environment in sync with the marketplace. The business world is hard. Getting a foothold in it and gaining a share of the market is the hardest part of all. This is why the competitive culture Travis fostered at Uber worked early on. The benefits of the hard-charging meritocracy fueled the rise of Uber and outweighed whatever the hidden costs might be. In just a few years the company expanded to some seventy countries, changing transportation worldwide. There was no doubt that Uber's business model scaled beautifully, and this created the illusion that its culture did, too. But in truth, Uber's culture didn't scale. And there is a lot we can learn from what went wrong.

I should cop to not being a stranger to the cage-match cultural style at the company, since I was accustomed to it. Academia can be just as cutthroat as the business world—prestige is what is at stake among academics, and often that can produce more desperation than money does—and the University of Chicago, in particular, is known for its no-holds-barred intellectual battleground. The first time I ever visited the school in 2002, before I worked there, I came prepared with what I thought was a brilliant lecture on the economics of discrimination. No sooner did I open my mouth than a man in the audience wearing a hospital gown and toting an IV plugged into his arm interrupted me with a barrage of penetrating questions that lasted nearly the entirety of my ninety-minute presentation. I flew home to the University of Maryland demoralized, only to receive a cordial email the next day from the man with the IV. He turned out to be the Nobel Prize–winning economist Gary Becker!

And yet, even though I was accustomed to the combative world of academia, something didn't sit right with me at Uber. Nearly every meeting was like my Gary Becker experience, except on steroids. At the time, some might have argued that it was meritocracy at its finest, but in truth, it could be viewed as meritocracy at its worst.

On its face, the concept of meritocracy is wonderful. People are rewarded on the basis of talent and effort, and the objective value of ideas determines which of those ideas win out. Privilege—or lack of privilege—and office politics play no role in success. In theoretical economic terms, this means that the brightest and hardest-working people will get ahead. Of course, we all know this is not how things play out in reality. Plenty of smart and hardworking people get passed over for promotions and earn little money, and plenty of not-so-smart and not-so-hardworking people climb the ladder and rake in cash. Meritocracies in workplaces don't live up to the principles of meritocracies in a vacuum.

If leaders aren't extremely thoughtful and disciplined about constructing workplace norms as their enterprise gets bigger—and Uber's weren't—privilege and other factors, like who talks the loudest or plays internal politics most skillfully, end up perverting and distorting meritocratic ideals. As a result, the best people and ideas don't always rise to the top. Naturally, then, employees begin to lose trust in leadership, and in those around them, which eventually bleeds into other behaviors and interactions and comes to define the overall work culture, much like fishing styles did in Bahia.

As Uber scaled, its purported commitment to meritocracy drifted further and further away from actual meritocracy, which relies on employees trusting that those running the show will assess effort and creativity fairly and objectively. Rather, Uber had scaled a fiction of meritocracy that merely paid lip service to its noble ideals. The best people and ideas, sadly, *didn't* always win out. This was because the culture at Uber made it acceptable to run people over if it was framed in the service of ideas, efficiency, and profit. As Travis himself later put it in an admirably lucid and deep self-critique, *"Meritocracy and toe-stepping can empower individuals to speak truth to power, but if weaponized can lead to people getting stepped on."* Travis had clearly learned what I learned during my time at Uber.

Where did Uber's culture leave those who were deep thinkers but slow talkers? Introverts who prioritized listening over grandstanding? People who didn't feel comfortable jousting? They got run over, and this led to them being silenced—and often to the loss of talented employees whose style didn't fit into Uber's hyperaggressive culture. As Uber grew, the human damage and wasted potential did, too. Inevitably, the more it scaled, the more people were affected by the company's take-no-prisoners culture, from corporate employees to drivers. Thus the number of people who got tired of being overlooked or hurt and jumped ship multiplied. Eventually, it even led to the loss of *potential* employees: it was stunning how many vacancies at the company went unfilled while I was there, as if the culture's reputation were a repellent to people who understood that profit wasn't everything.

"I favored logic over empathy, when sometimes it's more important to show you care than to prove you're right," Travis later reflected. "I focused on getting the right individuals to build Uber, without doing enough to ensure we're building the right kind of teams." Travis was right. When an organization is small, it is by its very nature tight-knit. Much like a family, one can have a heated, even combative debate without doing permanent damage to the relationships because the trust and mutual respect have already been established. Bygones are more easily bygones between people with unconditional mutual trust and respect. However, once you begin to add people whose trust and respect you haven't earned yet (and vice versa), you can't really expect them to feel comfortable in such an environment. Toxicity with newcomers just doesn't scale well.

Research suggests that deep trust is a powerful factor in enabling organizations to scale, in part because it promotes cooperation and functional teamwork is essential for growth, but for other reasons as well. The lack of trust at Uber was in large part the natural endgame of an organization that was a meritocracy in name but not in spirit: people didn't trust that the objective value of their contributions (time, ideas, and effort) would be appreciated. In other words, employees didn't feel respected. And, in the most self-destructive move of all, Uber soon disrespected the other group it couldn't exist without: its passengers.

There were the high-profile riders and rivals Uber spied on with its "God view," a tool that allowed employees to track the location of Uber riders without their knowledge. Then came news of the woman in India who was raped by her Uber driver, only to have the company acquire her medical report in the hope of discrediting her account. And, in yet one more example of the company's seemingly wanton disregard for passenger loyalty, it spiked its fare prices during a taxi drivers' strike in New York. This type of attitude toward your customers will never, ever scale.

Sure, Uber was great at attacking complacent and lazy thinking, but here is the irony: the leaders at Uber were complacent in how they thought about scaling up the company culture. No one in a leadership position—myself included—forcefully questioned Uber's culture to the same extent employees were pushed to question its business ideas and practices. It was the invisible air everyone breathed, but no one in power seemed to notice or had the courage to speak up about the fact that the air was contaminated. When this happens, something eventually has to give. If it's impossible to reform a culture from the inside, then the only lever possible is pressure from the outside.

This is exactly what happened once Fowler's blog post about Uber's tolerance of sexual harassment went viral (an event that presaged much of the #MeToo whistleblowing that was to come in the wake of the Harvey Weinstein accusations). The public pressure only intensified with the revelations about the Greyball program and the dash-cam video of Travis yelling at a driver. Even though Travis apologized after Fowler's blog post and the leaked video—and I know he sincerely felt remorse and shame in both cases—it was too late.

The eventual fall was slow in the making, but when it happened, it happened suddenly, akin to when humidity rises slowly to a critical level and eventually a rainstorm ensues. All the small cultural problems that plagued Uber gradually accumulated, and eventually the scandals came raining down. The company had scaled up its mistakes, and when everything fell apart at scale, the whole world saw it.

Uber's culture had led to a voltage drop that threatened the very future of the company. So the man who had created that culture was pushed out by the board. Travis resigned as CEO in June 2017, though he maintained his board seat at Uber until December 2019. I remained in contact with Travis, in part for his guidance through my final months at Uber, but also to lend support and because I believed he had matured as a leader and entrepreneur. He knew he had made big mistakes, and he showed remorse, not just because he lost his job but because he felt that he had let his Uber team down. I don't believe Travis Kalanick is a bad person. He is a good person who made several bad calls . . . at scale.

In a letter a chastened Travis composed for employees in the midst of the company's series of crises in 2017—but which he never ended up sending—he admitted to how he had failed to institute scalable values as part of Uber's DNA to the same extent that he'd done with data: "Ultimately, we lost track of what our purpose is all about— people. We forgot to put people first and as we grew, we left behind too many of the inspiring employees we work with and too many of the amazing partners who serve our cities. . . . Growth is something to celebrate, but without the appropriate checks and balances can lead to serious mistakes. At scale, our mistakes have a much greater impact—on our teams, customers and the communities we serve. That's why small company approaches must change when you scale. I succeeded by acting small, but failed in being bigger."

Of course, Uber isn't the only company to ever tout a meritocratic culture that in fact fails many of the people it promises to reward. That type of culture abounds across industries; "meritocracy" has become a buzzy concept in the business world. But research reveals that an assortment of toxic norms and behaviors tend to grow out of such cultures, including biases that produce race and gender disparities in pay raises, performance scores, and other measures of career success. And in a very unfortunate irony, managers in such organizations are less prone to self-examination and accountability about these biases precisely because they are convinced their meritocracy works! Once again, trust and cooperation evaporate in such cultures, setting up problems at scale.

This leaves us with a big, big question: If meritocratic cultural norms don't scale, there must be others that do. But which?

The answer lies back on the Bay of All Saints, in Cabuçu.

Putting Trust and Teamwork First

Meritocracy is predicated on the idea of *individual* achievement. This clearly encourages employees to value individual gains over collective ones and establishes a culture of every person for themselves. So while an emphasis on individual performance above all else may foster healthy amounts of internal competition in a company's early days, it is (as we saw with Uber) not conducive to the kind of collaboration that becomes increasingly critical as the company grows. At Uber, the incentive structure at the company was built to reinforce this. You received a bonus when *you* innovated a new idea, *you* tested it out, and *you* pushed it to be implemented.

Recall that for the fishermen of Cabuçu, trust, generosity, inclusivity, and cooperation were deeply embedded in both their work and their culture. There was an invisible hand that emanated from the workplace to the village and guided people in their behaviors. We saw this in how they made economic choices in our experiments compared to their counterparts in Santo Estêvão, whose style of fishing resembled the individualistic culture created at Uber.

At Uber, there was no invisible hand, no overarching social fabric, and not even any team rewards to push employees to develop and ship innovations *together*. For the most part, you kept the fish that you caught; cooperation and sharing weren't incentivized, never mind trust and generosity across teams. The employees fished on the same lake, as it were, but rarely in the same boats. Their behavior reflected these values, from the way executives ignored Susan Fowler's reports about sexual harassment (so as not to inconvenience high-performing employees) to the way sparring matches in meetings were expected. These values were also reflected on a daily basis in how siloed the company was. In some instances, it was next to impossible to collaborate across groups, departments, and countries to solve a problem.

As you scale an enterprise, a lack of *cross-functional collaboration* is especially troublesome. This is because the opportunity cost of *not* collaborating increases at scale, since there is the potential for a greater number and assortment of good internal partnerships. Think of it this way: In a five-person firm, there are some instances where working together makes a lot of sense, but many others where going it alone is the best route because none of the other four employees have the right skill set to complement your own. But in a five-thousand-person firm, around every corner there is a good partner (or many good partners) who can make your life easier and with whom you can produce a much better product or service. Designing workplace incentives and culture to promote partnerships allows you to reap such high-voltage opportunities.

However, lest you think that all this rosy talk of cooperation will lead me to ignore the role of competition in driving high performance as you scale, fear not. An emerging body of research on "coopetition" shows that a healthy interplay of cooperation and competition, both inside and across departments in organizations, can drive improvements in everything from financial performance to customer satisfaction. If managers mediate incentives so that employees receive rewards based on individual as well as team and organization-wide performance, this balance between competition and cooperation facilitates "knowledge transfer," the sharing of valuable expertise that others might not have but will benefit from.

Netflix is a company whose culture is highly innovative, with high-performing employees, yet still centered around trust—a prime example of coopetition. The company doesn't track or limit employees' vacation days or expense spending, and many development executives for TV and film projects are allowed to make seven-figure acquisitions without the approval of their superiors. Managers assume that their employees will exercise good judgment, leading to Netflix's famous culture of "freedom and responsibility." Micromanaging is a no-no; confident delegation is a yes-yes. Instead of bonuses based on individual performance, employees can choose how much of their paycheck they wish to receive in equity, which in effect ties their compensation to the success of the company as a whole. These policies lead to small problems once in a blue moon, but the culture of high-performing trust is self-regulating, meaning that people quickly learn to fit in and want to uphold the norms. Importantly, such cultures are self-fulfilling in the sense that once they are in place, they attract like-minded individuals and repel those who won't thrive or fit in. The invisible hand operates efficiently to shuffle the right workers in and the wrong workers out. And while employees are encouraged to challenge each other's ideas, they aren't rewarded for steamrolling colleagues to get their own ideas heard; Netflix CEO Reed Hastings doesn't tolerate, as he puts it, "brilliant jerks." Trust and competition aren't mutually exclusive at Netflix.

For a workplace to be cooperative *and* simultaneously high-performing at scale, you have to build teamwork into the structure of the organization. For instance, when building teams, one approach is to ensure that each employee is part of at least two different teams, and preferably teams in different departments. This opens up more opportunities for teamwork and promotes cross-fertilization of ideas. And it incentivizes employees to invest in the success of more than just a single team. To create a collaborative and high-performing culture, it should go without saying that you also need the best teams—as in the right human beings to carry out important job functions.

Recruiting at Scale

Several years ago, my friends Jeff Flory, Kara Helander, Andreas Leibbrandt, and Neela Rajendra cofounded a wonderful organization called the Science of Diversity Initiative, or SODI, for which I am an original board member. The premise of the group, which partners companies with academics from a range of disciplines, is to promote a truth of organizational success that, in recent years, a robust body of scientific research has made impossible to ignore: diversity matters. And by this I mean diversity in all senses: race, sex, age, ethnicity, religion, class background, sexual orientation, gender identity, neurotype, and other characteristics. Diversity in people's backgrounds equates to *cognitive* diversity when they are together, which produces not just greater innovation but also greater resilience. Research shows that diverse groups generate better decisions and problem-solving skills, more complex thinking, and higher profits. One study showed they even invest in better stocks!

Achieving the level of diversity that drives high-performing teams, however, is often easier said than done, especially at scale. Often this is not just for the reasons that might initially come to mind, like conscious or unconscious bias, or because the best diverse candidates get snatched up by someone else before you can hire them. My research shows that things can in fact go wrong even earlier in the hiring process—with *recruitment*.

One area where well-intentioned efforts to attract a more diverse pool of candidates can go surprisingly awry is the posting of job advertisements. Equal employment opportunity (EEO) regulations have become a norm in many countries around the world as countries seek to reduce inequality in job markets. In the United States, companies and organizations must uphold requirements imposed by federal codes, and EEO statements attesting to compliance with these requirements have become a common practice when employers post a job advertisement. Essentially, this just means that employers include a line in every job description stating their commitment to diversity. The logic behind this is straightforward: if you want to broadcast your commitment to equal opportunity and also attract a more diverse set of applicants, then making your policy of inclusivity explicit should be a surefire way to do so. This intuitively makes sense. And yet, as Andreas Leibbrandt and I discovered, this practice often produces some unintended consequences.

Partnering with an existing organization that agreed to lend us their good name for our field experiment, Andreas and I posted a job opening for an administrative assistant position in ten different U.S. job markets. We selected cities with different racial compositions, including several with white majority populations (Denver, Dallas, Houston, Los Angeles, and San Francisco) alongside more racially diverse ones (Chicago, New York City, Philadelphia, Washington, D.C., and Atlanta). As usual, we had a treatment group of potential applicants, who saw a posting with an EEO statement, and a control group, who saw a posting with no such statement. Nearly 2,500 people applied. We also offered potential job-seekers a $10 Amazon gift certificate to take a short survey, which would allow us to collect more qualitative data about what drew an applicant to this particular ad. Our hypothesis was that more racial minorities would apply to postings that carried the EEO statement. The bump would likely be small, but we felt sure there would be an increase, or at worst no effect.

Boy, were we wrong. It turned out that the EEO statement *discouraged* racial minorities from applying, and by as much as a shocking

30 percent. In other words, the statements completely backfired, and in very telling ways.

Interestingly, the effect was particularly pronounced in cities with less diverse populations, and for more highly educated applicants. The evidence from our survey illuminated why this was the case: *minority applicants feared tokenism.* The EEO statement triggered their mental antennae, an inner warning system tuned by past experiences of racism and discrimination, suggesting that the work environment might be one in which people of color were perceived as perfunctory or symbolic hires, rather than one in which people were hired on their own merits. In other words, the job seekers worried that the stated commitment to diversity and inclusivity was cosmetic, and not truly baked into the cultural DNA. The effect was particularly pronounced for applicants in cities with predominantly white populations and highly educated minorities because it is in those cities where they presumably have experienced tokenism throughout their education and careers. Their skepticism was not unfounded; whether they knew it or not, prior research found that employers who use EEO statements are *not* in fact less likely to discriminate against racial minorities!

Thanks to the thousands of participants who responded to our posting and survey, we gained an invaluable insight about the recruitment process. It is not enough to tell applicants that you're committed to diversity. You have to *show* them that your declared workplace values are also the actual lived ones that employees will experience and contribute to if they are hired. The good news is that when you do reach a critical level, diversity is easier to scale because of the "flywheel effect." Once in motion, the data on the racial and ethnic composition of your workforce (very often publicly available online) will begin to tell your story and spin further gains. A person of color will simply look up a company and see what percentage of employees are people of color, where employees of color stand in the company org chart, and more.

Yet the nuances of recruiting a diverse workforce at scale reach beyond just data and numbers. Other surprising avenues can help, too: for example, it turns out that including certain information *unrelated to diversity* in a job posting can nevertheless increase diversity.

The Hidden Benefits (and Costs) of Virtue-Signaling

Over the last several decades, the growing concern about corporate social responsibility (CSR) has changed the way most companies present themselves to the world. In advertisements, mission statements, and other public-facing contexts, brands love to tout the worthy causes they support, showcase the work of their charitable foundations, and generally sell the idea that while they care about profits, they also care about the world. This is why so many large firms have entire branches dedicated to ensuring socially responsible practices and/or planning and executing charitable activities, and it's why hundreds of billions of dollars annually are budgeted for such programs.

While CSR is undoubtedly sincere in many cases and often reflects a culture of corporate generosity, it is often employed less sincerely as a marketing technique. Interestingly, though, research shows that this isn't actually as effective as most presume. That is, CSR isn't a surefire approach to stimulate consumer demand. Indeed, the data suggest that most people are indifferent to most philanthropically oriented marketing and choose brands for different reasons. This isn't to say that companies should sunset their do-gooder policies. However, they might be surprised to learn that such policies don't exert a warm, fuzzy tug on consumers that leads to better sales. Yet could an emphasis on CSR help with recruiting top-notch talent? Or might it backfire just like EEO statements? Our hunch was that CSR could indeed play a subtle yet integral virtue-signaling role—that when applicants learn that a company cares about social issues (sustainability, giving back to local communities, et cetera), they may infer that this is a company with a prosocial culture that is also committed to an inclusive, fair, and equal workplace.

To explore this question, two wonderful economists (Daniel Hedblom and Brent Hickman) and I ran a field experiment similar to the one on EEO statements. This time, however, we created our own legitimate company—a data-entry firm, called HHL LLC, that compiled data from Google Street View photos. Our goal was to examine not only the applicant pool but also how productive the applicants were after we hired them. (Data entry was ideal for this experiment, as it is a job for which it is fairly easy to measure productivity and other performance metrics.)

We posted ads on Craigslist in twelve major U.S. cities, with a salary that was on par with the typical compensation for data-entry jobs. Of the thousand applicants who reached out to us, one group (the control group) received an email response containing standard information about the position, while another group (the treatment group) received an email that included the same standard information as well as this CSR paragraph: "We provide services for a variety of different firms and organizations. Some of them work in the nonprofit sector with various charitable causes. For example, with projects aimed at improving access to education for underprivileged children. We believe that these organizations are making the world a better place and we want to help them doing so. Due to the charitable nature of their activity, we only charge these clients at cost."

Next, we hired job-seekers who had seen the CSR posting along with applicants who had not. All of them were then put to work inputting information about the Google Street View images, giving us a rich data set that measured the productivity of each worker.

It turned out that the CSR language in the ad had the exact opposite effect of the EEO statement. It increased the number of applicants by 25 percent, while also generating a significantly more diverse pool of potential employees for us to choose from—in other words, it was vastly more inclusive than saying we were inclusive! But our results didn't end there. We also found that the CSR-recruited group of employees were considerably more productive and did higher-quality work than those not recruited with CSR, likely because they felt more motivated by the company's prosocial mission—that is, *I'm going to work harder to benefit the world*. Which is to say, the CSR posting attracted not only a more diverse pool of candidates but actually *better* ones!

Outside the recruiting process, however, organizations need to take care in how they scale CSR programs as a part of their culture. While billboarding prosocial causes helps to recruit more diverse and more valuable workers, presenting philanthropic practices as a defining aspect of an enterprise's mission can produce negative spillovers if applied to the wrong population of people.

In another field experiment, the brilliant Fatemeh Momeni and I once again created a business—only this time, instead of data entry, we employed participants to do transcription tasks. After they had been working awhile for the firm, we introduced CSR messaging to a portion of the three thousand employees. As anticipated, we witnessed an overall increase in productivity among those who received messages about our company's mission—but we also saw a dramatic uptick in *misbehavior:* 20 percent more employees shirked on their primary job duty, and we even saw an 11 percent uptick in cheating. What incited this counterintuitive result?

The explanation for why a prosocial commitment can produce negative individualistic behavior like cheating has to do with a psychological phenomenon called *moral licensing*. This ethical short-circuiting in our minds occurs when we feel that doing a good thing gives us permission to later do a not-so-good thing. For example, we make a donation to a charity in the morning, and in the afternoon we use this act of generosity to mentally justify cutting in line at the grocery store. Or we work late one night to help out a stressed coworker, then the next morning steal supplies from the office for our home. In this fashion, some of our employees felt that the good deed of working for a socially responsible firm earned them the right to cheat.

Managers can fall prey to moral licensing as well. When it comes to diversity and inclusiveness, for example, our results offer a cautionary tale for the manager who makes a couple of diversity hires and subsequently believes (consciously or not) that they now have the license to underinvest in other diversity / inclusion initiatives. This approach will not scale.

So CSR messaging can lead to voltage gains *and* voltage drops at scale, depending on how it is deployed. When used in the context of recruiting new employees, such messaging enhances your applicant pool. This approach scales well. However, when directed at existing employees, CSR needs to be applied with care, because while it will be motivating to some, there may be others who use it to justify bad behavior—an unintended consequence that will only be amplified at scale. This does not mean that CSR is to be avoided; rather, my advice is simply to be aware of such possibilities and monitor them closely.

Emphasizing a commitment to corporate social responsibility in a job posting isn't the only way to attract a more diverse applicant pool. Another field experiment I conducted with Andreas, again with approximately 2,500 job-seekers, revealed the importance of mentioning the negotiability of salary in job postings—specifically, the effect this has on women applicants.

The ugly truth is that far fewer women become CEOs or reach the highest positions in government than men, women working full-time take home roughly 80 cents on the dollar compared to men, and only about 6 percent of the five highest-paid types of positions in U.S. firms are occupied by women. And while there are many reasons for this disparity, it certainly doesn't help that, as research has revealed, women are significantly less likely to engage in salary negotiations, while men are *eight times* more likely to negotiate on salary offers.

However, as our field experiment showed, there are steps managers and recruiters can take to reverse this trend. We found that not only do more women apply to job postings that clearly state that wages are negotiable, but they are also willing to negotiate as hard as men, and in many cases even harder. Men, on the other hand, are more drawn to postings in which the rules around compensation are ambiguous, likely because this is where they reap disproportionate rewards relative to women. And most troubling of all, low-performing men bargain the most when the salary is vague, whereas the most exceptional women tend to hold back!

Crucially, these findings cut across job tasks, making this a phenomenon potentially relevant to all types of positions and industries. This is why it's essential to explicitly state in a job posting that salary is negotiable. If a woman takes the job but doesn't believe she can negotiate, she will start with a lower salary compared to her male peers. This disparity may linger for years or even decades after being hired—and it all started with that initial job posting. Organizations intent on scaling diversity through inclusive recruiting should be cognizant of these patterns and tailor their recruitment efforts accordingly.

Even so, women still have every reason to fear inequities during the hiring process. For example, a 2021 study found that informal short lists for candidates dramatically favor men. This is because, as the authors wrote, the shortlists "dually suffer from the *systemic* bias of informal, network-based recruitment and from the *implicit* bias of selecting top-of-mind candidates in gendered roles." The solution? Longer shortlists! Not only do deeper final interview shortlists— say, increasing the list by 67 percent, from three to five candidates— include more diverse candidates, but once given the chance, the diverse applicants are more likely to secure the position.

All this matters because not only is recruitment key to building a trusting, cooperative, and scalable workplace culture from day one, it's also one of the best tools for sustaining it at scale. The more you grow, the more positions you will have to fill, and it's impossible to scale for high voltage without good people to scale with you.

The Art and Science of Apologies

So, let's say you've done everything right. You've cannily phrased your job ads and descriptions and enhanced your short list to recruit the best and most diverse employees. And you've instilled organizational or team norms and values of trust and cooperation. You've built your own Cabuçu: a high-voltage, scalable culture.

But you will still mess up. While there is much science informing how to build trust, relatively less is known about the consequences of violating that trust. What actions can be taken to avoid the deterioration of your culture when trust has been compromised? Here, the simplest and perhaps most obvious answer is the correct one: you can apologize.

The practice of apology is an action as old as humankind. This is because all people and enterprises inevitably mess up. And this is especially true at scale, simply because as you hire more employees, serve more customers, and/or reach more communities, there will be more ways to inadvertently upset those you aim to help. But not all apologies are created equal. In fact, my research suggests that there are right and wrong ways to ask for forgiveness.

In January 2017, in the middle of the #DeleteUber campaign, I stepped out of my house in Chicago, pulled out my phone, and requested an Uber. I was giving a keynote address at an economics conference across town, and since I still had to polish my speech, I decided I would work on it en route rather than drive myself. My driver arrived promptly; I said hi and hopped into the car, and then immediately opened up my laptop. No time to waste—I had slides to create.

Twenty minutes later, just moments before I was expected to arrive at the conference, I looked up, expecting to see Chicago's chrome skyline alongside the deep blue of Lake Michigan. Instead, all I saw out my window was . . . *my house.* My driver had been driving this whole time, but somehow we were back where we started. Panicked, I asked her what was going on. She said the app had given her confusing directions that took her back to my home and she hadn't said anything about it because she didn't want to disturb me.

I was furious, but my more urgent concern was getting to the conference, as I was now going to be nearly a half hour late for my keynote. I gave her directions as she sped down Lake Shore Drive again. Thankfully, once I finally arrived, the organizers and audience were understanding, and I did my best to collect myself and give an engaging talk. But the whole time I was fuming about how Uber had let me down.

And that was that, it seemed. As I drove home (in a Lyft) I wondered if I would ever receive an acknowledgment from the company about the screw-up, or perhaps an automated apology.

I wasn't slated to visit Uber's headquarters in San Francisco for a few more weeks, so later that evening, still feeling peeved about the incident, I called Travis Kalanick and told him what had happened. An isolated mistake like this was one thing, but if similar mistakes were being made at scale, it was another thing entirely: a pattern, a problem, a whole lot of angry customers. And if Uber had caused me to arrive late for an important engagement and failed to offer any sort of apology, similar things had surely happened to tens of thousands of other people. The last thing the company needed right then was to give more riders a reason to delete the app.

Travis heard me out and then flipped the script, suggesting I take matters into my own hands and correct the problem—if indeed there was one.

I liked this approach and agreed. "But," I added, "if I find there is a problem, then I want to run a field experiment to determine the best way for Uber to apologize to passengers when they have a bad ride." This would be an example of real meritocracy in action: giving an employee the opportunity to prove the worth of their idea and empowering them to execute on that idea if they do so.

"Deal," Travis said.

My Ubernomics team got to work. Our first hurdle was to test whether Uber's reputation or bottom line was materially harmed by trips like the one I'd had. Of course, this couldn't be the old scientific experimental approach where one person gets a treatment and the other a control. This was business, and it just wasn't prudent to randomly give some people bad trips (not in the psychedelic sense, of course!). So what we did was find statistical "identical twins" in the data: two consumers who were identical up to a point in time, but then at that point one of them received a bad trip whereas the other received a good one. Because Uber executes nearly 15 million rides per day, there were plenty of statistical twins to explore. Analyzing the data across millions of riders, it was clear that bad trips mattered a lot. We found that a rider who experienced one spends 5–10 percent less on the platform over the next ninety days relative to their statistical twin. This amounted to millions and millions in lost revenues.

The second step was determining how to stem these losses. Given the sheer scale of the company, it was unrealistic to think we could eliminate bad trips altogether. But we could provide some solace for the customers who experienced them. The only question was how.

So in yet another field experiment, we sent different apologies to the 1.5 million people we identified as having experienced a bad trip: some received a basic apology, others received a more thoughtful one that acknowledged our responsibility, and another group got one expressing our desire to avoid future mishaps (we also had a control group, to whom we sent nothing). And with some of these apologies, we also included a $5 coupon for a future ride. Then we tracked the riders' usage of Uber.

After we analyzed the data, the first lesson we extracted was that the efficacy of an apology depends on *how* it is delivered. If you've ever had someone apologize to you by saying "I'm sorry you feel that way" instead of "I'm sorry for what I did," you won't be surprised to learn that riders who received the more contrite apologies were more likely to continue using Uber than those who received the basic apology. Our second finding, however, was more intriguing. For all types of apologies, money spoke louder than words. Or rather, words combined with money were the most effective means of retaining riders after a bad trip. Any type of apology that included a coupon was the best strategy, not because the $5 coupon was so valuable but because a gesture of remorse paired with a small material sacrifice demonstrated to customers that they were worth fighting for.

A third finding, perhaps our most provocative, is that too many apologies can backfire. In fact, apologizing for three or more transgressions within a short period is actually worse than not apologizing at all. When it happens the first time, an apology can temporarily restore a customer's loyalty after an adverse outcome. However, that apology acts as a promise that the customer should expect better outcomes in the future. So when those higher expectations go unmet, the company's reputation suffers more than if no apology had been tendered at all. Apologies should therefore be used strategically, and ideally only after unexpectedly bad outcomes that are unlikely to repeat again in the near future. *Caveat venditor* should be the rule when considering apologies.

Uber changed its apology policy after our experiment, and while this of course didn't address the trust issues that plagued the company's culture, I hope that it at least helped win back the trust of frustrated riders like me who arrived late somewhere. More importantly, the experiment yielded generalizable insights about how to handle screw-ups that any enterprise can scale. You need to demonstrate to the people you serve that you are willing to pay a price for their forgiveness—not just the price of a spoken apology, but a financial one, too. I haven't conducted an experiment inside a workplace culture to measure how best to apologize to employees who have been hurt; however, it stands to reason that a thoughtful apology alongside a gift or bonus is the best recipe.

*   *   *

THE IMPLICATIONS OF these insights reach well beyond the workplace. As we saw with the fishermen from Cabuçu and Santo Estêvão, when it comes to scaling culture, the stakes are much higher than our endeavor's individual success or failure. The culture we create at work has the potential to influence the greater web of behaviors in which we exist. And whether we are in a position of power or leadership in our organization or not, we have the ability to shift the culture toward trust and cooperation, or toward distrust and selfishness.

Research shows that organizational culture crucially affects the attitudes and choices of people *outside* the workplace, and there is even persuasive evidence that it subtly plays into the formation of human societies big and small. Indeed, the pull of workplace norms on broader interpersonal and societal ones is so profound that there is evidence suggesting that these norms correlate with economic growth and the quality of democracy. The story of Cabuçu and Santo Estêvão reveals that scaling any enterprise is inevitably also about scaling values. Not only will the culture you foster as you scale affect the choices and lives of your employees—and help your enterprise achieve high voltage—but it has the potential to bleed into society at large and shape the choices and lives of people you will never meet.

And it can also help for catching fish on the Bay of All Saints.

CONCLUSION:

TO SCALE OR NOT TO SCALE?

When I began working on this book in February 2020, I thought I had my year more or less figured out: monthly visits to Lyft in San Francisco, some invitations to give talks here and there, a summer conference I was putting together in Chicago, and a few fun trips with my family. Needless to say, things did not turn out as planned. A month after I started organizing the material that would become *The Voltage Effect,* the spread of Covid-19 led to lockdowns around the world, and life as we know it radically changed. Now a year has passed, and as I write this, we are still living through one of the strangest and most devastating periods in recent memory. Yet as hard as the pandemic has been in too many ways to count, I can't imagine a better time to have written this book—because at no other moment has the importance of scaling ever been so evident.

The collective response to Covid-19 arguably represents the biggest scaling challenge in human history: informing the public about safety protocols, producing an adequate supply of N95 face masks to protect essential workers, equipping hospitals with enough ventilators and other medical devices, not to mention ensuring Covid-19 tests could be made available to anyone who needed them, the production and distribution of vaccines, and many, many other things. This mobilization at scale has been singular and massive.

Some things have scaled very well. While there were significant growing pains, the infrastructure and mechanics for Covid-19 testing improved steadily over the first few months, then rapidly after six months. Hospitals quickly expanded their capacities and improved their efficacy of treatment. Messaging campaigns about wearing masks and social distancing (including some of my own work on this issue) reached billions of people. Economic stimulus packages were passed to aid individuals and prop up businesses and local and state governments. And several highly effective vaccines for a novel virus were created and brought to market in less than a year! That is a veritable scientific miracle.

Other things, however, have not scaled so well. Contact tracing in the United States was a bust; while it worked in certain places with certain people, those people and situations turned out not to be representative of the nation at large. Some Covid-19 tests were unreliable; early assessments of their effectiveness proved to be a false positive. Many people didn't receive their second stimulus payment and will only get it after filing their 2020 tax returns, while $1.4 billion in initial stimulus payments was accidentally sent to deceased individuals, representing a real marginal loss for the $2.2 trillion federal aid package.

Most disappointing of all, the initial rollout of vaccines at scale was slow and bumpy, due to problems ranging from limited refrigeration capacities to short supplies of doses, poor messaging about eligibility and availability, and insufficient medical personnel to administer the shots (the efficient distribution achieved on a smaller scale wasn't representative of nationwide distribution). And spillovers . . . don't get me started! We have seen and will surely be feeling for years the effects of a whole web of unintended consequences, from mask mandates spurring unrest and deepening political divides to an economy that will likely need real watching to avoid underperformance or perhaps even overheating.

Scaling the response to Covid-19 has, indisputably, produced voltage gains. But it has also been rife with voltage drops.

Many people would argue that a number of these problems were the result of inept responses worldwide by our leaders—former President Trump being a central target of this criticism—and to a certain extent I wouldn't disagree. But scaling so many parallel endeavors at the magnitude and speed that the pandemic demanded, and across a population of some 330 million people in the United States and nearly 8 billion people globally, was likely to produce voltage drops no matter who was in charge.

There are two key lessons here, both of which we have touched on, but which are both worth restating. One: If an enterprise has any weaknesses, they will reveal themselves at scale, often painfully so. Two: Scalable ideas and solutions remain our most valuable resource for addressing the world's most urgent problems.

Leo Tolstoy began his novel *Anna Karenina* with the famous opening line "Happy families are all alike; every unhappy family is unhappy in its own way." Out of this notion Jared Diamond popularized the "Anna Karenina principle," which holds that any one of several shortcomings can guarantee the failure of an idea, while success depends on avoiding all possible shortcomings. Scaling is, in the end, a weakest-link problem: the endeavor is only as strong as the weakest link in the chain. This applies to everything from biodiversity to conservation to migration policies. Many networks also have this feature—take, for example, encryption, IT infrastructure, cybersecurity, and even airport security. If you watch football, you even see it right in front of your eyes in the NFL: the offensive line is only as good as its weakest member. If one lineman is a sieve, the team is doomed.

The Anna Karenina principle undoubtedly applies to scaling too: successfully scaled ideas are all alike; every idea that fails to scale fails in its own way. An honest assessment of any idea demands a determination of the idea's vitality before scaling. The responses to Covid-19 vividly illustrate this rule. The secret to scaling isn't having any one silver bullet. There are multiple ways an idea can fail at scale, and to achieve high voltage, you must check each of the Five Vital Signs: false positives, misjudging the representativeness of an initial population or situation, spillovers, and prohibitive costs. Any one of these alone can sink your ship.

Once you clear these five hurdles, however, there is more you can do to improve your probability of success at scale. You can design the right incentives, use marginal thinking to make the most of your resources, and stay lean and effective as you grow. You can make decisions based on the opportunity cost of your time, discover your comparative advantage, and learn to optimally quit, allowing you to unapologetically cut your losses and move on to new and better ideas when appropriate. And you can build a diverse and dynamic organizational culture based on trust and cooperation, rather than competition and individualism.

By now, I hope the rules and principles I have outlined have convinced you that you don't have to be Steve Jobs or Elon Musk or Jeff Bezos to succeed at scaling. In spite of the contemporary obsession with the cult of personality, in its purest form scaling has nothing to do with personality. Of course, different character traits can help in different situations, but in most cases it is not the *who* that matters. It's the *what*.

It's also important to note that you don't need to be a start-up founder or entrepreneur or lead an organization to benefit from the lessons I've outlined in this book. Whether your sphere of influence is as a member of your condo board, an artist or writer, or a stay-at-home parent, the principles we've explored can lead to wiser decisions and better outcomes for you and others.

Not everyone dreams of building a giant company, starting a nationwide movement, or bringing their idea or innovation into every household in America, and that's just fine. Look at my grampa, my father, and my brother, with their small family trucking business. They never scaled up past a certain level, but they make good money, lead fulfilling lives, and make their families proud, me included. You can still make an impact even if your program or product or whatever your dream happens to be only works in some places with some people. And there are legitimate reasons for wanting to stay small or medium-sized, even if you have the potential to go bigger. Maybe massive national or international success sounds exhausting and stressful to you—it sure does to me! Decide what level of scale is ideal for you, and adapt the different lessons of this book to get there.

If you work in the realm of policymaking, my hope is that this book will help you spur more honest engagement about how programs perform at scale and how to develop truly effective policies—for closing the achievement gap in education and improving social mobility, for instance. Partisan politics, territorialism and infighting, and individualistic competition for funding must give way to objective metrics and replicable scientific data. It doesn't matter if we had high hopes for an intervention or program, or if we have already sunk resources into studying or developing it; if the data say it will not work, we must not waste more valuable resources trying to scale it (and we must abandon it ASAP if it is already implemented). And researchers must understand that the evidence-based policy mindset of two decades ago is woefully outdated. Today we need to create policy-based evidence. The opportunity cost of failing to do so is simply too high.

You will experience setbacks and failures as you grow your ideas, just as I did when scaling our curriculum at the Chicago Heights Early Childhood Center. However, with a commitment to scientific rigor, we have a real opportunity to learn from our missteps and redirect our energy toward scaling up programs with the potential to actually make a difference in people's lives, instead of throwing money at ones that appeared promising but turn out to be merely mirages of success. And we must constantly continue learning, evaluating, and analyzing data; only this way will we gain new insights for current and future scaling enterprises. While the barriers to social change are as varied and diverse as our society itself, the invisible barrier that unites them all is the scaling barrier—the inability to properly evaluate initiatives in order to choose those that will impact the largest number of people.

In this sense—and please excuse me for plugging my profession—data scientists are the world's greatest untapped resource in both for-profit and nonprofit environments. Through partnerships between businesses and academics, scientists and policymakers, we can build practices that align the pursuit of both progress and profits in ways that benefit us all.

Back in 2016, Silicon Valley was a new world to me. Now it's one of the several worlds I straddle, stretching from business to governments around the globe, and back again to education in my beloved Chicago. If my work in all of these different spheres has taught me one thing, it's that there is only one way to meaningfully change the world: at scale.

Acknowledgments

The seed for *The Voltage Effect* was fertilized years ago, when my parents would urge me to be curious and resilient. Back then, when I couldn't pronounce a word correctly, there was no "googling it," but there was a "try it out a few times and see if it works." When I did, and was invariably wrong, my parents' continual encouragement invited me to "keep working hard to dig deeper within yourself to find the correct answer."

The actual contents of this book revolve around a few decades of scientific work. The first part of the book draws heavily from my recent research with Omar Al-Ubaydli and Dana Suskind. Research with various other co-authors chipped in to help shape the Five Vital Signs of a scalable idea, including Fatemeh Momeni, Yves Zenou, Robert Metcalfe, Anya Samek, Min Sok Lee, Danielle LoRe, Claire Mackevicius, Zacharias Maniadis, Fabio Tufano, Pat Euzent, Charles Bailey, and the late Thomas Martin, among others. The second part of the book draws from various academic studies that I co-authored with Andreas Leibbrandt, Uri Gneezy, Jeffrey Flory, Tanjim Hossain, Roland Fryer, Sally Sadoff, Steven Levitt, Ian Muir, Basil Halperin, Benjamin Ho, Greer Gosnell, Seda Ertac, Lester Tong, Karen Ye, Kentaro Asai, Howard Nusbaum, Ali Hortacsu, Erwin Bulte, Daan van Soest, Daniel Rondeau, Amanda Chuan, Alec Brandon, Christopher Clapp, Michael Price, Alex Imas, Alexander Cappelen, Bertil Tungodden, Yang Xu, Jeffrey Livingston, Xiangdong Qiu, Ernst Fehr, Kenneth Leonard, Brent Hickman, Daniel Hedblom, Michael Haigh, Jon Alevy, Susanne Neckermann, Chad Syverson, Tova Levin, and Amee Kamdar, among others' work.

Without my mentors over the years, my students and colleagues, as well as my University of Chicago, Lyft, and Ubernomics teams, there would be no *Voltage Effect* (there are too many of you to name, but Diana Smith is an immediate person I must name as are lifelong mentors Shelby Gerking and Aart de Zeeuw). Working with all of you has been a great privilege. I hope this book allows other people to benefit from your wisdom the way that I have. Beyond being loyal friends, Kenneth Griffin and Anne Dias gave their minds and resources to improve and fund the education research discussed in this book, and the Griffin Incubator was a key resource for developing elements of this book.

James Levine, my literary agent, shared my vision for *The Voltage Effect* and enhanced the work at every step. Aaron Shulman started out as my writing coach and ended up becoming a deep friend, confidant, and investigative journalist *extraordinaire*. He taught me how to write for a broad audience, unlocked my "economese" to detail key secrets to scaling success, touched up my prose when necessary, but most important bludgeoned my writing when apropos. He was a full partner in getting the manuscript to its current state in every sense of partnership. I cannot imagine a better partner to have on this journey. Talia Krohn, my editor at Penguin Random House, was a dream to work with. Discerning, patient, smart, inquisitive, and empathic, she championed *The Voltage Effect* from the moment we began collaborating and never stopped. Her perceptive line edits and gentle encouragements to scale back here and go deeper there transformed the manuscript. I'm eternally grateful we had the opportunity to work together. I hope we get to do it again soon.

Thinking about all the people who contributed to *The Voltage Effect* is moving. Stephen Dubner is the busiest person I know. Yet he always returned my emails and provided comments on my very early outlines of this book. Logan Green and Travis Kalanick believed in me enough to give me a shot as chief economist at Lyft and Uber, respectively. Various colleagues at both firms were wonderful partners and colleagues. Without them, *The Voltage Effect* would not be what it is. In particular, Ian Muir managed both my Ubernomics team and the Department of Economics at Lyft with a steady hand and unwavering spirit. Likewise, Glenn Hubbard and the Council of Economic Advisers hired me to work in the White House (and Jason Shogren and Greg Mankiw provided their sage wisdom once I was in the White House), which provided deep policy perspectives and general learnings.

I have been deeply fortunate to work with colleagues who truly want to change the world for the better. In particular, the numerous people at firms, both nonprofit and profit, and governments who have partnered with me to help answer "big" questions that matter is breathtaking. Without their support, much of the research I talk about in *The Voltage Effect* would not have been possible. I am particularly grateful to Thomas Amadio, from the Chicago Heights School District, who opened up an exploration that I never imagined possible. Jeffrey Lachman, Nathan Durst, Jeremy Haber, and other colleagues with the Chicago White Sox opened my eyes to what really scales in professional sports. A deep thanks to my family, including my parents (Joyce and August), parents-in-law (Leslie and Robert), my eight children, my sister and brother (Dawn and Augie), and all of my in-laws (you know who you are!), who were patient enough to listen to my scaling adventures and brave enough to tell me when something didn't work. Without all of you, *The Voltage Effect* would have never seen its current form. Finally, my life and scaling partner, Dana Suskind, provided much inspiration, love, and wisdom from her very first research challenge on scaling to co-authoring multiple research studies to helping this book get across the finish line. Without Dana, there is no Voltage.

Notes

Introduction: Built to Fail or Built to Scale?

3 **Chicago Heights:** U.S. Census Bureau, 2019, https://www.census.gov/quickfacts/fact/table/IL,chicagoheightscityillinois/PST045219.

10 **women aren't inherently less competitive than men:** Uri Gneezy, Kenneth L. Leonard, and John A. List, "Gender Differences in Competition: Evidence from a Matrilineal and a Patriarchal Society," *Econometrica* 77, no. 5 (2009): 1637–1664.

10 **a charity will attract more donations:** Amee Kamdar, Steven D. Levitt, John A. List, Brian Mullaney, and Chad Syverson, "Once and Done: Leveraging Behavioral Economics to Increase Charitable Contributions," working paper, Science of Philanthropy Initiative, 2015, https://spihub.org/site/resource_files/publications/spi_wp_025_list.pdf.

10 **the fear of losing a reward:** Roland G. Fryer Jr., Steven D. Levitt, John List, and Sally Sadoff, "Enhancing the Efficacy of Teacher Incentives Through Loss Aversion: A Field Experiment," NBER Working Paper, 2012.

11 **Here's a true story:** Omar Al-Ubaydli, Min Sok Lee, John A. List, Claire L. Mackevicius, and Dana Suskind, "How Can Experiments Play a Greater Role in Public Policy? Twelve Proposals from an Economic Model of Scaling," *Behavioural Public Policy* 5, no. 1 (2020): 2–49, doi:10.1017/bpp.2020.17.

13 **The term "voltage drop":** Amy M. Kilbourne, Mary S. Neumann, Harold A. Pincus, Mark S. Bauer, and Ronald Stall, "Implementing Evidence-Based Interventions in Health Care: Application of the Replicating Effective Programs Framework," *Implementation Science* 2, no. 42 (2007).

13 **According to Straight Talk on Evidence:** "How to Solve U.S. Social Problems When Most Rigorous Program Evaluations Find Disappointing Effects (Part One in a Series)," Straight Talk on Evidence, March 21, 2018, https://www.straighttalkonevidence.org/2018/03/21/how-to-solve-u-s-social-problems-when-most-rigorous-program-evaluations-find-disappointing-effects-part-one-in-a-series/.

15 **roughly 10 percent of American women:** Anjani Chandra, Casey E. Copen, and Elizabeth Hervey Stephen, "Infertility and Impaired Fecundity in the United States, 1982–2010: Data from the National Survey of Family

Growth," National Health Statistics Report No. 67, U.S. Centers for Disease Control, 2013, https://www.cdc.gov/nchs/data/nhsr/nhsr067.pdf.

15 **Big data is now used at scale:** E.g., Ovia Fertility, https://www.ovia health.com/.

Chapter 1: Dupers and False Positives

21 **"Not you, not me, and certainly not our children":** Ronald Reagan, "'Just Say No' Speech," September 14, 1986, University of Virginia Miller Center, https://millercenter.org/the-presidency/presidential-speeches /september-14-1986-speech-nation-campaign-against-drug-abuse.

22 **In 1983, Los Angeles chief of police:** Jim Newton, "DARE Marks a Decade of Growth and Controversy," *Los Angeles Times*, September 9, 1993, https://www.latimes.com/archives/la-xpm-1993-09-09-mn-33226-story .html.

22 **Over the next twenty-four years:** 2007 D.A.R.E. Annual Report, https:// web.archive.org/web/20090320022158/http://www.dare.com/home /documents/DAREAmericaAnnual07.pdf.

22 **In the decades since Nancy Reagan:** Reagan, "'Just Say No' Speech."

22 **numerous studies have demonstrated:** Steven L. West and Keri K. O'Neal, "Project D.A.R.E. Outcome Effectiveness Revisited," *American Journal of Public Health* 94 (2004): 1027–1029.

22 **One study even found:** Earl Wysong, Richard Aniskiewicz, and David Wright, "Truth and DARE: Tracking Drug Education to Graduation and as Symbolic Politics," *Social Problems* 41 (1994): 448–472.

23 **For example, when I visited:** Tanjim Hossain and John A. List, "The Behavioralist Visits the Factory: Increasing Productivity Using Simple Framing Manipulations," *Management Science* 58, no. 12 (2012).

23 **consider a 2005 study:** Erwin A. Blackstone, Andrew J. Buck, and Simon Hakim, "Evaluation of Alternative Policies to Combat False Emergency Calls," *Evaluation and Program Planning* 28, no. 2 (2005): 233–242.

23 **In the case of D.A.R.E.:** M. J. Manos, K. Y. Kameoka, and J. H. Tanji, "Project Evaluation of Honolulu Police Department's Drug Abuse Resistance Education," program/project description, University of Hawaii at Manoa, 1986, https://www.ojp.gov/ncjrs/virtual-library/abstracts /evaluation-honolulu-police-departments-drug-abuse-resistance.

23 **a subsequent study conducted soon after:** William DeJong, "A Short-Term Evaluation of Project Dare (Drug Abuse Resistance Education): Preliminary Indications of Effectiveness," *Journal of Drug Education* 17, no. 4 (1987): 279–294, doi:10.2190/N2JC-9DXB-BLFD-41EA.

23 **Yet numerous scientific analyses:** Susan T. Ennet, Nancy S. Tobler,

Christopher L. Ringwalt, and Robert L. Flewelling, "How Effective Is Drug Abuse Resistance Education? A Meta-Analysis of Project DARE Outcome Evaluations," *American Journal of Public Health* 84, no. 9 (1994): 1394–1401.

25 **Studies suggested that employee wellness programs:** T. DeGroot and D. S. Kiker, "A Meta-analysis of the Non-monetary Effects of Employee Health Management Programs," *Human Resources Management* 42 (2003): 53–69.

27 **it's the worst form of government:** Richard Langworth, *Churchill by Himself: The Definitive Collection of Quotations* (New York: PublicAffairs, 2011), 573.

27 **"Judgment Under Uncertainty":** Amos Tversky and Daniel Kahneman, "Judgment Under Uncertainty: Heuristics and Biases," *Science* 185, no. 4157 (1974): 1124–1131, doi:10.1126/science.185.4157.1124.

27 ***Thinking, Fast and Slow:*** Daniel Kahneman, *Thinking, Fast and Slow* (New York: Farrar, Straus and Giroux, 2011).

27 ***Predictably Irrational:*** Dan Ariely, *Predictably Irrational: The Hidden Forces That Shape Our Decisions* (New York: Harper Collins, 2008).

27 ***The Undoing Project:*** Michael Lewis, *The Undoing Project: A Friendship That Changed Our Minds* (New York: W. W. Norton, 2017).

28 **confirmation bias prevents us:** E. Jonas, S. Schulz-Hardt, D. Frey, and N. Thelen, "Confirmation Bias in Sequential Information Search After Preliminary Decisions: An Expansion of Dissonance Theoretical Research on Selective Exposure to Information," *Journal of Personality and Social Psychology* 80, no. 4 (2001): 557–571; P. C. Wason, "On the Failure to Eliminate Hypotheses in a Conceptual Task," *Quarterly Journal of Experimental Psychology* 12, no. 3 (1960): 129–140; P. C. Wason, "Reasoning About a Rule," *Quarterly Journal of Experimental Psychology* 20 (1968): 273–281; R. E. Kleck and J. Wheaton, "Dogmatism and Responses to Opinion-Consistent and Opinion-Inconsistent Information," *Journal of Personality and Social Psychology* 5, no. 2 (1967): 249–252.

28 **This is because science has taught us:** Daniel Kahneman and Amos Tversky, "Subjective Probability: A Judgment of Representativeness," *Cognitive Psychology* 3, no. 3 (1972): 430–454; Tversky and Kahneman, "Judgment Under Uncertainty"; Ariely, *Predictably Irrational;* Thomas Gilovich, Dale Griffin, and Daniel Kahneman, *Heuristics and Biases: The Psychology of Intuitive Judgment* (New York: Cambridge University Press, 2002).

29 **The British psychologist Peter Wason's:** Wason, "Reasoning About a Rule."

29 **In 1951, the pioneering social psychologist:** Solomon E. Asch, "Effects of Group Pressure upon the Modification and Distortion of Judgments,"

in *Groups, Leadership and Men: Research in Human Relations,* edited by Mary Henle (Berkeley: University of California Press, 1961).

30 **the top-selling basketball jerseys:** Interbasket, "The Best NBA Jerseys of All-Time," n.d., https://www.interbasket.net/jerseys/nba/best-selling/, accessed May 10, 2021.

32 **the widespread acceptance:** Lawrence Cohen and Henry Rothschild, "The Bandwagons of Medicine," *Perspectives in Biology and Medicine* 22, no. 4 (1979): 531–538, doi:10.1353/pbm.1979.0037.

33 **oftentimes pays more:** Barry Lind and Charles R. Plott, "The Winner's Curse: Experiments with Buyers and with Sellers," *American Economic Review* 81, no. 1 (1991): 335–346.

34 **she explained that he had poured milk:** R. A. Fisher, *The Design of Experiments* (Edinburgh: Oliver and Boyd, 1942); David Salsburg, *The Lady Tasting Tea: How Statistics Revolutionized Science in the Twentieth Century* (New York: Holt Paperbacks, 2002).

36 **medical errors:** M. A. Makary and M. Daniel, "Medical Error—the Third Leading Cause of Death in the US," *BMJ* 353 (2016): i2139, doi:10.1136/bmj.i2139.

37 **Several years ago:** Janette Kettmann Klingner, Sharon Vaughn, and Jeanne Shay Schumm, "Collaborative Strategic Reading During Social Studies in Heterogeneous Fourth-Grade Classrooms," *Elementary School Journal* 99, no. 1 (1998).

37 **only to fail miserably:** John Hitchcock, Joseph Dimino, Anja Kurki, Chuck Wilkins, and Russell Gersten, "The Impact of Collaborative Strategic Reading on the Reading Comprehension of Grade 5 Students in Linguistically Diverse Schools," U.S. Department of Education, 2011, https://files.eric.ed.gov/fulltext/ED517770.pdf.

37 **This emerging pattern even spurred one psychologist:** Open Science Collaboration, "Estimating the Reproducibility of Psychological Science," *Science* 349, no. 6251 (2015), doi:10.1126/science.aac4716.

37 **"file drawer problem":** Eliot Abrams, Jonathan Libgober, and John A. List, "Research Registries: Facts, Myths, and Possible Improvements," NBER Working Paper, 2020, doi:10.3386/w27250.

38 **that grocery shopping:** Aner Tal and Brian Wansink, "Fattening Fasting: Hungry Grocery Shoppers Buy More Calories, Not More Food," *JAMA Internal Medicine* 173, no. 12 (2013): 1146–1148, doi:10.1001/jamainternmed.2013.650.

38 **eating from a bigger bowl:** Brian Wansink and Matthew M. Cheney, "Super Bowls: Serving Bowl Size and Food Consumption," *JAMA* 293, no. 14 (2005): 1727–1728, doi:10.1001/jama.293.14.1727.

38 **the classic cookbook *The Joy of Cooking*:** Brian Wansink and Collin R.

Payne, "The Joy of Cooking Too Much: 70 Years of Calorie Increases in Classic Recipes," *Annals of Internal Medicine* 150, no. 4 (2009).

39 **As of this writing, nineteen of:** Retraction Watch, http://retractiondatabase.org/, accessed May 11, 2021.

39 **In 2018, the *Journal of the American Medical Association*:** "JAMA Network Retracts 6 Articles," September 19, 2018, https://media.jamanetwork.com/news-item/jama-network-retracts-6-articles-that-included-dr-brian-wansink-as-author/.

39 **Cornell launched an investigation:** Michael I. Kotlikoff, "Cornell University Statements," September 20, 2018, https://statements.cornell.edu/2018/20180920-statement-provost-michael-kotlikoff.cfm.

39 **Unfortunately, such behavior is more common:** J. List, C. Bailey, P. Euzent, and T. Martin, "Academic Economists Behaving Badly? A Survey on Three Areas of Unethical Behavior," *Economic Inquiry* 39 (2001): 162–170.

40 **Of course, we now know:** *Securities and Exchange Commission vs. Elizabeth Holmes and Theranos, Inc.*, 5:18-cv-01602, United States District Court, Northern District of California San Jose Division, March 14, 2018, https://www.sec.gov/litigation/complaints/2018/comp-pr2018-41-theranos-holmes.pdf.

41 **At one point:** Matthew Herper, "From $4.5 Billion to Nothing: Forbes Revises Estimated Net Worth of Theranos Founder Elizabeth Holmes," *Forbes,* June 1, 2016, https://www.forbes.com/sites/matthewherper/2016/06/01/from-4-5-billion-to-nothing-forbes-revises-estimated-net-worth-of-theranos-founder-elizabeth-holmes/.

41 **then threatened with lawsuits:** Taylor Dunn, Victoria Thompson, and Rebecca Jarvis, "Theranos Whistleblowers Filed Complaints out of Fear of Patients' Health," ABC News, March 13, 2019, https://abcnews.go.com/Business/theranos-whistleblowers-filed-complaints-fear-patients-health-started/story?id=61030212.

Chapter 2: Know Your Audience

46 **for instance, its net earnings would top:** "Costco Wholesale Corp.," MarketWatch, https://www.marketwatch.com/investing/stock/cost/financials, accessed 2021.

49 **paper on "two-part tariffs":** W. Arthur Lewis, "The Two-Part Tariff," *Economica* 8, no. 31 (1941): 249–270, doi:10.2307/2549332.

55 **Ashley Madison:** Dean Takahashi, "Ashley Madison 'Married Dating' Site Grew to 70 Million Users in 2020," Venture Beat, February 25, 2021, https://venturebeat.com/2021/02/25/ashley-madison-married-dating-site-grew-to-70-million-users-in-2020/.

58 **In the mid-1990s, McDonald's:** Tabitha Jean Naylor, "McDonald's Arch Deluxe and Its Fall from Grace," Yahoo, August 13, 2014, https://finance .yahoo.com/news/mcdonalds-arch-deluxe-fall-grace-190417958.html.

59 **However, it turned out that the fortified salt:** Abhijit Banerjee, Sharon Barnhardt, and Esther Duflo, "Can Iron-Fortified Salt Control Anemia? Evidence from Two Experiments in Rural Bihar," *Journal of Development Economics* 133 (2018): 127–146.

59 **the Nurse-Family Partnership:** David L. Olds, Peggy L. Hill, Ruth O'Brien, David Racine, and Pat Moritz, "Taking Preventive Intervention to Scale: The Nurse-Family Partnership," *Cognitive and Behavioral Practice* 10, no. 4 (2003): 278–290.

60 **Opower carried out:** Hunt Allcott, "Site Selection Bias in Program Evaluation," *Quarterly Journal of Economics* 130, no. 3 (2015): 1117–1165.

61 **On average, our Parent Academy:** John A. List, Fatemeh Momeni, and Yves Zenou, "Are Measures of Early Education Programs Too Pessimistic? Evidence from a Large-Scale Field Experiment," working paper, 2019, http://conference.iza.org/conference_files/behavioral_2019/momeni _f28001.pdf.

62 **what motivates people:** Uri Gneezy, Andreas Leibbrandt, and John A. List, "Ode to the Sea: Workplace Organizations and Norms of Cooperation," *Economic Journal* 126, no. 595 (2016): 1856–1883.

62 **the inner workings of markets:** John A. List, "Does Market Experience Eliminate Market Anomalies," *Quarterly Journal of Economics* 118, no. 1 (2003): 41–71.

62 **why people discriminate:** John A. List, "The Nature and Extent of Discrimination in the Marketplace: Evidence from the Field," *Quarterly Journal of Economics* 119, no. 1 (2004): 49–89.

62 **This finding raised a question:** Joseph Henrich, Steven J. Heine, and Ara Norenzayan, "Most People Are Not WEIRD," *Nature* 466, no. 29 (2010).

63 **Under the right conditions:** Uri Gneezy, Kenneth L. Leonard, and John A. List, "Gender Differences in Competition: Evidence from a Matrilineal and a Patriarchal Society," *Econometrica* 77, no. 5 (2009): 1637–1664.

65 **As of this writing:** Gopuff, "About Us," https://gopuff.com/go/about -us, accessed May 11, 2021.

65 **In 2019, the Japanese conglomerate:** Cory Weinberg and Amir Efrati, "SoftBank's Secret $750 Million Investment in GoPuff," The Information, January 17, 2020, https://www.theinformation.com/articles/softbanks -secret-750-million-investment-in-gopuff.

66 **in 2018, Taco Bell introduced:** Sarah Whitten, "Taco Bell's Nacho Fries Are the Most Successful Launch in the Chain's History," CNBC, March 13, 2018, https://www.cnbc.com/2018/03/13/taco-bells-nacho-fries-are-the

-most-successful-launch-in-the-chains-history.html; Jordan Valinsky, "Taco Bell Is Bringing Back Nacho Fries After Trimming Its Menu," CNN, December 16, 2020, https://www.cnn.com/2020/12/16/business/taco-bell-nacho-fries-menu/index.html.

66 **When I partnered:** Daniel Rondeau and John A. List, "Matching and Challenge Gifts to Charity: Evidence from Laboratory and Natural Field Experiments," *Experimental Economics* 11 (2008): 253–267.

Chapter 3: Is It the Chef or the Ingredients?

70 **It received an admiring review from *The Guardian:*** Matthew Norman, "Restaurant Review: Jamie's Italian," *The Guardian,* July 25, 2008, https://www.theguardian.com/lifeandstyle/2008/jul/26/restaurants.review.

70 **Oliver's new chain:** This story was put together from a variety of sources, including: Jamie Oliver Group, "News," 2020, https://www.jamieolivergroup.com/news/jamie-oliver-group-launches-new-international-dining-concept/; Sean Farrell, "Not So Fresh: Why Jamie Oliver's Restaurants Lost Their Bite," *The Guardian,* February 17, 2018, https://www.theguardian.com/lifeandstyle/2018/feb/16/not-so-fresh-why-jamie-oliver-restaurants-lost-their-bite.

71 **one-of-a-kind El Bulli:** Matt Goulding, "The End of El Bulli?," *Wall Street Journal,* January 27, 2010, https://www.wsj.com/articles/SB10001424052748704094304575029580782188308.

73 **"We were opening too many restaurants":** Debra Kelly, "The Real Reason Jamie Oliver's Restaurant Empire Is Collapsing," Mashed, May 22, 2019, https://www.mashed.com/153506/the-real-reason-jamie-olivers-restaurant-empire-is-collapsing/.

74 **By the time the influential *Sunday Times:*** Marina O'Loughlin and Camillo Benso, "The Food Isn't Actively Bad, Just Defiantly Mediocre," *Sunday Times,* December 16, 2018.

74 **At the start of 2019, the chain:** Amie Tsang, "Jamie Oliver's U.K. Restaurants Declare Bankruptcy," *New York Times,* May 21, 2019, https://www.nytimes.com/2019/05/21/business/jamie-oliver-uk-restaurants-bankruptcy-administration.html.

80 **As my colleagues Robert Metcalfe:** Steven Levitt, John List, Robert Metcalfe, and Sally Sadoff, "Engaging Parents in Parent Engagement Programs," Society for Research on Educational Effectiveness, 2016, https://eric.ed.gov/?id=ED567211.

81 **Starting with sixty-eight programs:** U.S. Administration for Children and Families, "Early Head Start Turns 25 in 2020," February 6, 2020, https://eclkc.ohs.acf.hhs.gov/video/early-head-start-turns-25-2020; U.S. Admin-

istration for Children and Families, "The Origins of Early Head Start," February 7, 2020, https://eclkc.ohs.acf.hhs.gov/video/origins-early-head -start.

81 **However, when the program scaled:** Lori A. Roggman, Gina A. Cook, Mark S. Innocenti, Vonda Jump Norman, Lisa K. Boyce, Katie Christian-sen, and Carla A. Peterson, "Home Visit Quality Variations in Two Early Head Start Programs in Relation to Parenting and Child Vocabulary Out-comes," *Infant Mental Health Journal* 37 (2016): 193–207.

82 **The consequence was:** Lori A. Roggman, Gina A. Cook, Carla A. Peter-son, and Helen H. Raikes, "Who Drops Out of Early Head Start Home Visiting Programs?," *Early Education and Development* 19, no. 4 (2008): 574–599, doi:10.1080/10409280701681870.

83 **what the author Paul Midler:** Paul Midler, "'Quality Fade': China's Great Business Challenge," Wharton School, July 25, 2007, https://knowledge .wharton.upenn.edu/article/quality-fade-chinas-great-business -challenge/.

83 **nonprofit groups try to support:** AARP, "2019 AARP Annual Report," 2019, https://www.aarp.org/content/dam/aarp/about_aarp/annual _reports/2019/2018-aarp-form-990-public-disclosure.pdf.

84 **Inexplicably, the anticipated energy savings:** Alec Brandon, Christopher Clapp, John A. List, Robert Metcalfe, and Michael Price, "Smart Tech, Dumb Humans: The Perils of Scaling Household Technologies," 2021, https://cclapp.github.io/ChrisClapp.org/Files/Manuscripts/Brandon ,%20Clapp,%20List,%20Metcalfe%20&%20Price%20-%20Smart%20 Tech,%20Dumb%20Humans-The%20Perils%20of%20Scaling%20House hold%20Technologies.pdf.

Chapter 4: Spillovers

89 *Unsafe at Any Speed:* Ralph Nader, *Unsafe at Any Speed: The Designed-In Dangers of the American Automobile* (New York: Grossman, 1965).

89 **Flash forward to 1975:** Sam Peltzman, "The Effects of Automobile Safety Regulation," *Journal of Political Economy* 83, no. 4 (1975).

90 **Give a biker a safety helmet:** Lei Kang, Akshay Vij, Alan Hubbard, and David Shaw, "The Unintended Impact of Helmet Use on Bicyclists' Risk-Taking Behaviors," 2018, https://www.unisa.edu.au/siteassets/episerver -6-files/global/business/centres/i4c/docs/kang-et-al-2018.pdf; Ian Walker and Dorothy Robinson, "Bicycle Helmet Wearing Is Associated with Closer Overtaking by Drivers: A Response to Olivier and Walter, 2013," 2018, PsyArXiv, doi:10.31234/osf.io/nxw2k.

90 **NASCAR drivers:** Adam T. Pope and Robert D. Tollison, "'Rubbin' Is Racin'": Evidence of the Peltzman Effect from NASCAR," *Public Choice* 142 (2010): 507–513.

90 **political scientist Scott Sagan:** Scott D. Sagan, "The Problem of Redundancy Problem: Why More Nuclear Security Forces May Produce Less Nuclear Security," *Risk Analysis* 24, no. 4 (2004): 935–946, doi:10.1111/j.0272 -4332.2004.00495.x.

93 **When economists Jonathan Hall:** Jonathan V. Hall, John J. Horton, and Daniel T. Knoepfle, "Pricing in Designed Markets: The Case of Ride-Sharing," 2021, https://john-joseph-horton.com/papers/uber_price.pdf.

95 **In 2014, a group of noteworthy economists:** Dennis Egger, Johannes Haushofer, Edward Miguel, Paul Niehaus, and Michael W. Walker, "General Equilibrium Effects of Cash Transfers: Experimental Evidence from Kenya," NBER Working Paper, 2019, doi:10.3386/w26600.

99 **In 2017, two crafty economists:** Zoë Cullen and Ricardo Perez-Truglia, "How Much Does Your Boss Make? The Effects of Salary Comparisons," NBER Working Paper, 2021, doi:10.3386/w24841.

101 **The wonderful work of economist Bruce Sacerdote:** Bruce Sacerdote, "Peer Effects in Education: How Might They Work, How Big Are They and How Much Do We Know Thus Far?," in *Handbook of the Economics of Education*, vol. 3, edited by Eric A. Hanushek, Stephen Machin, and Ludger Woessmann, 249–277 (Amsterdam: Elsevier, 2011).

102 **But first we would have to be sure:** John A. List, Fatemeh Momeni, and Yves Zenou, "The Social Side of Early Human Capital Formation: Using a Field Experiment to Estimate the Causal Impact of Neighborhoods," NBER Working Paper, 2020, doi:10.3386/w28283.

104 **The extra time:** Amanda Chuan, John List, and Anya Samek, "Do Financial Incentives Aimed at Decreasing Interhousehold Inequality Increase Intrahousehold Inequality?," *Journal of Public Economics* 196 (2021): 104382.

Chapter 5: The Cost Trap

107 **Arivale was going to revolutionize:** This story is put together from a variety of sources, including Jeffrey Bland, "Arivale Is Gone but Not Forgotten: What Did We Learn?," *Medium*, May 21, 2019, https://medium .com/@jeffreyblandphd/arivale-is-gone-but-not-forgotten-what-did-we -learn-6c37142f5f80; Paul Roberts, "Closure of High-Tech Medical Firm Arivale Stuns Patients," *Seattle Times*, April 26, 2019, https://www.seattletimes .com/business/technology/closure-of-high-tech-medical-firm-arivale -stuns-patients-i-feel-as-if-one-of-my-arms-was-cut-off/; Todd Bishop and

James Thorne, "Why Arivale Failed: Inside the Surprise Closure of an Ambitious 'Scientific Wellness' Startup," GeekWire, April 26, 2019, https://www.geekwire.com/2019/arivale-shut-doors-inside-surprise-closure-ambitious-scientific-wellness-startup/.

108 **a peer-reviewed observational study:** Niha Zubair, Matthew P. Conomos, Leroy Hood, Gilbert S. Omenn, Nathan D. Price, Bonnie J. Spring, Andrew T. Magis, and Jennifer C. Lovejoy, "Genetic Predisposition Impacts Clinical Changes in a Lifestyle Coaching Program," *Scientific Reports* 9 (2019): art. no. 6805.

109 **The book is most famous:** Adam Smith, *An Inquiry into the Nature and Causes of the Wealth of Nations,* book 4, ch. 2. You can read the whole text for free here: https://www.gutenberg.org/files/38194/38194-h/38194-h.htm.

113 **We founded Arivale:** Arivale website, http://www.arivale.com, accessed 2021.

115 **early demand suggested:** Rachel Lerman, "Lee Hood's Arivale Raises $36M to Personalize Your Health Care," *Seattle Times,* July 13, 2015, https://www.seattletimes.com/business/technology/lee-hoods-arivale-raises-36m-to-personalize-your-health-care/.

115 **As Picariello would later recall:** Jim Picariello, "My Company Grew Too Fast—and Went Out of Business," CBS News, August 11, 2012, https://www.cbsnews.com/news/my-company-grew-too-fast-and-went-out-of-business/.

117 **This can be seen vividly:** The official video from SpaceX is no longer up on YouTube, but you can see it at "SpaceX Falcon Heavy STP-2 Launch and Booster Landing—FULL VIDEO," YouTube, posted by NASASpaceflight, June 26, 2019, https://youtube/f6GfeT_MIOo?t=530.

117 **Indeed, using reusable rockets:** Matthew C. Weinzierl, Kylie Lucas, and Mehak Sarang, "SpaceX, Economies of Scale, and a Revolution in Space Access," Harvard Business School Case 720-027, April 2020 (revised June 2020).

121 **In the 1950s, the poliovirus:** Lauro S. Halstead, "A Brief History of Post-polio Syndrome in the United States," *Archives of Physical Medicine and Rehabilitation* 92, no. 8 (2011): P1344–1349.

123 **For instance, in the 1990s, California:** Christopher Jepsen and Steven Rivkin, "Class Size Reduction and Student Achievement: The Potential Tradeoff Between Teacher Quality and Class Size," *Journal of Human Resources* 44, no. 1 (2009): 223–250, doi:10.3368/jhr.44.1.223.

124 **after Zermelo published his theorem:** Ernst Zermelo, *Über eine Anwendung der Mengenlehre auf die Theorie des Schachspiels* (Berlin: Springer, 1913).

Chapter 6: Incentives That Scale

131 **the "dropped wallet" experiment:** "Dropped wallet" experiments are numerous, done in the field (as in M. D. West, *Law in Everyday Japan: Sex, Sumo, Suicide, and Statutes* [Chicago: University of Chicago Press, 2005]) and in the lab (Martin Dufwenberg and Uri Gneezy, "Measuring Beliefs in an Experimental Lost Wallet Game," *Games and Economic Behavior* 30, no. 2 [2000]: 163–182).

134 **the #DeleteUber campaign:** Mike Isaac, "What You Need to Know About #DeleteUber," *New York Times,* January 31, 2017, https://www.nytimes.com/2017/01/31/business/delete-uber.html.

136 **We weren't sure exactly:** Ofer H. Azar, "The Economics of Tipping," *Journal of Economic Perspectives* 34, no. 2 (2020): 215–236, doi:10.1257/jep.34.2.215.

142 **In 2013, Virgin Atlantic:** Greer K. Gosnell, John A. List, and Robert Metcalfe, "A New Approach to an Age-Old Problem: Solving Externalities by Incenting Workers Directly," NBER Working Paper, 2016, https://www.nber.org/system/files/working_papers/w22316/w22316.pdf.

144 **This was likely thanks to:** Steven D. Levitt and John A. List, "Was There Really a Hawthorne Effect at the Hawthorne Plant? An Analysis of the Original Illumination Experiments," *American Economic Journal: Applied Economics* 3, no. 1 (2011): 224–238, doi:10.1257/app.3.1.224.

149 **Humans' extreme aversion:** See, e.g., Daniel Kahneman, Jack L. Knetsch, and Richard H. Thaler, "Experimental Tests of the Endowment Effect and the Coase Theorem," *Journal of Political Economy* 98, no. 6 (1990).

149 **This seemingly irrational effect:** Ziv Carmon and Dan Ariely, "Focusing on the Forgone: How Value Can Appear So Different to Buyers and Sellers," *Journal of Consumer Research* 27, no. 3 (2149): 360–370.

149 **I had the opportunity to explore:** Tanjim Hossain and John A. List, "The Behavioralist Visits the Factory: Increasing Productivity Using Simple Framing Manipulations," *Management Science* 58, no. 12 (2012).

151 **For example, in the suburbs:** Erwin Bulte, John A. List, and Daan van Soest, "Toward an Understanding of the Welfare Effects of Nudges: Evidence from a Field Experiment in the Workplace," *Economic Journal* 130, no. 632 (2020): 2329–2353.

151 **that people with vast experience:** John A. List, "Does Market Experience Eliminate Market Anomalies?," *Quarterly Journal of Economics* 118, no. 1 (2003): 41–71.

151 **over time will begin to encode losses:** Lester C. P. Tong, Karen J. Ye, Kentaro Asai, Seda Ertac, John A. List, Howard C. Nusbaum, and Ali Hortaçsu, "Trading Modulates Anterior Insula to Reduce Endowment Effect,"

Proceedings of the National Academy of Sciences 113, no. 33 (2016): 9238–9243, doi:10.1073/pnas.1519853113.

152 **Alex Imas, Sally Sadoff, and Anya Samek:** Alex Imas, Sally Sadoff, and Anya Samek, "Do People Anticipate Loss Aversion?," *Management Science* 63, no. 5 (2016).

152 **They may even be particularly well suited:** Roland G. Fryer Jr., Steven D. Levitt, John List, and Sally Sadoff, "Enhancing the Efficacy of Teacher Incentives Through Loss Aversion: A Field Experiment," NBER Working Paper, 2012, doi:10.3386/w18237.

153 **In the year prior to our intervention:** Illinois State Board of Education, "2009–2010 School Year: Illinois State Report Card Data," https://www .isbe.net/pages/illinois-state-report-card-data.aspx.

154 **in looking at teacher quality:** Fryer et al., 2021. "Enhancing the Efficacy of Teacher Incentives Through Framing."

155 **To find out, we ran:** Steven D. Levitt, John A. List, Susanne Neckermann, and Sally Sadoff, "The Behavioralist Goes to School: Leveraging Behavioral Economics to Improve Educational Performance," *American Economic Journal: Economic Policy* 8, no. 4 (2016), doi:10.1257/pol.20130358.

156 **some research shows that rewards:** These four studies taken together tell the story: Levitt et al., "The Behavioralist Goes to School"; Alexander W. Cappelen, John A. List, Anya Samek, and Bertil Tungodden, "The Effect of Early Education on Social Preferences," NBER Working Paper, 2016, doi:10.3386/w22898; Uri Gneezy, John List, Jeff Livingston, Xiangdong Qin, Sally Sadoff, and Yang Xu, "Measuring Student Success: The Role of Effort on the Test Itself," *American Economic Review: Insights* (forthcoming); Steven D. Levitt, John A. List, and Sally Sadoff, "The Effect of Performance-Based Incentives on Educational Achievement: Evidence from a Randomized Experiment," NBER Working Paper, 2016, doi:10.3386/w22107.

Chapter 7: Revolution on the Margins

161 **The year before he became:** Stephen Breyer, *Breaking the Vicious Circle: Toward Effective Risk Regulation* (Cambridge, MA: Harvard University Press, 1993).

162 **This approach actually began:** A brief history of benefit-cost analysis can be found in David Pearce, "Cost Benefit Analysis and Environmental Policy," *Oxford Review of Economic Policy* 14, no. 4 (1998): 84–100.

169 **By its very nature:** William Niskanen, *Bureaucracy and Representative Government* (New York: Aldine-Atherton, 1971).

Chapter 8: Quitting Is for Winners

183 **two-time Academic All-American athlete:** I still have the plaques!

185 **coach Vince Lombardi, who famously said:** This quotation has been attributed to him.

188 **a body of influential psychological research:** Shane Frederick, Nathan Novemsky, Jing Wang, Ravi Dhar, and Stephen Nowlis, "Opportunity Cost Neglect," *Journal of Consumer Research* 36 (2009): 553–561, doi:10.1086/599764.

188 **In other words, we magnify:** T. D. Wilson, T. Wheatley, J. M. Meyers, D. T. Gilbert, and D. Axsom, "Focalism: A Source of Durability Bias in Affective Forecasting," *Journal of Personality and Social Psychology* 78, no. 5 (2000): 821–836.

188 **Experimental research suggests that policymakers:** Emil Persson and Gustav Tinghög, "Opportunity Cost Neglect in Public Policy," *Journal of Economic Behavior and Organization* 170 (2020): 301–312.

191 **An experiment conducted in the 1990s:** P. Legrenzi, V. Girotto, and P. N. Johnson-Laird, "Focussing in Reasoning and Decision Making," *Cognition* 49, nos. 1–2 (1993): 37–66.

191 **To develop this practice:** Shane Frederick, Nathan Novemsky, Jing Wang, Ravi Dhar, and Stephen Nowlis, "Neglect of Opportunity Costs in Consumer Choice," 2006, https://www.researchgate.net/publication/228800348_Neglect_of_Opportunity_Costs_in_Consumer_Choice.

191 **Perhaps the best example:** X Company, https://x.company/, accessed May 10, 2021.

192 **As the research lab's chief, Astro Teller:** Eric "Astro" Teller, "The Unexpected Benefit of Celebrating Failure," TED2016, February 2016, https://www.ted.com/talks/astro_teller_the_unexpected_benefit_of_celebrating_failure.

192 **In 2011, when Netflix:** Brian Stelter, "Netflix, in Reversal, Will Keep Its Services Together," *New York Times,* October 10, 2011, https://mediadecoder.blogs.nytimes.com/2011/10/10/netflix-abandons-plan-to-rent-dvds-on-qwikster/.

193 **Doing so doesn't mean:** Angela Lee Duckworth and Patrick D. Quinn, "Development and Validation of the Short Grit Scale (Grit–S)," *Journal of Personality Assessment* 91 (2009): 166–174.

193 **These were the two commercial goods:** You can read the full text of *On the Principles of Political Economy, and Taxation* for free here: https://www.gutenberg.org/files/33310/33310-h/33310-h.htm.

195 **One example from the start-up world:** Claire Cain Miller, "Why Twit-

ter's C.E.O. Demoted Himself," *New York Times*, October 30, 2010, https://
www.nytimes.com/2010/10/31/technology/31ev.html.

196 **In 1998, the company started:** Conner Forrest, "How the 'PayPal Mafia'
Redefined Success in Silicon Valley," Tech Republic, June 30, 2014, https://
www.techrepublic.com/article/how-the-paypal-mafia-redefined-success
-in-silicon-valley/.

198 **Back in 2013, Steve Levitt and I:** "Would You Let a Coin Toss Decide
Your Future?," *Freakonomics Radio* podcast, episode 112, January 31, 2013,
https://freakonomics.com/2013/01/31/would-you-let-a-coin-toss-decide
-your-future-full-transcript/.

199 **As tech entrepreneur, investor, and author:** Reid Hoffman, June Cohen,
and Deron Triff, *Masters of Scale* (New York: Currency, 2021), 179.

Chapter 9: Scaling Culture

202 **This was the question my friend:** Uri Gneezy, Andreas Leibbrandt, and
John A. List, "Ode to the Sea: Workplace Organizations and Norms of
Cooperation," *Economic Journal* 126, no. 595 (2016): 1856–1883.

203 **CEOs of coffee mills:** Ernst Fehr and John A. List, "The Hidden Costs and
Returns of Incentives—Trust and Trustworthiness Among CEOs," *Journal
of the European Economic Association* 2, no. 5 (2004): 743–771.

203 **professional traders:** Jonathan E. Alevy, Michael S. Haigh, and John A.
List, "Information Cascades: Evidence from a Field Experiment with Financial Market Professionals," *Journal of Finance* 62, no. 1 (2007).

203 **members of the Masai ethnic group:** Uri Gneezy, Kenneth L. Leonard,
and John A. List, "Gender Differences in Competition: Evidence from a
Matrilineal and a Patriarchal Society," *Econometrica* 77, no. 5 (2009): 1637–
1664.

205 **First, a twenty-five-year-old engineer:** Susan J. Fowler, "Reflecting on
One Very, Very Strange Year at Uber," February 19, 2017, https://www
.susanjfowler.com/blog/2017/2/19/reflecting-on-one-very-strange-year
-at-uber.

205 **A week later, Waymo:** "A Note on Our Lawsuit Against Otto and Uber,"
Waymo website, February 23, 2017, https://blog.waymo.com/2019/08/a
-note-on-our-lawsuit-against-otto-and.html.

205 **The week after that:** Eric Newcomer, "In Video, Uber CEO Argues with
Driver over Falling Fares," Bloomberg, February 28, 2017, https://www
.bloomberg.com/news/articles/2017-02-28/in-video-uber-ceo-argues
-with-driver-over-falling-fares.

205 **the *New York Times* exposed:** Mike Isaac, "How Uber Deceives the Au-
thorities Worldwide," *New York Times,* March 3, 2017, https://www.nytimes

.com/2017/03/03/technology/uber-greyball-program-evade-authorities
.html.

210 **Research suggests that deep trust:** Federico Cingano and Paolo Pinotti, "Trust, Firm Organization, and the Pattern of Comparative Advantage," *Journal of International Economics* 100 (2016): 1–13.

210 **functional teamwork is essential:** Rafael La Porta, Florencio Lopez de Silanes, Andrei Shleifer, and Robert W. Vishny, "Trust in Large Organizations," *American Economic Review* 87, no. 2 (1997): 333–338, https://www.jstor.org/stable/2950941.

210 **There were the high-profile riders:** Mike Isaac, "Uber Fires Executive over Handling of Rape Investigation in India," *New York Times,* June 7, 2017, https://www.nytimes.com/2017/06/07/technology/uber-fires-executive.html.

213 **However, lest you think:** Xueming Luo, Rebecca J. Slotegraaf, and Xing Pan, "Cross-Functional 'Coopetition': The Simultaneous Role of Cooperation and Competition Within Firms," *Journal of Marketing,* April 1, 2006.

214 **The company doesn't track:** Josef Adalian, "Inside the Binge Factory," *Vulture,* June 2018, https://www.vulture.com/2018/06/how-netflix-swallowed-tv-industry.html; Patty McCord, "How Netflix Reinvented HR," *Harvard Business Review,* January 2014, https://hbr.org/2014/01/how-netflix-reinvented-hr.

214 **Micromanaging is a no-no:** McCord, "How Netflix Reinvented HR."

214 **Netflix CEO Reed Hastings:** Maria Konnikova, "What if Your Company Had No Rules?," *Freakonomics Radio* podcast, September 12, 2020, https://freakonomics.com/podcast/book-club-hastings/.

215 **Several years ago, my friends:** Check us out at http://sodi.org/.

215 **Research shows that diverse groups:** John E. Sawyer, Melissa A. Houlette, and Erin L. Yeagley, "Decision Performance and Diversity Structure: Comparing Faultlines in Convergent, Crosscut, and Racially Homogeneous Groups," *Organizational Behavior and Human Decision Processes* 99, no. 1 (2006): 1–15.

215 **problem-solving skills:** Lu Hong and Scott E. Page, "Groups of Diverse Problem Solvers Can Outperform Groups of High-Ability Problem Solvers," *Proceedings of the National Academy of Sciences* 101, no. 46 (2004): 16385–16389, doi:10.1073/pnas.0403723101.

215 **higher profits:** Paul A. Gompers and Sophie Q. Wang, "And the Children Shall Lead: Gender Diversity and Performance in Venture Capital," NBER Working Paper, 2017, doi:10.3386/w23454.

215 **One study showed they even:** Gompers and Wang, "And the Children Shall Lead."

216 **And yet,:** Andreas Leibbrandt and John A. List, "Do Equal Employment

Opportunity Statements Backfire? Evidence from a Natural Field Experiment on Job-Entry Decisions," NBER Working Paper, 2018, doi:10.3386/w25035.

217 **Their skepticism:** Marianne Bertrand and Sendhil Mullainathan, "Are Emily and Greg More Employable than Lakisha and Jamal? A Field Experiment on Labor Market Discrimination," *American Economic Review* 94, no. 4 (2004): 991–1013, https://www.jstor.org/stable/3592802; Sonia K. Kang, Katherine A. DeCelles, András Tilcsik, and Sora Jun, "Whitened Résumés: Race and Self-Presentation in the Labor Market," *Administrative Science Quarterly* 61, no. 3 (2016): 469–502.

217 **(very often publicly available online):** For example, the publisher of this book: https://www.penguinrandomhouse.com/about-us/our-people/.

218 **That is, CSR isn't:** Daniel Hedblom, Brent R. Hickman, and John A. List, "Toward an Understanding of Corporate Social Responsibility: Theory and Field Experimental Evidence," NBER Working Paper, 2019, doi:10.3386/w26222.

219 **To explore this question:** Hedblom, Hickman, and List, "Toward an Understanding of Corporate Social Responsibility."

220 **In another field experiment:** John A. List and Fatemeh Momeni, "When Corporate Social Responsibility Backfires: Theory and Evidence from a Natural Field Experiment," NBER Working Paper, 2017, doi:10.3386/w24169.

221 **Another field experiment I conducted:** Andreas Leibbrandt and John A. List, "Do Women Avoid Salary Negotiations? Evidence from a Large Scale Natural Field Experiment," NBER Working Paper, 2012, doi:10.3386/w18511.

221 **The ugly truth:** A good rundown of the various domains of leadership that women are underrepresented in can be found here: Judith Warner, Nora Ellmann, and Diana Boesch, "The Women's Leadership Gap," Center for American Progress, November 20, 2018, https://www.americanprogress.org/issues/women/reports/2018/11/20/461273/womens-leadership-gap-2/.

221 **women working full-time:** Francine D. Blau and Lawrence M. Kahn, "The Gender Wage Gap: Extent, Trends, and Explanations," *Journal of Economic Literature* 55, no. 3 (2017): 789–865, doi:10.1257/jel.20160995.

221 **only about 6 percent:** David A. Matsa and Amalia R. Miller, "Chipping Away at the Glass Ceiling: Gender Spillovers in Corporate Leadership," *American Economic Review* 101, no. 3 (2011): 635–639, doi:10.1257/aer.101.3.635.

221 **And while there are many reasons:** See, for example, Linda Babcock and Sara Laschever, *Women Don't Ask: Negotiation and the Gender Divide* (Princeton: Princeton University Press, 2009); L. Babcock, M. Gelfand,

D. Small, and H. Stayn, "Gender Differences in the Propensity to Initiate Negotiations," in *Social Psychology and Economics*, edited by D. De Cremer, M. Zeelenberg, and J. K. Murnighan, 239–259 (Mahwah, NJ: Lawrence Erlbaum Associates, 2006); Deborah Small, Michele Gelfand, Linda Babcock, and Hilary Gettman, "Who Goes to the Bargaining Table? The Influence of Gender and Framing on the Initiation of Negotiation," *Journal of Personality and Social Psychology* 93, no. 4 (2007): 600–613, doi:10.1037/0022-3514.93.4.600; K. G. Kugler, J. A. M. Reif, T. Kaschner, and F. C. Brodbeck, "Gender Differences in the Initiation of Negotiations: A Meta-analysis," *Psychological Bulletin* 144, no. 2 (2018): 198–222.

221 **We found that not only:** Leibbrandt and List, "Do Women Avoid Salary Negotiations?"

222 **For example, a 2021 study:** Brian J. Lucas, Laura M. Giurge, Zachariah Berry, and Dolly Chugh, "Research: To Reduce Gender Bias in Hiring, Make Your Shortlist Longer," *Harvard Business Review*, February 2021, https://hbr.org/2021/02/research-to-reduce-gender-bias-in-hiring-make-your-shortlist-longer.

225 **Any type of apology:** Basil Halperin, Benjamin Ho, John A. List, and Ian Muir, "Toward an Understanding of the Economics of Apologies: Evidence from a Large-Scale Natural Field Experiment," NBER Working Paper, 2019, doi:10.3386/w25676.

227 **Indeed, the pull of workplace norms:** Stephen Knack and Philip Keefer, "Does Social Capital Have an Economic Payoff? A Cross-Country Investigation," *Quarterly Journal of Economics* 112, no. 4 (1997): 1251–1288; La Porta et al., "Trust in Large Organizations."

Conclusion: To Scale or Not to Scale?

230 **Some Covid-19 tests were unreliable:** Nadia Drake, "Why Unreliable Tests Are Flooding the Coronavirus Conversation," *National Geographic*, May 6, 2020, https://www.nationalgeographic.com/science/article/why-unreliable-tests-are-flooding-the-coronavirus-conversation-cvd.

230 **while $1.4 billion:** Greg Iacurci, "IRS Sends Coronavirus Stimulus Checks to Dead People," CNBC, April 17, 2020, https://www.cnbc.com/2020/04/17/irs-sends-coronavirus-stimulus-checks-to-dead-people.html.

231 **Leo Tolstoy:** Leo Tolstoy, *Anna Karenina*, translated by Richard Pevear and Larissa Volokhonsky (New York: Penguin Classics, 2004).

Index

About the Author

JOHN A. LIST is the Kenneth C. Griffin Distinguished Service Professor in Economics at the University of Chicago. He has served on the Council of Economic Advisers and is the recipient of numerous awards and honors including the Kenneth Galbraith Award. His work has been featured in the *New York Times, The Economist, Harvard Business Review, Fortune, Slate,* and the *Washington Post,* and on NPR, NBC, and Bloomberg. List has authored over 250 peer-reviewed journal articles, several academic books, and, with Uri Gneezy, the international bestseller *The Why Axis*.

About the Type

This book was set in Dante, a typeface designed by Giovanni Mardersteig (1892–1977). Conceived as a private type for the Officina Bodoni in Verona, Italy, Dante was originally cut only for hand composition by Charles Malin, the famous Parisian punch cutter, between 1946 and 1952. Its first use was in an edition of Boccaccio's *Trattatello in laude di Dante* that appeared in 1954. The Monotype Corporation's version of Dante followed in 1957. Though modeled on the Aldine type used for Pietro Cardinal Bembo's treatise *De Aetna* in 1495, Dante is a thoroughly modern interpretation of that venerable face.